MARTIN MILLS

NEXUS

ENGLISH FOR ADVANCED LEARNERS

Balm (plant, ½; branch, ⅓ natural size).

Mundul & Co.
Estd 1860
(Calcutta)

HEINEMANN

Heinemann International
A division of Heinemann Publishers (Oxford) Ltd
Halley Court, Jordan Hill, Oxford OX2 8EJ

OXFORD LONDON EDINBURGH
MADRID PARIS ATHENS BOLOGNA
MELBOURNE SYDNEY AUCKLAND SINGAPORE TOKYO
IBADAN NAIROBI GABORONE
PORTSMOUTH (NH)

ISBN 0 435 28202 6

© Martin Mills 1990

First published 1990

The author would like to express his gratitude to
the following for their contributions to the course:
Ben Duncan; Paul Cane; Eileen Miller; Yvonne
Harvey; Dave Chumbley; John Gillow; Dr Hugh
King; Martin Parrott; Malcolm Hebden; Psyche
Kennett; Jan McCarry; Tony Robinson; David
Boyd.

Text acknowledgements

Our thanks are due to the following for their kind
permission to reproduce a text:

International House (pp. 2 and 3); Steve Elsworth
(p. 7); Newsweek (pp. 14 and 15); Department of
Health and Social Security (Crown Copyright)
(pp. 18 and 19); The Guardian (pp. 26 and 27);
Jacquie Hughes (pp. 30 and 31); Prentice Hall
Trade Division, a division of Simon & Schuster,
Inc. (pp. 38 and 39); Time Inc. (pp. 42 and 43);
Oxford University Press (pp. 50 and 51); The
Independent (p. 55); Pan Books Ltd (p. 64); The
Sunday Times (pp. 68 and 69); Constable
Publishers (pp. 76 and 77); Her Majesty's
Stationery Office (Crown Copyright) (pp. 80 and
81); The Observer (pp. 86 and 87); Martin Walker
(pp. 90 and 91); Curtis Brown (Aust.) Pty Ltd,
Sydney (pp. 98 and 99); Encyclopaedia Britannica,
Inc. (pp. 102 and 103); New English Library,
Hodder and Stoughton Ltd (pp. 110 and 111);
Coronet (pp. 116 and 117); Newsweek (pp. 124
and 125); International Herald Tribune (p. 129);
The Observer Colour Supplement (pp. 134 and
135); Fiat Auto (UK) Ltd, Citroën Cars Ltd,
Subaru (UK) Ltd, VAG (United Kingdom) Ltd,
Suzuki GB (Cars) Ltd (pp. 140 and 141); Fanfare

Publications (p. 146); Prentice Hall Trade
Division, a division of Simon & Schuster, Inc.
(p. 147); The Observer Colour Supplement
(pp. 150 and 151); Cambridge University Press
(pp. 154 and 155).

Photograph acknowledgements

We would also like to thank the following for
permission to reproduce photographs:

The Bell Educational Trust (p. 1); Liz Somerville
(p. 4); © Henry Moore Foundation. Reproduced
by kind permission of the Henry Moore Foundation
and the Tate Gallery, London (p. 13); Aspect
Picture Library (p. 19); David Hoffman/Camera
Press, London (p. 19); Nigel Coke/Science Photo
Library (p. 19); Cath Tate (p. 25); Mary Evans
Picture Library (p. 37); Barry Lewis/Network
(p. 43); Windsor Castle Royal Library © Her
Majesty The Queen (p. 61); Mary Evans Picture
Library (pp. 68 and 69); British Heart Foundation
(p. 70); Electronic Graphics Ltd (p. 73); The
Kobal Collection. A First National Production
(p. 76); The Mansell Collection (p. 85); Rex
Features Ltd (p. 88); G. & G. Attwell/Aquila
Photographics Ltd (p. 97); J. J. Brooks/Aquila
Photographics Ltd (p. 99); Octopus Publishing
Group Library (p. 101); Mary Evans Picture Library
(p. 109); Camera Press Ltd (p. 110); Zefa (p. 117);
Fay Godwin/Barbara Heller Photo Library
(p. 121); WWF/Save the Rhino Trust (p. 124);
Andreas Ramer/Rex Features Ltd (p. 124); Andes
Press Agency (p. 129); Chris Honeywell (p. 131);
Winnebago Industries Inc., Iowa, U.S.A.
(p. 134); Fiat Auto (UK) Ltd (p. 140); Subaru
(UK) Ltd (p. 141); VAG (United Kingdom) Ltd
(p. 141); Mary Evans Picture Library (p. 145);
Christine Osborne (pp. 146 and 147).

Illustrations by:

Matthew Buckley	Ian Kellas
Paul Campion	David Mostyn
Barbara Crow	Chris Price
Rob Fowler	John Pugh
Steve Fricker	Trevor Ridley
Val Hill	Paul Slater
Keith Hume	Billy Stevenson

Typeset by Tradespools Ltd, Frome, Somerset
Printed and bound in Great Britain by
Thomson Litho Ltd, East Kilbride, Scotland

91 92 93 94 95 10 9 8 7 6 5 4 3 2

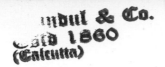
Introduction

In general

Nexus is a course for students of English whose level is approximately equivalent to pass standard at Cambridge FCE. By the end of the course, the English of such users should be most of the way to the level required for a Cambridge Proficiency candidate. However, the course is a general one, not a specific preparation for any examination.

The aims of *Nexus* are to broaden and enrich your English, and to help you to use it more correctly, creatively and fluently. An equally important aim is to help you to be an adult, autonomous learner of English, for whom time spent in the classroom is only a part of your studies. Students who think for themselves and take their English out of the classroom when they leave it are much more likely to be successful learners. To this effect, *Nexus* contains practical advice on how to organise your learning effectively, and a varied selection of voluntary projects and assignments, to be tackled creatively outside class time. In addition, at every stage of the course you, the students, are encouraged to bring your own knowledge, ideas and experience to the work in hand, and to discuss them with each other and with your teacher.

The structure of the course

Nexus consists of thirteen units, each divided into seven sections. There are two sections for reading, and one each for listening, speaking, writing, grammar and vocabulary.

Reading

In the Reading sections you will read, analyse and discuss a variety of written material, ranging from literary extracts to advertisements. The exercises aim not only to check your understanding but also to improve your reading in various ways. The following are some of the subskills practised: predicting while reading; guessing words from context; identifying words with given meanings; appreciating stylistic features; reading for gist; scanning for specific information.

Speaking

The Speaking sections are of two types. In one type you use your English freely and creatively, in an organised discussion, a game, or a role play. In another, you study and practise useful items of spoken English, selected according to functional criteria, through a series of guided exercises.

Listening

You will hear a fairly long piece of authentic spoken English, with from one to four people speaking. The exercises test your comprehension, and also ask you to listen hard for certain useful words and expressions.

Writing

The Writing sections aim to help you write in a more organised and thoughtful way. Study of the organisation and language used in model texts is followed by controlled writing exercises. There are also many opportunities for free writing.

Grammar

The aim of the Grammar sections is to clear up your doubts about the basics of English grammar, to introduce you to more advanced language points, and to provide varied practice. In every Grammar section you will have the opportunity to discuss and share what you already know about the grammar before studying a description of the language area in question, and then going on to practice activities.

Vocabulary

Advice about how to expand and store your vocabulary in your own time is given in the Organising your learning sections in the Study pages. The Vocabulary sections aim to teach you new words in class time. Each section teaches a vocabulary set in an integrated and systematic way. Your own knowledge is activated and then a variety of activities strengthen your understanding of the new words.

The Study pages

These pages, at the back of your Coursebook, are an essential and integral part of your work in the course. They contain: language descriptions for the Grammar sections; some back-up vocabulary exercises; answer keys for re-ordered texts; transcripts of dialogues; information for role plays and information-exchange activities.

▭ This cassette symbol tells you when to switch on your cassette and listen to recorded material.

Nexus aims to offer a balanced, stimulating and challenging programme, and it is hoped that the users of the course will benefit from it not only in terms of language improvement, but also through the opportunities it offers for communication and interaction with other users of English.

Contents

Mundul & Co.
Estd 1860
(Calcutta)

Contents

Mundul & Co.
Estd 1860
(Calcutta)

Contents

Contents

UNIT 1 Learning and teaching English

A Reading 1

Discussion

● Note down the problems which a British teacher of English new to your country would face.
● What could a language school do to help with these problems?

Reading exercises

1 You are going to read an extract from a practical manual. At ten points, fragments have been removed. What do you think was in each gap? Discuss this in groups. Cover the list of fragments underneath the article.

2 Study the list, which contains the missing fragments from the extract plus three additions. Choose the ten correct items, and decide where they go in the extract. Check with your teacher, then fill the gaps in the extract.

3 By what sort of organisation do you think the manual was produced? For whom is it intended?

4 To what do the words in italics refer?
a . . . failure to *do so* . . . (introduction)
b . . . even if *it* does not . . . (introduction)
c . . . such *extreme results* . . . (introduction)

d . . . Anyway, *it* is your fault . . . (suggestion 4)
e . . . *something* merely to be coped with (suggestion 6)
f . . . who fail to do *it* . . . (suggestion 6)
Check your answers with another student.

5 Find words or expressions in the completed extract with the following meanings.
a are originally caused by
b dealt with, talked about
c temporary accommodation
d be careful about
e improve an unsatisfactory situation
f concerning
g strange, foreign
h persuade people to change their mind about

Helping new teachers

It is very much in the interests of schools to give new staff the maximum possible help, rather than merely to observe the minimal conditions mentioned in the Affiliation Agreement or in the local contract. Failure to do so may well lead to (1) _____ _____ — always a major inconvenience for school and students alike! Even if it does not have such extreme results, failure to help teachers will almost certainly cause them to adopt such negative attitudes that full

2

adaptation (and thus the chance of a second year) is effectively ruled out. As annual IH visitors know well, many staff complaints stem from negative attitudes to schools rather than from specific incidents or problems. And these attitudes often stem from a teacher's belief that he or she was not given sufficient help on arrival in the school. It is gratifying to note that over the last five years (2) _____, and that teachers seem to be very appreciative of this assistance.

Some suggestions

1 Even if social, legal and practical problems are covered in an orientation course, advice on them should also (3) _____. This might contain details of entertainments and shops, addresses of doctors etc.

2 Assume that teachers will forget much of what they are told initially, and that they will lose their booklets! This can cause problems at times of emergency (e.g. sickness) and may be partially counteracted by pinning up real survival information in the staffroom.

3 If long-term accommodation is not provided, the school should do more than arrange a few days' lodgings and tell teachers to find flats as soon as possible. At worst, information should be given on where to look for flats, what to watch out for, how much to pay etc. Much better, someone (4) _____ _____.

4 Where accommodation is provided, try to ensure that it is in a reasonable state of repair and decoration before new staff move into it. Also, that it is really adequately furnished, with a heater, etc. (I know — last year's staff (5) _____. That is hardly the fault or concern of new teachers. Anyway, it is your fault for not having made the old teachers put things to rights before they left.)
  How about laying on a few flowers; and perhaps a few drinks, etc. in the fridge? Totally unnecessary, of course, and not to be found in any employment contract. But very cheap and unbelievably good PR. Schools which have adopted this type of approach (e.g. Heliopolis) have found that (6)_____ _____.

5 Whatever the accommodation arrangements, encourage and help teachers to make their flats comfortable and attractive. Persuade them that this need not be expensive nor take a great effort. It will, however, (7) _____ _____. After all, everyone needs a pleasant home-base.

6 Try to make new arrivals feel welcome, both to the school and to the country. Show them around, introduce them to the rest of the staff, take them around the town, invite them for drinks, etc. (preferably with some local people there). Talk to them about local culture as something to be explored, appreciated and enjoyed, rather than as (8) _____.
  Again, making people feel welcome cannot be specified in a contract or in the Affiliation Agreement, nor can it be enforced. However, directors and directors of studies who fail to do it will inevitably pay for their failure in the end, even if they do not always recognise the fruits of this failure.

7 Keep an eye on people who are having obvious problems in adapting or in socialising with colleagues/staff.

8 Take particular care of people who are ill. True, they may be hypochondriacs and giving you immense problems re stand-bys, etc. However, (9) _____, and people need considerable moral support at such times.

9 Avoid going on the defensive when criticisms or complaints are made. If the points are unjustified, talk people out of them. If they are justified (and whether they are the result of accident, local incompetence or mistakes by London), (10) _____ _____.

International House

---

a there is little worse than being ill in an alien environment
b it really does help to boost morale among new teachers
c apologise for them and try to find remedies
d should go round with the teacher on their search for housing

e unhappiness on the part of the teacher
f managed very well without such things
g something merely to be coped with
h be contained in a booklet for new teachers
i make sure that they are receiving proper medical care

j the amount of assistance given to new teachers in our schools has increased tremendously
k the breaking of contracts by teachers
l left it in a mess and broke everything
m tend to make them feel happier and more settled

B Speaking

Role play

Finding a flat

1 Discussion

In Reading 1, Directors of Studies are advised to help new teachers with finding long-term accommodation. The writers recommend that 'information should be given on where to look for flats, what to watch out for, how much to pay, etc.' What do you think are the things that should be watched out for in renting a flat in your own country? If you know Britain, what things do you think one should bear in mind in flat-hunting there? Are they any different from in your own country?

2 Role play situation

Imagine that two foreign students are in London to study English. They don't want to stay with a 'host family' so, like the British teacher abroad, they have to find somewhere to live. In groups of three, you are going to improvise a conversation between the two students (Students A and B) and a clerk in an accommodation agency (Student C). To prepare, Students A and B should read on. Student C should turn to Study page 157.

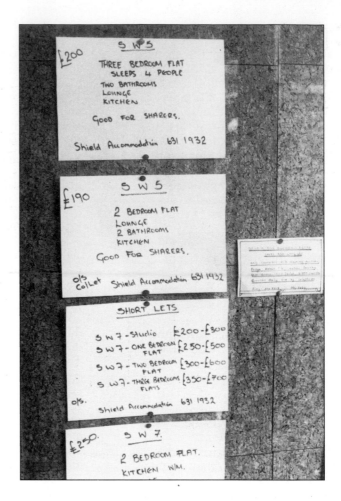

Students A and B

You will be in London for three or four months. After paying school fees you have about £400 per month each. Your school is in the central area. Before you visit an accommodation agency, discuss the relative importance to each of you of the following points.

- living in a quiet, attractive area
- living in a safe area
- living close to the centre (for your school, going out, etc.)
- having money left over after rent for travelling, entertainment etc.
- having your own room each
- being able to invite people over to your flat
- a telephone
- a TV
- a garden
- a luxurious modern bathroom
- central heating
- living close to a tube station

Bear in mind the following information:
- Taxis are very expensive.
- Tube fares in the central fare zone are 50p, flat fare, but fares get a lot higher once you leave this zone. Tubes stop around midnight.
- Eating out will probably cost you at least £7 or £8 per person.
- Cinemas cost about £4 per person, but West End theatres cost far more.

Regarding areas of London, you've heard that:
- Ealing is a pleasant residential suburb, where nothing exciting happens;
- Streatham is similar, but a bit nearer;
- Chelsea is an exciting, central area, with lots going on;
- Islington is a pleasant area, fairly close to the centre;
- Stockwell is a rather run-down area, fairly close to the centre, but not very safe at night.

---

3 Acting the role play

Improvise the conversation in the accommodation agency, as the clerk tries to interest the students in the accommodation s/he has. The two students should arrange to see any of the accommodation which interests them, but may also decide not to bother with any of it.

C Listening

EFL teachers talk

Discussion

● Why do you think people become teachers of English?

● What do you think might be the good things and the bad things about the job?

● Why are you studying English? (Be honest!)

Listening exercises

1 You are going to hear an extract from an interview with two teachers of English as a Foreign Language (EFL), Ben and Paul. Listen, take notes, and answer the following questions as fully as possible.

a What made each of them join the profession?

b What careers had Ben had before taking up teaching? In what ways were they unsatisfactory?

c What does Ben like about his work?

d What difference does Ben see between the work of state school teachers and teachers of EFL?

e Why does he prefer EFL teachers to most of the people he worked with before?

f What is the important difference between the school where he works and the majority of language schools?

g In what way does he hope English language schools might change in the future?

h In what way are both Paul and Ben critical of EFL teachers?

i What does Paul like about his work?

2 Listen again, filling the gaps in the following. Each line represents a word or contraction. Sometimes one extract is a direct continuation of another, so pay attention!

a . . . I was very poor. I couldn't earn enough to _____ _____.

b And when I was working as a journalist, I _____ _____ write an article about English language schools.

c Almost all the teachers I know are in some way exploited by somebody else. _____ _____ _____ _____ that these are people who have all the ability that's needed to be running their own lives . . .

d Perhaps what we should be doing is actually organising ourselves better, and going out, _____ _____ _____ an institution or starting our own . . .

e So, I don't think anyone's going to suddenly _____ _____ places to us . . .

f . . . perhaps we need to _____ _____ _____ _____ ourselves.

g . . . in management positions.' 'Yes, _____ _____ to something you said, Ben, we're back onto the type of person . . .'

3 Match the following meanings to five of the expressions above:

i initiate, begin a process

ii gaining possession of . . .

iii buy what is necesssary, in order to live

iv I very often have the impression . . .

v give, without resistance

D Reading 2

Discussion

● In B Speaking, you imagined being in London and looking for long-term accommodation. Have you ever really been to London? If so, tell your group the good things and bad things about your stay.

● If you have never been to London, would you like to go? Why/Why not?

● You are going to read a letter written to a British newspaper. The writer is rather critical of London (perhaps unreasonably so), and mentions four things: language schools, finding a bed for the night, flat-hunting, and the immigration service. What do you think he will say about each topic?

Reading exercises

1 Read the text of the letter. The paragraphs have been jumbled up. Working in pairs, try to put the paragraphs in the right order. As you work, pay attention to the content of each paragraph and the words which in any way link one paragraph to another.

For example, **d** must be the first paragraph, because it begins with 'Sir' and is clearly an introduction; **f** is the second, linked to the first by 'another reason'.

Check your answer against the original letter on Study page 157.

2 Discuss the following questions in groups:

a What is the writer's purpose (perhaps more than one purpose) in writing the letter?

b Which adjectives describe how he feels?
furious   critical   desperate
confused   concerned
amused   astonished
pessimistic   sad   irritated

c The writer is being rather sarcastic when he says *And next, the 'language' schools* (para. i). How does he make it clear that he is being sarcastic? Look for other sarcastic remarks in paragraphs 4 to 7.

d What is the writer suggesting by imagining a school called the *Me Tarzan, You Jane School English*? (para. i)

e What does *'no-one would blink an eyelid'* mean? (para. 1)

3 Complete the following summary of the letter.

The basic reason why tourist figures in London are declining is _____. There are four main reasons for this. The first is _____. The second is that _____. It is also very difficult _____. The fourth problem is the language schools: you don't need _____, so _____.

What is needed in London _____. In this way prices and conditions could be checked regularly, and tourists _____.

4 Now working alone, write a letter to the same newspaper, expressing your reaction to the letter.

London: a tourist trap that lives up to its name

a I worked at a language school once where the principal was a retired actor with no educational qualifications; the teachers were completely untrained, the students were not graded into different language levels (so you had nearly fluent students in the same class as people who could just say 'Hello, how are you?') and the language laboratory, though advertised, didn't exist. And the students were each paying £110 a month.

b Until we have a similar system in London, or until we at least make an effort towards looking after our tourists, then the numbers coming to London will continue to decline. The word is being passed back along the line: 'Don't go to London — it stinks.'
Yours,
Steve Elsworth
London N5

c The Germans (and myself) found it amazing that there was no useful information service available — not even some central clearing house we could telephone to find a bed for a night. Surprising though it may seem, trains and planes do arrive outside office hours.

d Sir,
There is much alarm about the declining tourist figures in London this year: various reasons have been put forward including the strength of the pound and the oil shortage.

e If the tourist manages to find an accommodation agency, the next hurdle is the price. I spent an hour telephoning agencies advertised in the Evening Standard trying to find a small flat for an Argentinian student, whose maximum was £50 a week. 'Oh no,' said the agencies, 'we haven't got anything for £50: don't you know this is the tourist season?' One agency offered me a double bedsit for £40. I know the floors of London are paved with gold but this is ridiculous.

f I spend my working hours with tourists and foreign students, and I can give another reason for the tourist decline: it's a growing awareness among foreigners of what a voracious and insatiable tourist trap London is.

g Do you remember the feeling of relief when you're abroad, on guard against being ripped off and you see the sign on the wall of a restaurant or hotel 'This establishment is subject to Touristic Control'; in other words, the price and conditions offered are regularly checked?

h When the tourist has fought his way through Immigration control, his next problem is accommodation. If he arrives after 9 p.m., then he's just had it. All the hostels and B&B places are full.

i And next, the 'language' schools. A lot of people come here because they want to learn English since in many countries a sound knowledge of English is very useful for job promotion. But you don't need a licence to open a language school; there are 100 language

schools in London, some of which are quite reputable and others which are downright atrocious. Tarzan could come over to London and open the 'Me Tarzan, You Jane School of English' and no one would blink an eyelid.

i If you look at London from a foreigner's point of view, it isn't really a holiday city, more a type of steeplechase in which the tourist has to jump over a set of hurdles at the same time as fighting off the clutches of some of the more unscrupulous inhabitants.

k I arrived with two German students at Euston at 11 p.m. last Thursday. After half-an-hour's working through Yellow Pages, we still hadn't found them anywhere to stay. We tried the BR information office: 'Ask a policeman,' they said.

l The first hurdle is Immigration, a service not renowned among foreigners for its tact and diplomacy. The UK and the USA apparently have the worst reputation in the West for the belligerence of their Immigration officers.

The Guardian

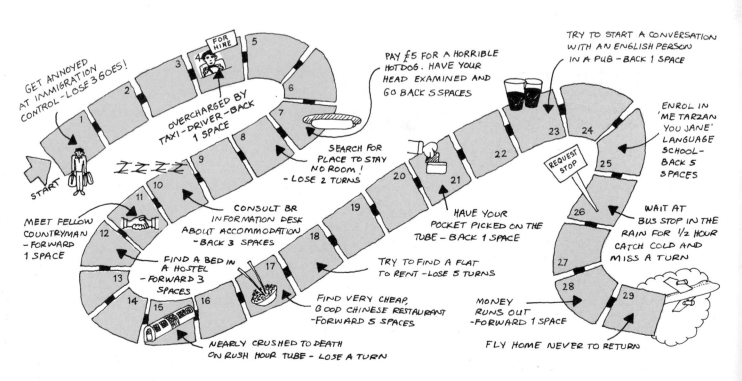

E Vocabulary

Neutral and strong adjectives

1 Study the following language items from D Reading 2, and discuss the questions below them. Check your answers on Study page 158.

Adverbs	Adjectives
quite	reputable
very	useful
downright	atrocious

a Which adverb is strongest and which weakest?
b Which adjective is strongest?
c Which of the following adverbs could replace which of the adverbs in the first column with little change of meaning?
absolutely   fairly   extremely   utterly
d Fill in the table, using the adjectives beneath it.

surprising	amazing
	atrocious
	indispensable
angry	
	ridiculous
hungry	starving

silly   useful   bad   furious

e What is the difference between the adjectives on the left and those on the right?
f Which adjectives follow adverbs like *downright*? Which follow *very*, etc.?

2 Working in groups, fill in the table with neutral or strong adjectives. Keep the list below the table covered. When you have filled in as many words as you can, uncover the list and fit all the words into the table.

Neutral Used with *very, extremely/ quite*, etc.	**Strong** Used with *absolutely*, etc.
good	
bad	
hot (*weather*)	
cold	
big	
	tiny, minute
	hideous
annoying	
hard to believe	

	fascinating,
	enthralling
interested	
tired	
	moronic
	essential, crucial
pretty (*girl*)	
pretty (*view*)	
	brilliant
	disgusting, revolting
	deplorable
	delighted
strange, unusual	
	delicious
funny	
scared	

tremendous   incredible   regrettable
fascinated   huge   small   terrible   icy   ugly
infuriating   fantastic   awful   pleased
marvellous   exhausted   gorgeous   terrified
hilarious   petrified   tasty   enormous
scorching   unpleasant   interesting   freezing
important   breathtaking   remarkable   clever
stupid   amusing

Note: *beautiful* could go in either column.

3 Listen to the pronunciation of the strong adjectives in the following dialogues, and mark the stressed syllables. Pronunciation can also intensify.

Dialogue 1
Is it important?
It's absolutely essential.

Dialogue 2
Has it been hot, then?
It's been absolutely scorching.

Dialogue 3
Silly, isn't it?
Absolutely ridiculous.

Repeat each dialogue after the cassette.

4 Improvise similar dialogues, using the word columns. Use emphatic stress and intonation like that in the model dialogues.

Expressions using 'have'

The following sentence is from D Reading 2.
If he arrives after 9pm, then **he's just had it**.
The expression in bold is an idiomatic expression,
which in this case means *He has no chance.*
It is also used when it seems certain that something
bad is going to happen.
Example:
Oh, no, we've had it, look at those storm clouds!
The expression can also mean that something is old
and worn out.
Example:
These shoes have had it, I'm going to throw them away.
It is always in the present perfect simple tense.
There are many more, equally useful expressions
using *have*.

5 Have (a) (*noun*)
All the following nouns may be used with *have* to
speak of activities. Working with a partner, put as
many as you can into groups according to
meaning. Use your dictionaries if necessary.
*a listen a heart a dance a meeting a holiday
a go a nice day a good time
a discussion a drink breakfast a cigarette
a break an affair a bath dinner an argument
a shower a taste a look a wash a party
a swim a smell a fight a game a chat
a relationship a conversion a haircut
an operation a word a nap*

6 Which expression(s) might be connected with
each of the following situations?
a Two angry men in a bar.
b Somebody is being cold and unfeeling.
c A child is showing her new toy to a friend.
d Someone is very tired.
e Someone is using stereo headphones.
f Interrupting someone's conversation.
g Saying goodbye to someone.
h A divorce.

7 There are other expressions using *have* and an
abstract noun (usually with *no*), which speak of
feelings and attitudes in a rather formal way. They
are usually followed by a verb. Replace the
following utterances with such expressions.

Example:
I'm not sorry I moved to London.
I have no regrets about moving to London.
a I don't intend to wait any longer.
b It's hard for her to express herself clearly.
c I can't remember signing this form.
d I don't mind if you go.
e I don't want to be rude.
f He isn't at all interested in the rest of his family.

8 Idiomatic Expressions using 'have'
There are a number of idiomatic expressions,
including phrasal verbs, which make use of the
word '*have*'. Read the following expressions in
context, and discuss their meanings in groups. For
the moment, cover the list of definitions at the
bottom of the page.
a You can't go on like this, suspecting the worst and
not knowing. I think you should *have it out with*
her, and find out what the situation really is.
b You've been rude to me twice in public lately, and
I'm telling you now, *I won't have it*, do you
understand?
c All right, all right, *have it your own way*, Napoleon
invaded Russia in 1815. I'm tired of arguing with
you!
d You'd better renew the road tax on your car, it's out
of date. You can *be had up* for that, you know.
e You paid how much for this bike?! Well, I'm sorry
to have to say this, but I reckon *you've been had!*
f The world has always been divided into two groups
of people: *the haves*, and *the have-nots*.
g We must *have you over* some time. How about this
weekend, why don't you come over for drinks on
Saturday?
h He said what? That can't be true, he must have
been *having you on.*

9 Match the definitions below to the expressions
above.
i   the rich and the poor
ii   to openly discuss a secret worry with somebody
iii to say something untrue to someone (if they
     believe it they'll look silly)
iv   believe what you want, even if it's silly
v   to get into trouble with the law
vi   to tolerate something
vii to be cheated or tricked
viii to have someone in your house for dinner, etc.

F Writing

Guided work: listing and adding; recommending; explaining purpose

Discussion

● The letter in D Reading 2 was very critical of London language schools, but it didn't mention all the good ones. What do you think a good British language school should offer its students? For the moment, cover the essay below.

1 Read the following essay and do the exercise which follows it.

What makes a good language school?

Every year, thousands of young people come to Great Britain to learn English. They come from a range of backgrounds, and have varying expectations of what their stay in the country will be like. Two things they all have a right to expect, however, are that their stay in Great Britain will be reasonably enjoyable, and that they will return to their countries speaking English a lot better than when they left them. How can a language school ensure that these expectations are not disappointed?

Clearly, the first objective is that what students do in the classroom should improve their English. First of all, the teachers should be capable and qualified. That is to say, they should know what the students need to learn, and be able to help them learn it. On top of that, the school should provide students with efficient material to work with. Lastly, a school ought to try to keep up with technological developments in language learning, in order to be able to offer these facilities to students.

The second question is school facilities. Apart from good-sized classrooms, the school must offer a comfortable place for students to meet and talk between lessons. Furthermore, it is convenient for students if the school provides meals, coffee and so on. Some schools even contain a bar for socialising among students and staff.

The final way in which schools can help students is by making sure that they enjoy themselves outside schooltime. The most important question here is accommodation, and a responsible school will not only find students somewhere to stay, but also take care that accommodation continues to meet high standards. In addition, it is part of a school's responsibilities to inform students about places to go in the town, so that students don't sit

at home all the time. Last but not least, in one or two very good schools there is a welfare officer, whose job is to look after the well-being of students, and to give advice when needed.

Few schools meet all these requirements, and one cannot expect the cheaper ones to do so. However, any school that meets most of them is doing a pretty good job.

The recommendations in the text in paragraphs 2, 3 and 4 are represented in the flow diagram. Fill in the boxes with short notes. Some have been done for you.

2 The textual organisation which is shown in the diagram by boxes and lines is achieved in the essay by sensible paragraphing and by the use of connecting expressions. Re-read the text, marking words or expressions which have the following functions.
a List or add items:
by connecting paragraphs;
by connecting sentences;
by connecting information within one sentence.
b Explain purpose (why something is done).
c Make recommendations
directly or indirectly.
Check your findings on Study page 158.

3 The following ideas were left out of the text.
a The school should be well-heated in winter.
b Materials should be suitable for the level of the students.
c Examples of equipment are language laboratories, video, computers.
d The school should arrange parties, excursions, entertainments.
e Students should be graded into groups of similar language ability.
f Classrooms should be attractive and well-lit.
Expand the items as you like (thinking particularly of purpose). Say where you would fit each into the text and the connecting expression you would use.

4 Write a similar essay entitled: 'What makes a good language teacher?'.
a Before you start decide which of the following points you would like to include, and add any others. Note that some points may automatically exclude others.
preferred teaching method (e.g. a lot of pairwork or the teacher being the centre of the lesson; close control of language used by students or encouragement of a lot of free use by students).
profound understanding of the language
patient person
entertaining person

strictness about students' punctuality, homework, etc.

friendly, 'human', easy-going person

handsome or pretty person

smart, neat appearance

dynamic person

extremely high intelligence

willingness to meet students socially

punctual, well-organized person, marks homework on time, etc.

quiet person, letting students dominate lessons

native English speaker

able to use modern equipment

highly-trained for teaching

university degree

b Decide how many paragraphs to use, and what is to be in each.

Please be reasonable! You are asked to describe a good teacher, not the perfect one!

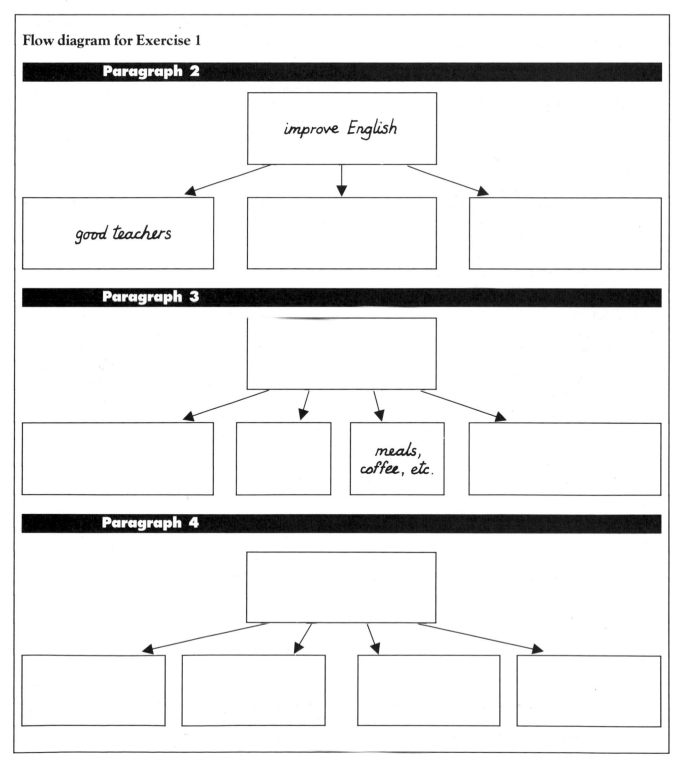

Flow diagram for Exercise 1

Paragraph 2

improve English

good teachers

Paragraph 3

meals, coffee, etc.

Paragraph 4

G Grammar

Used to do; be (get) used to doing; present simple with frequency adverbs

These structures are employed to talk about habits and customs. This section deals with the differences in meaning between them.

1 Imagine you are studying English in Britain, living with a British family, or a new teacher from Britain in your own country.

a Write five sentences about yourself, using the structures in focus.

b Read each other's sentences. Are they all correct?

2 Discuss the differences in meaning between the structures.
Check your ideas on Study page 159.

3 Read what an imaginary Brazilian student has to say about living in England. Some of the italicised pieces of language are used incorrectly. Correct them or replace them with a suitable structure.

'Do you like staying with an English family, Antonio? (**a**) *Have you got used to* our habits?'

'Well, some things are OK. I don't mind the food as much as some students do, for example; in Brazil my family has a cook who can't even boil an egg, so (**b**) *I'm used to eating* horrible dinners. Breakfast is awful, though. In Brazil, people (**c**) *are used to having* coffee in the mornings, and (**d**) *I don't get used to drinking* tea or instant coffee with my breakfast. Driving can sometimes be a problem, too, since you English drive on the left. (**e**) *I'm used to drive* on the right, of course, because that's the way (**f**) *I would drive* in Brazil, and I've nearly had an accident a couple of times. Also, people in Brazil (**g**) *use to drive* more aggressively than here, and (**h**) *I'm not used to having* to behave myself on the road. Generally, though, I think (**i**) *I'm finally getting used to* English ways.'

'What do you do at weekends?'

'(**j**) *I use to play* football on Saturday mornings, and then in the afternoon (**k**) *I usually go* for a walk if the weather's nice, or if it's raining I stay in and do my housework or listen to music. On Saturday evenings (**l**) *I'm used to going out* to see a film or a play with my English girlfriend. On Sundays (**m**) *I used to stay* in bed until late and then (**n**) *I use to*

pick up my girlfriend and drive down to visit her parents to have Sunday lunch with them. After that (**o**) *we're usually watching* TV for a while before driving back to London. I drop my girlfriend off, and then (**p**) *I generally do* my homework on Sunday evening, unless I go to the pub for a pint or two of English beer, which I'm trying hard (**q**) *get used to*. I must say my weekends were quite different in Brazil. There, (**r**) *I used to spend* most of my time at the beach during the summer, and in winter (**s**) *I was used to going* to my family's house in the hills for weekends. In fact my whole life (**t**) *would be* completely different, to tell you the truth.'

4 The implied meaning of sentences like *I'm used to working nights* varies according to which word carries the main sentence stress.
Examples:
i *I'm 'used to working nights.*
Here, the word *used* is stressed.
ii *I'm used to working 'nights.*
Here the word *nights* is stressed.

a Listen, and match the two sentences you hear to the sentences above.
Repeat each sentence after the tape.

b Match the sentences above to the following situations.
A I've got a new job, working nights. I've worked nights so often before that it's no problem.
B In my new job I start work at 6 a.m. It's difficult because I've always worked nights before.

5 Listen. You will hear ten sentences. Repeat each, and discuss the situation in which it might be said.

6 Working in pairs, write two short dialogues between a foreign student and her/his host 'mother', or yourself and a new British teacher at a school in your country.
One dialogue should concern something new and strange, the other something which is not strange. Practise your dialogues, paying attention to pronunciation, until you can perform them naturally. Perform your dialogues for another pair. Listen to their dialogues. Is the language being used correctly? Use your teacher as a consultant.

A Reading 1

Discussion

- At what age do young people in your country usually leave home? Are they tending to leave home earlier than before, or stay at home longer?
- What factors are important in deciding to leave home?
- What are the advantages and disadvantages for parents of young people staying at home?

Reading exercises

1 Read the first two paragraphs of the article opposite. What is 'post-adolescence'?

2 Scan the article. Put the people below into the following categories.

a experts
b mothers
c post-adolescents

Alain Audirac   Sophie Boissonnat
Ulf Clausen   Christianne Collange
Christine de Solliers
Natasha Chassagne
Alexis de Solliers

3 Read the article carefully, noting down the following points.

a the reasons for post-adolescence
b the reasons why it will probably continue
c the bad things about it

4 Find words or phrases with these meanings.

a absolute
b tendency
c found everywhere
d have been influential
e arrogantly unconcealed
f under constant attack
g assume
h too well-looked after
i to end (*transitive*)
j to end (*intransitive*)

5 Using your notes from Exercise 3, summarise the reasons for post-adolescence, and its probable continuation. Use about ten sentences.

The stay-at-

There was an old woman who lived in ... She had so many children she didn't kr...

At 25, Alfred Hennemann seems to have it made. A law student at the University of Bonn, he lives in a spacious four-room apartment in his parents' home. He comes and goes as he wishes and as a rule cooks for himself. But when he's 'not in the mood to cook', he has a place waiting at the family table. As for the laundry, Alfred sorts his dirty clothes into piles and leaves them by the washing machine. His mother does the rest. Says Alfred: 'She doesn't mind - yet.'

Alfred Hennemann is one of the hundreds of thousands of Europeans over the age of 20 who still live in their parents' home. Some do so out of sheer necessity, when they have lost a job or are unable to find one. Some seek the perpetuation of a warm and supportive parent–child relationship. Some find it is just easier and cheaper to stay in the nest. Whatever their reasons, increasing numbers of young Europeans, especially well-educated, middle-class young adults, are simply not leaving home. The pattern is beginning to worry some parents — and sociologists as well. 'Post-adolescence' has emerged as a term to describe the phenomenon, which is now rampant in France, Spain, Italy, West Germany and Sweden.

The current trend is an abrupt reversal of the pattern of the 1970s. At that time, says Alain Audirac of the French national demographic institute, 'One census after another showed young people leaving home earlier and earlier. Recently, though, it's been just the opposite.' In France, half the population between the ages of 18 and 25 still live 'at home'; for those who have not married, the figure is three out of four. Italian studies in three cities (Padua, Bari and Matera) indicate that just over 30 percent of the 25 to 34 age group live with their parents. Statistics for West Germany are less

home kids

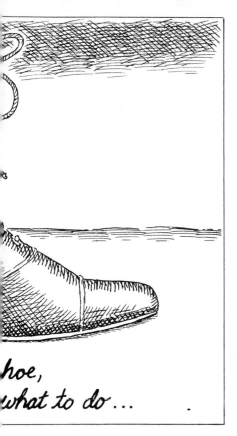

*hoe,
what to do...*

dramatic, but as Ulf Clausen, a German psychologist, points out: 'There are 450,000 youngsters between 20 and 25 in this country who are jobless. They are forced to stay at home.'

While the economic crisis and widespread youth unemployment of the last 10 years have undoubtedly played a part in keeping post-teenagers at home, the principal motivations have been sociological and psychological. Franco Ferrarotti, professor of sociology at Rome University, believes it is parents, rather than their children, who have changed. 'Once, parents were seen as oppressors,' Ferrarotti argues. 'But today, parental authority has softened. Before 1968, leaving home represented winning freedom. Now, a generation of permissive parents has made it easy for the generation of ex-rebels to return to the fold.'

Sociologists and post-adolescents agree that shifting parental attitudes toward sex have revolutionized the living-at-home scene. Christine de Solliers, a 45 year-old divorcee in the Paris suburb of Evry, does everything possible to tempt her son Alexis, 21, back to the family homestead. Every Tuesday, Alexis and his girlfriend, Maud, also 21, come for dinner and spend the night — together. 'The sexual revolution has changed everything in 20 years,' says Christi-anne Collange, author of a best-selling book, 'I Your Mother,' on the changing relations between parents and grown children. Evelyne Sullerot, a French demographer says that the stay-at-homes are 'undergoing a semi-initiation into a socio–sexual state. It is, in fact, a second adolescence.'

Loneliness, too, is tending to push parents and their post-teen children closer together. Sophie Boissonnat, a 20 year-old Paris student, tried living in a well-equipped studio apartment, but she quickly found that she missed the lively atmosphere at home and the company of her younger twin brothers. She has now moved back. She remarks philosophically: 'I wanted to be independent, but I find it's better being independent at home.' De Solliers, the mother of three children, admits that she 'never imagined the day when the children would all be gone.' She is now considering buying a small house in an effort to tempt them back.

Some parents, though, have begun to rebel at what they see as flagrant exploitation by their own children. Collange, whose book has made her a kind of spokesperson for beleaguered parents, complains that 'children aren't even *embarrassed* at being completely dependent. They use the house like a hotel, with all services. They treat parents as moneybags and then ignore them or just plain insult them.' Natasha Chassagne, a French working mother with a 21-year old daughter and a 22 year-old son at home, says: 'They take it for granted that the fridge will always be well stocked and the closet full of clean clothes. To get them to do anything around the house, you have to yell bloody murder.' A group of parents in Bremen, West Germany, has formed a self-help and counselling group called 'Toughlove,' where they trade stories about their pampered post-teen children.

Professional observers see some even deeper dangers in the emerging situation. 'Today,' says Ferrarotti, 'we have grown men with the behaviour patterns of teenagers. They are failing to mature, losing their masculinity, turning into what the French call *vieux jeunes hommes*, old young men.' Benoît Prot, who edits a magazine for French students, says today's youngsters are 'suffering from too much security and are becoming soft. One day, we may yearn back to the old fighting spirit of the 1968 rebels. At least they knew how to tell the world to go to hell.'

The trend toward later and later separation between European parents and children looks like it will last for some time to come. Youth unemployment on the Continent exceeds 15 per cent in every country and is not expected to fall for a number of years. More and more European young people go to universities and take more and more advanced degrees. Official student housing ranges from nonexistent to inadequate. European boys and girls marry three or four years later than they did a generation ago — if they marry at all. Those who do marry, or break off a less formal relationship, often head for 'home' when the relationship breaks up.

Much as parents may complain about the overgrown louts hanging about their houses, many of them actually relish the situation. Mothers, especially divorcees and widows, want their kids at home for company. Working mothers, ridden with guilt that they may have neglected their children in infancy, go on trying to atone for it when the 'children' are in their 20s. On the kids' side, as well, the attractions of protracted adolescence are unlikely to diminish soon. 'Nowadays,' writes Collange, 'they don't have to move out to make love. They have no problems of bed and board, no taxes and no bills and no serious points of difference with Mom and Dad.' What post-adolescent in his right mind could turn down that kind of deal?

Sullivan, Dissly, Seward and Bompard
Newsweek

B Grammar

Conditional sentences

Review

1 Note down the four main types of conditional sentence in English, and the differences in meaning between them. Check your ideas on Study page 160.

2 Working in pairs, write three short dialogues, using a variety of conditional sentences. Practise until you can perform them naturally. Perform your dialogues for another pair. Listen to theirs. Is the language being used correctly?

3 In groups of four, write five open-ended questions. Use various conditional sentences.
Examples:
What will John do if he doesn't get the job?
What would you do if you were the leader of your country?
Write each sentence on a piece of card. Pass your questions to another group. Give short answers on separate pieces of card to the questions you get.
Examples:
He'll keep looking for another one, I suppose.
I would make every Friday a national holiday.
Return your cards to your teacher, who will mix up all the cards from all the groups and give you ten. Exchange cards with other groups so that you have five question/answer pairs.

Mixed conditional sentences

We can use sentences which are a mixture of the second and third types for the following purposes.
When imagining how a different (unreal) past would affect the present state of affairs.
Example: *If **I hadn't missed** that plane, **I'd be** dead now.*
When supporting a statement about the present by mentioning a past fact.
Example: *Of course I love you, darling. If **I didn't love** you, **I wouldn't have married** you, would I?*

4 Produce mixed conditional sentences from the following prompts.
a But I don't know the answer! That's why I asked you!
b We're in this mess now because you didn't warn me in time.
c You spent hours choosing a tie to wear, so we're standing here in the cold, waiting for the next bus.
d You're so insensitive; you didn't notice he was upset.
e You weren't invited because you're always so rude to people.

f You didn't listen to my advice, so now you're in prison.
g You've got no sense. For example, you didn't take that job last year.
h I'm not a rich man now because I didn't buy those shares when they were cheap.

Wish

Wish has two uses. The first is to express regret, either for a present state of affairs or for a past action or state of affairs.
Examples:
I wish I had some money (present)
I wish I'd gone to university. (past)
There is a strong connection between these *wish* sentences and conditional sentences. This can be shown by following the examples with amplifying sentences.
*I wish I **had** some money. If I **had** some money I could go to the cinema.* (In fact, I don't have any money).
*I wish **I'd gone** to university. If **I'd gone** to university, I could have got a good job.* (In fact I **didn't go** to university.)
Note that these sentences accept the situation, and do not express any desire or intention.

The second use of *wish* is to express a desire that something should happen, or irritation with a present situation.
Examples:
I wish you would come. Please change your mind!
I wish you wouldn't do that, it really annoys me.
Wish . . . would is similar in meaning to an imperative, and can only be used in the sort of situation in which an imperative would be possible. We cannot say. *Be thinner!*, and we cannot say, *I wish you would be thinner.* However, we can say, *Go on a diet*, and so we can say, *I wish you would go on a diet.*
Similarly, it would not make sense to say, *I wish I would go on a diet.* If I want myself to go on a diet, there's nothing to stop me! If I can't do it, then I should say, *I wish I could go on a diet.*

5 Make sentences with *wish*, based on the following prompts.
a I can't understand this.
b For Heaven's sake, shut up!
c I'm sorry I came to this party.
d It really annoys me that you smoke in the bedroom.
e It's raining, and I want to go out.
f I have to work, but I'd prefer not to.
g I regret having said that.
h I'm not on a tropical beach now, which is a pity.
i I can't help you, sorry!
j This inflation is terrible, and the Government does nothing about it!

C Listening

Counselling

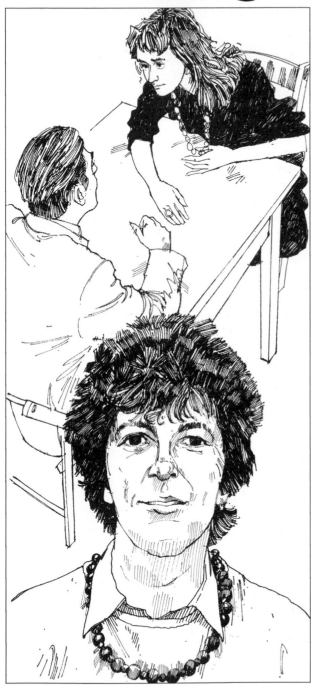

Discussion

● Note down any causes you can think of for the increasing number of broken marriages nowadays.

● Should marriages always be saved from breaking up? Why/Why not?

● Marriage Guidance Counsellors offer help to people whose marriages are in trouble. Is it a job that would interest you? Why/Why not?

● What form do you think the help might take?

Listening exercises

1 Eileen Miller works as a Marriage Guidance Counsellor for an organisation called Relate. Listen, take notes and answer the following questions as fully as possible.

a What type of person is suitable for the job?

b Why does Eileen say a counsellor is not 'someone with a stick of glue'?

c What is the basic problem most clients have?

d What is the first task Eileen mentions? Why would she set this task to a couple?

e What was the second task? Why did she set it to the couple she mentions?

f What does she mean by a 'contract'?

g What will she normally talk about in the first few sessions?

h What might cause her to depart from the contract? Explain her reference to tissues.

i Why does Eileen find that the word 'counsellor' is not a very good name?

j Why does she mention the postcard she received?

2 Listen again, filling in the following with prepositional expressions. Each line represents a word.

a Quite often it _____ _____ that in fact they stay together.

b The underlying problem which my clients often have _____ _____ is a lack of communication.

c Could you _____ _____ that a bit — the tasks?

d I _____ _____ a first session, which I suppose is essentially an assessment.

e And then we will _____ _____ from there to deal with the problems that seem to be around.

f Quite often the contract has to _____ _____ _____ _____ _____ .

g You have to deal with what I would call the 'here and now' problems which _____ _____ .

h We _____ _____ a lot of tissues.

i And that actually for me _____ _____ successful counselling.

3 Match these meanings to the expressions above.

i happens, in the end

ii progress (to another stage, step)

iii shared

iv use up, consume

v be abandoned (a plan, idea, policy, etc.)

vi say more about

vii occur unexpectedly (usually problems, situations, etc.)

viii expressed the essential point about

ix organise, arrange (meetings, etc.)

D | Reading 2

Discussion

● 'The drug problem' is big news these days, but what is it? Is there only one, in fact?

● Why do you think people take drugs?

● What can be the dangers of using drugs?

● If you were a parent who found one of your children was taking drugs, what would you do?

● What should governments do about the drug problem(s)?

Reading exercises

The three extracts are from a government booklet concerning drug use among young people.

1 Extract 1 has been jumbled. Put the fragments back in the right order. Fragment **h** is the first, and fragment **b** is the last. Check your answer against the complete extract on Study page 160.

2 At seven places in Extract 2, parts of sentences have been removed. What was written in each gap? Check your answers against the complete extract on Study page 161.

3 Extract 3 concerns the dangers of drugs. Which of them did you think of before? Which seem to you the most important?

DRUGS—
WHAT YOU CAN DO AS A PARENT

Extract 1

THE DRUG PROBLEM

a Often it's a time when we don't get on with our parents.

b Because the most important people when it comes to coping with the drug problem may not be the police, doctors or social workers.
They could be parents ... like YOU.

c Cigarettes and alcohol are, of course, the most common ones.
But many of us also turn to sleeping tablets, tranquillisers or anti-depressants to help relax and cope with the stress and tension of everyday life.

d There are also many pressures at school, from parents, and from friends.
It is a period of change when many choices must be made.

e Fortunately, most children say 'No'.

f Most children grow out of it. Or simply decide they don't like it and then stop. But a few go on to have a serious drug problem.
That's why we all need to tread carefully when talking to a child we suspect may be taking drugs.
A wrong word at the wrong time can sometimes make a child even more rebellious.

g All of which means that when someone, perhaps a friend, offers a child something which is supposedly 'fun' and 'everyone else' is taking it, the pressures and curiosity are so great they may try it themselves.

h Just because someone takes a drug it does not mean they will become addicted to it.
At times in our life, almost all of us turn to drugs of one sort or another.

i In many ways children turn to their drugs for just the same reasons.
Adolescence, as we all know, can be a difficult period.

j And at a time when work can be a major problem, there is also frustration and boredom.

k Unfortunately, though, a disturbing number are saying 'yes'.

l But the right words of understanding can reinforce their decision not to take drugs.
This booklet hopes to help you find those right words, and to make you better informed.

Government officials burning seized heroin *Aspect Picture Library*

Extract 2

HOW PARENTS CAN HELP

It is natural for parents to feel hurt and angry when they discover that their child is taking drugs.

The problem is that these reactions won't solve anything.

So here we'd like to (1) _____ _____ _____.

Mike, for example, told his parents how a friend had been caught smoking cannabis at school and how he'd been offered a joint once or twice.

Understandably worried, Mike's parents (2) _____ _____ _____.

As a result the school took action — (3) _____ _____ _____.

Helen, like many teenage girls, had become depressed after breaking with a boyfriend. So she started taking her mother's tranquillisers, which she knew her mother had taken on prescription for a short time following her grandma's death.

Discovering this, perhaps not surprisingly her mother and father reacted angrily. But this (4) _____ _____ _____.

So, shortly afterwards, when a friend offered her heroin, (5) _____ _____ _____.

On reflection Helen's parents realised that (6) _____ _____ _____.

The lesson of many similar stories from children of all kinds of background is that (7) _____ _____ _____.

Extract 3

WHAT CAN BE THE DANGERS OF DRUGS

The main dangers are as follows:
● Having an accident while under their influence.
● Some drugs may depress or stop breathing.
● Accidental overdoses can lead to unconsciousness or even death.
● Addiction or dependence, after regular use.

In addition to these dangers, drugs can also have nasty side effects.

They can also bring on confusion and frightening hallucinations.

They can cause unbalanced emotions or more serious mental disorders.

First-time heroin users are sometimes violently sick.

Regular users may become constipated and girls can miss their periods.

Later still, there may be more serious mental and physical deterioration.

And if a drug user starts to inject, infections leading to sores, abscesses, jaundice, blood poisoning and even AIDS virus infection may follow.

Department of Health and Social Security (Crown copyright)

E Vocabulary

Phrasal verbs 1

These expressions have appeared in the reading texts in this unit.

*They don't have to **move out**.*

We don't always ***get on with*** our parents.

Many of us also ***turn to*** sleeping tablets.

*Those who **break off** a less formal relationship.*

Such constructions, comprising a root verb and one or two particles (adverbial or prepositional) differ in important ways.

Firstly, the meaning of some is clear from the parts (e.g. *move out*), while the meaning of others is not clear, existing only when the parts are together (e.g. *get on with*).

Secondly, they behave differently, and can be classified accordingly.

Type 1   Transitive, inseparable

The object comes after the particle (e.g. *turn to, get on with*).

Type 2   Transitive, separable

The object can go before or after the particle.

A pronoun goes in the middle (e.g. *break it off*)

A long object (e.g. *a less formal relationship*) goes after the particle.

An object that is neither a pronoun nor very long can go in either position.

Type 3   Intransitive

Intransitive verbs have no object (e.g. *move out*).

Type 4   Separable three-part verbs

With a few three-part verbs the direct object goes in the middle (e.g. *Talk someone out of doing something*).

1 Note down all the phrasal verbs you know which could be connected in any way with children and their parents.

2 Working in groups, try to fill the spaces in the texts below with phrasal verbs, in the correct tense or form. Each line represents a word. A few words are given. For the moment, cover the list at the end of the exercise.

Bringing up a child is a tricky business. There are books on it, which (1) _____ _____ certain approaches, considered to be correct, while (2) _____ _____ others, considered to be incorrect; most parents tend to ignore books, however, and just (3) _____ it _____ for themselves as they go along.

When a child falls ill, her parents look after her until she has (4) _____ _____ the illness. If the illness is quite long, her studies may suffer, and she may (5) _____ _____ the rest of her class at school. In this case, or if a child is not (6) _____ _____ very well for some other reason, parents who are concerned that she should be successful at school will help with her work, so that she can (7) _____ _____ _____ her classmates. This concern can be destructive, however, when the child is desperate to (8) _____ _____ _____ her parents' expectations, and becomes terrified of (9) _____ them _____ .

In poor countries, when there isn't enough food to (10) _____ round, parents may have to (11) _____ _____ food, so that their children can eat.

Very often children (12) _____ _____ one of their parents, inheriting a similar personality, but even so they may find it difficult to (13) _____ on _____ them, especially in adolescence. Some children go through a phase of (14) _____ _____ , and (15) _____ for the day when they can leave home for good, and not have to come back.

'Johnny! Eat that up! What do you mean, you've (16) _____ _____ fish! When you (17) _____ _____ you can eat what you like. Till then you'll eat what you're given!'

'Fred, don't you think you're being a bit hard on him? You seem to be (18) _____ him _____ all the time lately!'

'What do you mean? I'm being firm, that's all. He's too fussy, and disobedient, too, and I won't (19) _____ for it. If a child does something wrong he has to be told, and punished if necessary. If you keep (20) _____ him _____ and being soft on him, he'll think he can (21) _____ away _____ anything.

3 The missing verbs are listed below. Use them to fill more gaps.

run away   get on with someone
stand for something   put something forward
getting on   let someone off   get over something
(not enough to) go round   grow up
frown on something   catch up with someone
live up to something   tell someone off
long for something   go without something
let someone down   work something out
fall behind someone   take after someone
get away with something   go off something

Now turn to Study page 161, where the verbs are matched with their meanings, and fill any remaining gaps.

4 Working in pairs, write a short dialogue containing six of the phrasal verbs you have been using. Practise your dialogue, then perform it for another pair. Listen to the other pair's dialogue. Are the phrasal verbs being used correctly? Use your teacher as a consultant.

F | Speaking

*Focus on function: informal criticism;
critical exclamations; criticising;
accepting criticism; making excuses;
apologising; promising; accepting or
rejecting apologies*

1 Listening comprehension

Listen to two dialogues, and answer the following
questions.
a What has John done to make his mother angry?
b What excuse does he give?
c What else does he do to make her angry?
d Does he make her angry very often?
e What is the difference between the way John's
   mother speaks to him and the way his father does?

2 Pronunciation

Listen to the eight utterances below, and mark the
syllables which carry the main stress.
a Oh no, I don't believe it!
b I wish you wouldn't leave your mess lying
   everywhere.
c Why couldn't you have put some newspaper down!
d I'm terribly sorry, Mum. Shall I try and clean it
   up?
e Oh Mum, have you pressed my suit yet?
f It was a bit thoughtless of you, you must admit.
g You really should be more careful.
h I'm sorry to have to say this, but you're becoming a
   very difficult person to live with.
   Repeat each utterance, trying to match the
   pronunciation on the tape.

3 Reproduction

Using the flow diagram to help you, act out the
dialogues with a partner, using the original
language where possible, but improvising when
necessary.

4 Improvisation

In pairs, improvise dialogues for the following
situations. Before you begin each dialogue,
consider your role carefully, and think about what
you are going to say. Also consider whether the
criticism is going to be calm or angry. You may
modify or add to each situation as you like.
Naturally, it is hoped that you will use some of the
language you have been studying, but it is equally
important that your dialogues should be as natural
and spontaneous as possible.

a A daughter has made some soup and left the
   kitchen in a mess. During the ensuing row, she
   asks if her mother has mended a hole in her blouse.
b A son has borrowed his father's car and damaged it
   very slightly, without telling him. His father
   discovers the damage.
c A son stays out late every night and makes a lot of
   noise when he comes home. Tonight is worse than
   usual (how?), leading to a huge row.
d A daughter's room is always in a mess, and her
   mother is always having to tidy it up (she is
   fanatical about tidiness). This annoys the
   daughter, who can never find anything she wants
   after her room has been tidied. They have a row.
   Later her father talks to her about this.
e A son hangs around the house all day, getting in
   the way and making a mess, rather than going out
   and getting a job. There is a row, during which he
   asks if he can borrow some money.
f A daughter is in work, and spends a lot of time out
   of the house. She spends a fortune on clothes,
   etc., but contributes nothing to bills, and hardly
   ever helps around the house.
g A daughter is going out every night with a new
   boyfriend, and neglecting her university studies.
   She is very defensive, because she thinks her
   parents don't like him because he is out of work and
   a punk. Her mother tries to reason with her.

Flow diagrams for Exercise 3

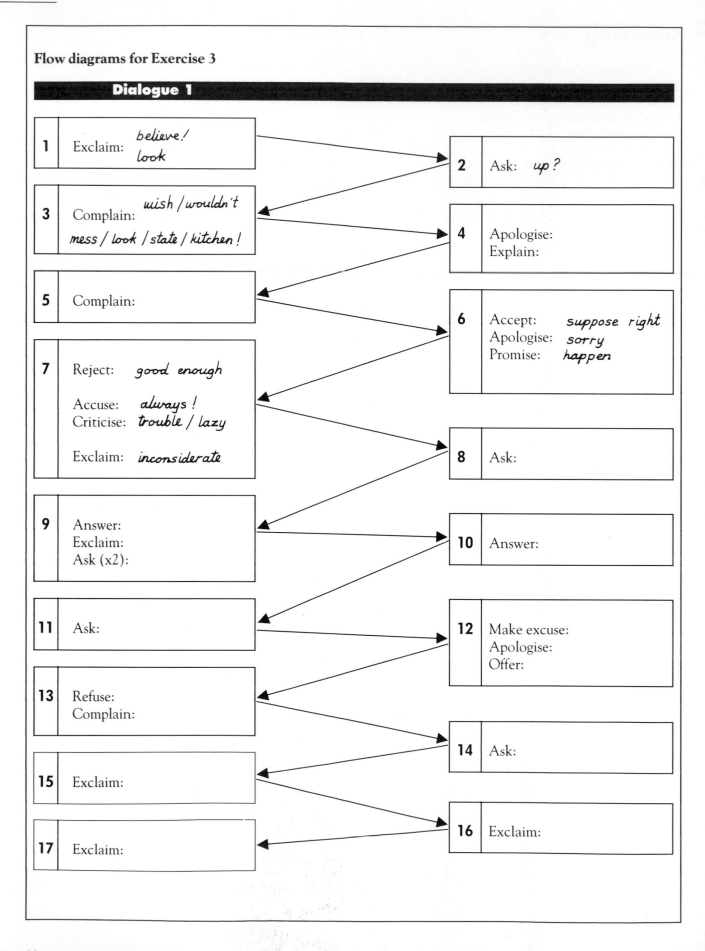

Dialogue 1

1 Exclaim: *believe!* *look*

2 Ask: *up?*

3 Complain: *wish / wouldn't* *mess / look / state / kitchen !*

4 Apologise: Explain:

5 Complain:

6 Accept: *suppose right* Apologise: *sorry* Promise: *happen*

7 Reject: *good enough* Accuse: *always !* Criticise: *trouble / lazy* Exclaim: *inconsiderate*

8 Ask:

9 Answer: Exclaim: Ask (x2):

10 Answer:

11 Ask:

12 Make excuse: Apologise: Offer:

13 Refuse: Complain:

14 Ask:

15 Exclaim:

16 Exclaim:

17 Exclaim:

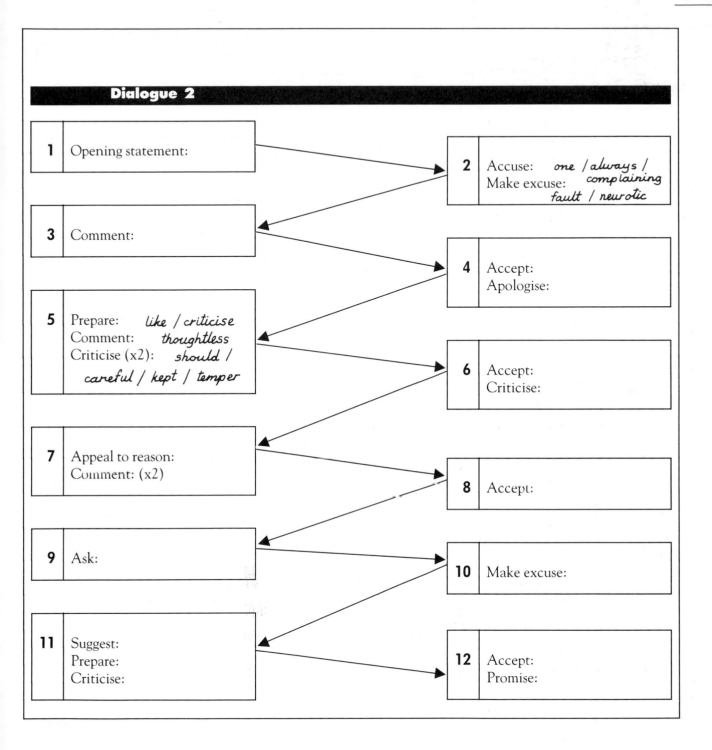

Dialogue 2

1 Opening statement:

2 Accuse: *one / always /*
Make excuse: *complaining*
fault / neurotic

3 Comment:

4 Accept:
Apologise:

5 Prepare: *like / criticise*
Comment: *thoughtless*
Criticise (x2): *should /*
careful / kept / temper

6 Accept:
Criticise:

7 Appeal to reason:
Comment: (x2)

8 Accept:

9 Ask:

10 Make excuse:

11 Suggest:
Prepare:
Criticise:

12 Accept:
Promise:

G Writing

Guided work: supporting a statement through amplification: exemplification; rephrasing

1 Read the language description on Study page 162, then do the exercises below.

2 Read the following essay, finding instances of exemplification and rephrasing. Mark each one you find with an E or an R, accordingly.

Does Nanny know best?

It is very difficult for a working couple to spend as much time as they should with their children. Take the case of a couple who work in the centre of London and live in the suburbs. Both will probably have to leave the house around 8 a.m. and will be lucky to get home before 6 p.m. Since school hours run from 9 a.m. to about 3.30 p.m., such a couple has no option but to pay for someone to look after their children, such as a childminder — that is to say someone who looks after the children whenever their parents cannot do so — or even a full-time nanny. Such services do not come cheap. A nanny, for example, will have to be paid a salary comparable to that of a receptionist or a typist, or even more. In other words, one of the partners in the marriage might well be working for practically nothing.

Of course this is not true all over the world. In such countries as Brazil or Malaysia — in other words countries which have a great many unemployed or underpaid workers — nannies can be employed for practically nothing. This can also have its disadvantages, of course, because these nannies are not always as reliable or capable as their famous English counterparts. Employing such people can also be extremely dangerous. A case in point was the Brazilian nanny who was overheard explaining the best way to keep her 6-month-old charge quiet for most of the day. Her method was to impregnate a cloth with gas from the cooker, then hold it over the mouth and nose of the baby. Another example was that of a nanny who took an exceptionally attractive baby out into the streets during the hottest part of the day and begged at traffic lights, using the child to arouse the pity of drivers.

But such stories are always a possibility if one employs people from shanty towns for minimal wages. To put it another way, when all is said and done, 'You get what you pay for'.

3 Below are three sentences which amplify statements in the text. Which statement does each amplify?

a There simply isn't enough time in the day to work, keep the household running efficiently, and also perform even the basic duties of a parent, such as taking the children to school and picking them up afterwards.

b They are usually from extremely poor homes, and simply do not know enough about anything to be of much use in a crisis.

c One cannot really be surprised at this sort of irresponsibility from people who have been brought up in the brutalising atmosphere of Third World slums.

4 Reproduce an essay from the following framework. You may use your own words, as long as the meaning of the original is preserved. Before you start, study the essay for a minute or two, but try not to refer to it as you do the exercise.

Paragraph 1
_____ very difficult _____ couple _____ time _____ children. There _____ time _____ work, _____ household _____, _____ also _____ duties such as _____ school _____ afterwards. *Take the case of* _____: 8 a.m. and _____ 6 p.m. Since _____, such a couple _____ look after _____, *such as* _____ — *that is to say* _____ — or even _____. Such services _____. A nanny, *for example*, _____ salary _____. *In other words* _____ partners _____ practically nothing.

Paragraph 2
_____ not true _____ world. In *such* countries *as* _____ — *in other words* _____ — nannies can be _____ nothing. This _____ disadvantages, because _____ not reliable or capable _____. They _____ poor homes _____ use in a crisis. _____ also dangerous. *A case in point* was _____ keep _____ quiet _____ cloth _____ gas _____ face. *Another example* was _____ attractive baby _____ streets _____ hottest _____ begged _____ pity _____ drivers.

Paragraph 3
But such stories _____ possibility _____ shanty town _____ minimal wages. One _____ surprised _____ irresponsibility _____ brought up _____ slums. *To put it another way* _____.

5 Write the following essay, using about 250 words:
'To use violence to punish a child is always wrong.' Discuss.
Before you begin, discuss your ideas with other students, and plan what you are going to write.

"IT'S SO PRACTICAL DARLING."

WHEN I'M NOT LYING ON CARS I'M A BRAIN SURGEON

FIAT
SETTING NEW STANDARDS

A Reading 1

Discussion

- Write a definition of the word 'prejudice'. Look the word up in a dictionary and compare the definition with yours.
- Which groups of people most often suffer from prejudice?
- Many men believe that women don't drive as well as men. How does this belief affect men's behaviour on the road? Do you know of any incidents?

Reading exercises

1 You are going to read a newspaper article entitled 'There's a man on my bumper'. Cover the article, and the three letters that follow. Look at the diagram which illustrates part of the article. In groups describe what happened in the diagram and what you think happened afterwards.

2 The sentences below are from the article, but they are in jumbled order. Some, but not all, follow each other consecutively in the article. Keeping the article covered, read the sentences carefully, asking your teacher about any vocabulary you don't understand, then try to put them in the right order. When you have finished, read the article and check your ordering. Do not read the letters yet.

a It was travelling quite slowly, between 35 and 40 m.p.h.

b The minibus increased speed also, so that we were travelling neck and neck at about 65 m.p.h.

c The minibus driver chased me to the centre of Otley, driving three feet away from my bumper.

d About fifteen minutes from Otley a white minibus pulled out in front of me.

e I was driving towards Otley in West Yorks after visiting a friend in a village near Wetherby.

f He grabbed me by the neck and tried to pull me out of the car.

g The driver of the minibus made no attempt to slow down and my only choice was to cut in front of him.

h A car appeared from the opposite direction.

i Then I think I must have screamed and sobbed a lot until I was found by a lady who telephoned the police.

j I pulled out and accelerated.

k As soon as the lights changed to green he ran back to his minibus, got in and drove off.

l Suddenly my car door was opened and there stood a small man in a flat cap — the minibus driver.

m When we came to a wide and clear stretch of road, I thought I would overtake.

3 Discuss the following questions.

a In what ways did the driver of the minibus behave badly?

b Did the writer do anything wrong herself?

c The three letters appeared in the same newspaper the following week. Two were written by men and one by a woman. What do you think they say?

4 Read the letters, and answer the following questions.

a What do all the letters say that the writer of the article should have done?

b Which letter agrees in principle with the article?

c Which letter is sarcastic?

d Both John Bailey's letter and Clare Hendley's letter say that, badly as the minibus driver behaved, the writer behaved badly too. Underline the part in each letter which says this. What is the difference in style between the two extracts?

There's a man on my bumper

SOMETHING unexpectedly nasty happened to me one Sunday evening recently. I was driving towards Otley in West Yorks after visiting a friend in a village near Wetherby. The weather had been bad, which was lucky because in good weather the roads around Otley can become clogged and slow with caravans and trippers who have grabbed a day out on the moors. This evening the roads were quite clear.

About 15 minutes from Otley a white minibus pulled out in front of me. There were a few children inside it. I followed the minibus for about 10 minutes. It was travelling quite slowly, between 35 and 40 mph. When we came to a wide and clear stretch of road, I thought I would overtake. I pulled out and accelerated. The minibus accelerated too. I put my foot right down. The minibus increased speed also, so that we were travelling neck and neck at about 65 mph. A car appeared from the opposite direction.

Letters to the Editor

Why be like a rogue male?

I HAVE seldom read a more frightening article than Philippa Lowthorpe's (First Person, September 23). I have stopped driving myself, being over 70. When I did drive, though a male, I always maintained that women were better drivers than men because, for the most part, they used their cars as a means of transport, not as a way to prove toughness and superiority. Ms Lowthorpe makes me wonder if this is still true.

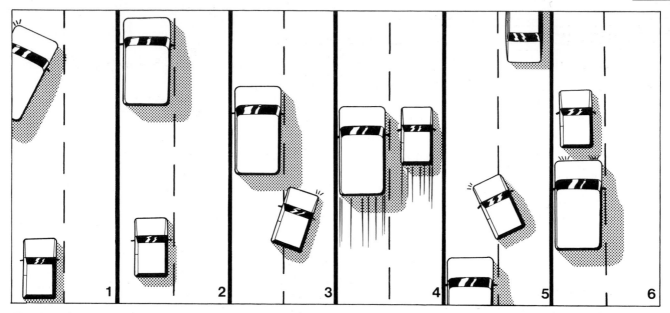

The driver of the minibus made no attempt to slow down and my only choice was to cut in front of him.

This has happened to me several times on the motorway, which I use a lot because of my job. Man in fast car is overtaken by me, a woman, in a small Fiat Panda. Man's pride is put out of joint and he's on for a race. Man number two (usually in a Ford Sierra) steams up behind flashing headlights wildly. I grip the wheel in terror, forced to drive at a shaky 95 mph to escape them both.

This, however, was not the end of the story. The minibus driver chased me to the centre of Otley, driving three feet away from my bumper. I was not only irritated by his behaviour, I was frightened.

We stopped at some traffic lights. Suddenly my car door was opened and there stood a small man in a flat cap – the minibus driver. He grabbed me by the neck and tried to pull me out of the car. When he could not get me out, he slapped me round the face three or four times, sending my glasses flying. He shouted abuse, pushing his face into mine.

As soon as the lights changed to green he ran back to his minibus, got in and drove off. I still do not know how I had the presence of mind to scribble down his number. Then I think I must have screamed and sobbed a lot until I was found by a lady who telephoned the police.

I have always experienced the worst chauvinism from behind the wheel of a car.

I have seen the meekest of males metamorphose into aggressive and bullying individuals who shout abuse out of their windows and make vulgar gestures in their mirrors. As for motorways, they are the showground for male machismo and I, in my little car, am the red rag for the bull.

But, resorting to physical violence? I now drive with all the doors locked so that no one else would be able to invade my space to let off steam.

Philippa Lowthorpe *The Guardian*

Why did she see a white minibus in front of her as a challenge? Why was it so necessary to overtake that she risked a nasty smash-up that would have involved children, rather than abandon her right to pass a commercial vehicle? Why should the bus driver slow down to let her pass and why did she not slow down and tuck herself in behind? Why, in short, does she find it necessary to drive like a stupid insensitive man, and why can she now not see that, deplorable as his behaviour was, her own was not impeccable?

Competitive driving like this, regardless of sex, will always produce irritation if not anger, and only too often leads to accidents. I hope that I am right and that most women still leave this sort of behaviour to men; and will rather lose face and stay alive, than prove their equality by risking their own, and far worse, other people's lives.
John Bailey, London

PHILIPPA Lowthorpe did have an alternative as the minibus she was trying to pass, accelerated. She could have braked and fallen back in line behind the minibus quickly. Granted, the driver of the minibus was acting childishly; all the more reason for someone to act like an adult.
Clare Hendley, London NW3

'CONFESSIONS of a road hog – nearly had a man on the bumper' should have been the heading for this story.

Frightened me to death reading it: 'Neck and neck at 65 mph. A car appeared in front ... only thing I could do was to cut in front of him.' ... Why not brake and pull behind?

Ninety-five mph in a Fiat Panda, phew. Somebody ought to lock her car doors before she gets in and throw the keys away.

Is she really serious or have I been taken for a ride?
R Hudson, Carlton, Yorkshire

B Grammar

Story-telling structures

Past tense review

Past tenses in a story show the relationship in time between situations, actions and events.

1 The following sentences are about Reading 1.
i   The weather had been bad.
ii She was driving towards Otley.
iii She had been visiting a friend in a village.
iv A minibus pulled out in front of her.
v   It was travelling quite slowly.
vi She pulled out and accelerated.
vii They were travelling neck and neck at about 65 m.p.h.
viii A car appeared from the opposite direction.
Discuss the following questions. Check your answers on Study page 163.
a Which sentences describe **events** in the story?
b Which sentences describe the **situations** in which the events happened?
c What are the differences between i, ii and iii?
d What are the names of the tenses exemplified here?

2 Put the verbs in italics into the correct past tenses.
It was a warm summer night, but a light rain (**a**) *fall*. I (**b**) *walk* home alone, in a good mood because I (**c**) *be* at a party. Suddenly I (**d**) *hear* a strange noise and (**e**) *look* up at the sky. There I (**f**) *be* astonished to see a large saucer-shaped object, hanging above the rooftops. No, it (**g**) *not hang*, it (**h**) *come* down to land!! I couldn't believe it. I (**i**) *drink*, it was true, but I (**j**) *not drink* that much. The spaceship (**k**) *land* and a door (**l**) *open*, but nothing (**m**) *come* out. I (**n**) *stay* motionless, unable to believe what (**o**) *happen*. Then, abruptly, I (**p**) *realise* that the door (**q**) *not open* to let something out, but to let someone in. And that someone (**r**) *be* me! They (**s**) *want* me! Maybe they (**t**) *watch* me all the time I (**u**) *walk* along the street! At this horrible thought I (**v**) *be* so terrified that I (**w**) *wake* up. I (**x**) *lie* in my bed at home, and it all (**y**) *be* a dream.

Ability in the past

To speak of ability in the present we use *can* or *can't*, or *cannot* (more formal).

3 Speaking of ability in the past is not so simple.

Study these sentences, most of which are about the first text in A Reading 1.
i   The man *could have driven* more quickly at first, then she wouldn't have had to overtake.
ii   Later, he *could have slowed down* to let her overtake.
iii She *could see* a car coming from the opposite direction.
iv   Finally, she *was able to overtake*.
v   She *couldn't get away* from the man.
vi   He *was able to open* her door because it wasn't locked.
vii He *couldn't get* her out, but he *was able to slap* her round the face.
viii I *could drive* when I was fifteen.
ix   The first cars that were invented *could* only *go* very slowly.
Discuss the following questions. Check your answers on Study page 163.
a Which of the above sentences refer to ability in a sequence of events and which refer to ability in a more general past period?
b In which sentences was something not done, although it was possible?
c In which sentences was something possible, and also done?
d Which form(s) could be replaced by *managed to*? What effect would this have on meaning?
e Sentence iii refers to ability at a particular time, but *see* is preceded by *could*, not *was able to*. What other verbs would be used with *could* in the same way?

4 Which of these sentences are correct and which incorrect? Put the incorrect ones right. Each may contain more than one error.
a I wasn't able to understand what he was talking about.
b Finally I was able to get the injured man into the car.
c I went to the theatre in my lunch hour and could buy four tickets before they sold out.
d She could smell something burning, and ran to the kitchen to find the frying pan in flames. However, she didn't panic, and was able to put the fire out without too much difficulty.
e Hello, John, is that you? Thank God I could have got in touch with you!
f If I'd known about this, I was able to save myself all this trouble!

C Listening

With God on our side

Discussion

● Note down anything you know about the 'troubles' in Northern Ireland. In what way are they connected with prejudice?

● You are going to hear Yvonne, who is from Northern Ireland, talking about the problems and prejudice there. What do you think she will say about the following?

a schools
b names
c prejudices or foolish ideas
d a wedding
e the true nature of the problem in Northern Ireland

Listening exercises

1 Before you listen, make sure you know what the following mean.
discrimination   segregation   bigoted
council housing

2 Listen, taking notes on anything important that is said about the points above.

3 Listen again, and answer the following questions.

a Why did Yvonne never witness 'anything really shocking'?

b What is Yvonne's religion in terms of firstly, personal inclination and secondly, background?
c Explain the joke about being Jewish.
d Where did most people who colonised Northern Ireland come from?
e 'It's all their fault.' Whose fault? Whose opinion is this?
f Did Yvonne's parents refuse to go to her sister's wedding because of their own prejudices or because of social pressures on them?
g Comment on the name of Yvonne's brother-in-law.
h How has moving to London improved things for Yvonne's sister?
i According to Yvonne who suffer more from prejudice, the Protestants or the Catholics?
j In which areas of life does Yvonne mention discrimination?
k With whom does Yvonne seem to sympathise more?

4 Listen again, filling the gaps in the following. Each line represents a word or abbreviation.
a . . . you just ____ ____ ____ ____ affected by it.
b . . . well I obviously met people, but I didn't ____ ____ ____ any Catholics till I went to university.
c . . . the schools are ____ ____ ____ , I think, practically totally segregated.
d . . . if you ____ ____ there, ____ ____ ____ ____ to say you're not a Protestant?
e . . . if you've got an Irish surname, ____ ____ ____ that you're Catholic.
f . . . you can ____ a Catholic, their eyes are too close together.
g . . . if ____ ____ all on a desert island, ____ ____ ____ ____ to the wedding?
h . . . how have you ____ ____ not being bigoted?
i . . . they're not ____ political.
j . . . I didn't want to know about it at all, I ____ ____ ____ get away each summer.
k . . . the Protestants are ____ ____ ____ in Northern Ireland.

5 Match the meanings to six words or expressions above.
i was very anxious/keen to
ii identify, recognise
iii can't avoid being
iv generally
v it's probable
vi particularly, especially

D | Reading 2

Discussion

- Are there religious or ethnic minority groups in your country? How are they treated?
- Do you know of any racist incidents, or evidence of racial prejudice, in Great Britain or in your country?
- You are going to read an article concerning the police, racism and trouble in restaurants. In what ways could customers in restaurants behave badly? How might racism be involved in the story?

Reading exercises

1 Read the article, making notes on these points.

a The sorts of problems Chinese restaurants have with customers.

b Evidence of the racism of the police and legal authorities.

c The actions of the local community regarding the latest incident.

2 The information needed to answer the following questions is in the text, but is not stated explicitly. You have to infer the answer.

a Why have Chinese restaurants

What do you do when you're a Chinese waiter attacked by a customer? You don't call the police. Jacquie Hughes tells the extraordinary tale of the Diamond Four.

Mr Cheung has worked as a waiter in London's Chinatown for over 20 years. With his white shirt sleeves rolled up, the multicolour bruises and deep gash on his left arm glare out. So do the cut on his forehead and the bruises around his thumb.

2 On duty last Saturday night at the Wong Kei restaurant in Wardour Street, Mr Cheung heard a row in the basement. A customer had gone down and tried to get behind the counter to get himself a glass of water and became aggressive. 'Then he threw a punch at the cleaner and I jumped between them to push him off. He punched me in the face and sent me flying into a row of teapots filled with hot tea ... I was burnt—and shocked. He picked me up by my waistband and hurled me over the counter onto the table.' When the

police came, they announced that as both parties had suffered hurt they wouldn't take any action, and suggested the two swop addresses if they wanted to take civil action.

3 At the Lido restaurant in Gerrard Street the previous Saturday, a party of 17 customers spent a rowdy three hours over a meal before throwing leftover bones and rice around the place, and refused to leave. The waiters called the police but the group hung around outside causing a scene, while one of them sneaked into the basement toilet and nicked the ballcock out of the cistern, sending water flooding over stored bags of rice and other dried food. 'But things like this happen every week,' said the Lido's Fu Yung Lam.

4 A waiter for 17 years, Fu Yung Lam tells a stream of stories of customers running out without paying their bills, of the police being called and, in stock response, suggesting the restaurant take the customer's name and pursue civil action for payment. His bar is framed with dozens and dozens of unpaid bills with customers names and addresses scrawled on the back. 'It is a joke. The cost of taking such action would be more than the bill.'

5 Mr Cheung and Mr Lam's experiences are far from unique, but the traditionally reserved workforce of Soho's Chinese eating houses is not usually given to shouting about itself. Now, shocked by a recent court case which saw four Chinese waiters who

were involved in a fight with a group of customers, sentenced to two years imprisonment for affray, the community is coming forward and speaking out.

6 In July Southwark crown court found the waiters—Peter Lee, Chung Fat Li, Frankie Lam and Kin Sun Chu—guilty of attacking members of a party from Essex who came into the Diamond late one Saturday night at the end of June.

7 Prosecution argued that the party had been sober and well behaved, but refused a number of dishes and drinks, and so decided to leave. When they asked for the bill, counsel said, they were violently set upon by the waiters.

8 But the waiters and their defence counsel told a different story. The group had been drunk and provocative, they said, used racially abusive language and drummed the table with bottles and dishes. When they were refused drink because it was after licensing hours, they attempted to leave without paying the bill.

9 When Mr Li tried to stop them, they launched into attack. Mr Li was kicked and punched and held down on the floor, other waiters came to his aid and a fight broke out. One of the waiters used a broken chair leg and one of the customers suffered a cut to the forehead.

10 Mr Chu called the police, who immediately took statements from the white customers only, before taking them to hospital. The four waiters

always had such trouble with customers?

b In the third and fourth incidents, did the customers leave without paying?

c In the fourth incident, why was the money knocked onto the floor?

d In the fourth incident, why did the customers leave without further trouble?

3 Find words or expressions which mean:

a exchange (para. 2)

b noisy, excited, aggressive (para. 3)

c went secretly (para. 3)

d stole (*colloquial*) (para. 3)

e written untidily (para. 4)

f the crime of fighting in public (para. 5)

g lawyer (para. 10)

h making life difficult for someone (para. 13)

i doesn't trust any more (para. 13)

4 Summarise the ways in which the police and legal authorities seem to have behaved in a racist way in the story of the Diamond Four. Use six sentences or so.

were taken straight to Bow Street police station, denied access to an interpreter or solicitor, and offered no medical attention until they had been charged.

11 When their families came to the station to see them the next day, they were told that would only delay the process. The police questioning of the four, recorded in their own accounts, constantly refers to the 'Europeans' and the 'Chinese', and has pre-conceived notions of who was guilty: *'Tell us which other Chinese were involved in the fighting …' 'were there just waiters or other Chinese in the fight?'* … When the four asked that their injuries be included in their statements—they were refused.

12 None of the men had any previous police record, and never before had such an incident led to such heavy custodial sentencing. The case raised serious questions about the partiality, and racism, of the police, and a campaign—the Diamond Four defence campaign—was launched with a set of basic demands, including an inquiry into the police's procedure.

13 'For years we have been saying that the police's complacent attitude to dealing with incidents of harassment and assault leaves a lot to be desired,' said Jabez Lam from the campaign. 'The Chinese community has lost faith in the police, experience has forced us to rely on our resources to protect ourselves and our workplaces. The Diamond restaurant incident merely

reflects everyday occurrences in our community. If one of the customers had not been injured, and had managed to get away without paying, then we would only have had to endure the usual situation—coping with the damage without any recourse in law.'

14 The Diamond Four campaign is supported by MPs and nine community centres around London. Every week it sets up a stall in Soho to collect funds and signatures for a petition. It's published a guide to legal rights, and made links with police monitoring groups around the capital. More importantly, it has started gathering information on other experiences of racism against the Chinese, with depressing results: people are coming forward with the same stories; expectations of trouble are regularly fulfilled, the police's response the same.

15 One waiter with 11 years' experience in Soho, said: 'Many times the police say, "this is a small matter—don't call us". What are we supposed to do? No waiter wants to start a fight, we open for business not fights. How can we earn a living here if customers know they can just raise a fist and walk out?"

16 One worker from the Wong Kei told another tale. A group of customers decided to pay their bill in coins, stacking them in towers on the table. When they got up to leave, one knocked the piles over, sending the money flying. When a waiter tried to stop them leaving until it had been counted, a woman in the group hit him over the

head. The waiter—who had his hands full of dishes—pushed back. She produced police ID, and said she was going to charge him with assault. Another customer objected, and offered to be witness for the waiter. He was told to shut up, it was none of his business. When he announced he was a journalist, the group apologised and left.

Jacquie Hughes   *City Limits*

Glossary
para. 3 *cistern*, the water tank of a w.c.,
para. 3 *ballcock*, a device which prevents the w.c. from overflowing;
para. 9 *charged*, formally accused by the police;
para. 11 *custodial sentencing*, punishment by sending to prison (*very technical language*);
para. 11 *partiality*, prejudice in favour of one side in a dispute;
para. 15 *ID*, identification documents/card.

E | Writing

Time expressions in story writing

In B Grammar we saw how tenses relate actions and events to one another. Time expressions are also important.

1 Study this list of expressions.

at last   after that   just then   first
at that point   in the end   at the end   finally
in next to no time   shortly afterwards
last of all   straight away   meanwhile
lastly   at the beginning   at first
after a while   at that moment

Which expressions talk about the following?

a The point in time when something happened/was happening.

b How long something took to happen.

c The order in which things happened.
Check your answers on Study page 164.

2 Complete the sentences.

a I waited for hours, but she still didn't come, so _____ I just went home.

b 'Certainly,' said the waiter, and in next to no time _____ .

c 'The killer is . . .' said Holmes, and paused dramatically. At that point _____ .

d Georgina's mouth was dry with excitement. At last, _____ .

e He went out, slamming the door, and _____ , I heard the sound of his car driving away.

f 'Surely nothing else can go wrong,' groaned Alistair desperately. Just then _____ .

g How do you write a good composition? Well, first, you _____ . _____ , you can get on with writing the composition itself. Last of all, you should _____ , before you give it to your teacher.

h One of the thieves held everyone in the bank at gunpoint. Meanwhile, the other one _____ .

i _____ of the lesson, the teacher checked that everyone was in the classroom.

j I don't mind driving in heavy traffic now that I've been driving for a while, but _____ , I was terrified.

k There's a chemist's _____ of the road.

l We sat down at our table, and _____ he began complaining. _____ , the table was too close to the door, so we had to move. _____ , he found a fork that was a little bit dirty, so the waiter had to change it. Next, it was the background music, which he said was too loud. It was so embarrassing! _____ , I had more sympathy for the waiters than for him!

Concession; balancing pros and cons; introducing unexpected facts

3 Continue the following sentence fragments.

a *It is true that* fewer people today are openly racist . . .

b *While* one can understand concern about the spread of AIDS, . . .

c *Although* she was the best applicant for the job . . .

d *Despite* statistics showing men cause more accidents than women . . .

e *Of course* there are differences between people from different cultures . . .

f It *might* be prejudiced to say that women are bad drivers . . .

All the items in italics have a similar effect on the way in which the fragments can be continued. They signal that the next fact (e.g. 'she was the best applicant', 'there are differences between people from different cultures') will be followed by something that contrasts with it in some way. Expressions like these are used for two main purposes.

Balancing one point against another
In weighing the pros and cons of something in one sentence, the following expressions can be used.
Example: a flat

It **might**   be small,
It's true that it's small, } **but** *the rent's quite low.*
Of course   it's small,
Although   it's small,   *the rent's quite low.*

We admit the first fact, but the second is more important. The facts are not contradictory. (It is not surprising that a small flat is cheap.) They are opposed only because one is considered good, and the other bad.
If there is too much information for one sentence, the second sentence (containing the more important fact), can be introduced by *on the other hand* or *however*.

Adding unexpected or contradictory facts
When a fact or idea is followed in the same sentence by something unexpected or contradictory, the following expressions can be used.
Example: complaints

Although   *we complained, nothing was done.*

Despite
In spite of } *our complaints, nothing was done*
Notwithstanding

Although precedes clauses (containing a finite verb).
Despite, In spite of, Notwithstanding precede nouns, noun clauses beginning with *what*, and gerunds.

The most formal is *Notwithstanding.*
When two sentences are used, the second can
begin with *Nevertheless, Yet, Even so, However, In
spite of this, Despite this.*

4 Study the following sentences.
Motorbikes **might** *be cheap,* **but** *they're very
dangerous.* (One sentence.)
*Motorbikes are pretty cheap, all things considered. To
start with, they don't cost that much to buy. On top of
that, they use very little fuel, and parts and
maintenance also tend to be reasonable.* **On the other
hand**, *they are a very dangerous way of getting about.*
(More than one sentence.)
Write single sentences weighing the pros and cons
of:
a pets;
b gardens;
c travelling by air.

5 Expand one of your sentences into two or more
sentences, as in the example.

6 Study the following sentences.
Despite *today's wet weather, thousands of holidaymakers flocked to the coast.* (One sentence.)
*The weather was horrible that morning, overcast and
chilly, with a strong wind.* **Nevertheless**, *we decided
to go to the beach as we had planned.* (More than one
sentence.)
Write single sentences, each containing one of the
following fragments plus some unexpected
information.
a . . . I'd never met him before . . . .
b . . . her unfriendly manner . . . .
c . . . an intensive advertising campaign . . . .
d . . . many people have grave doubts about nuclear
power . . . .
e . . . what I'd been told . . . .
f . . . the brochure claimed that the hotel was first-
rate . . . .

7 Expand three of your sentences into two or more
sentences, as in the example.

8 In the following sentences and short paragraphs,
connecting words and expressions which you have
studied in Units 1, 2 and 3 are printed in *italics.*
Some of the items are used correctly and some
incorrectly.

Working in pairs, correct those which are wrong.
a He's rich, *furthermore* he's famous, *however* he isn't
happy.
b *In spite of* his pronunciation problems, he makes
himself understood very well. *Nevertheless,* his
charm and his communicative nature help him to
get on with people even when his English lets him
down.
c They leave their children with a childminder *in
order to* both of them can work.
d *Despite* workers *for example* nurses and teachers do
very important jobs, *nevertheless* they are very
poorly paid in Britain.
e When the drug problem is mentioned, people
usually think of illegal drugs *such as* 'crack' and
heroin. *Furthermore,* the real drug problems in
many Western countries often concern substances
which is is quite legal to use. *For example,* many
thousands of British people are chronically
addicted to drugs which are prescribed by their
doctors.
f In his letter, Steve Elsworth complains that tourists
arriving late at night in London have difficulty in
finding a bed for the night. *Moreover,* he
continues, visitors who want to stay longer find it
impossible to secure cheap long-term
accommodation. I agree that London is far from
perfect, and do not usually find myself defending
it. *Indeed,* I think Mr Elsworth is being
unreasonably critical. *Of course* it's hard to find a
hotel room late at night in London, *nevertheless*
what busy city doesn't have this problem? *Indeed,*
in some European capitals the problem is even
worse. *However,* what the sensible traveller does,
rather than complain when it's too late, is reserve
accommodation in advance, *such as* these problems
won't happen. *Furthermore, it's true* that rents are
also high in London, *but* this is a problem *not only*
for visitors *but also* for Londoners. *On the other
hand,* it might be argued that the presence of so
many visitors in London itself has the effect of
forcing rents up! (*Take* areas like Earl's Court and
South Kensington, *for example*). *Of course* we
should all do everything we can *in order to* make
London more attractive to tourists, *in other words*
what is needed first is a more careful look at the
problems.

F Speaking

Focus on function: formal complaints; formal requests; exclamations; demands; excuses; apologies; promises; thanks; responses to thanks

1 Listening comprehension

🔲 Listen to the dialogue and answer the following questions.

a What is the problem?
b What is the excuse?
c Describe the manner of the reception clerk.
d Describe the manner of the manager.
e What does the guest suspect?

2 Pronunciation

🔲 Listen to the eight utterances below and mark the stressed syllables.

a Are you telling me my air conditioner won't be repaired until tomorrow?
b This is ridiculous!
c I'm very sorry but there's nothing I can do.
d I'll see what I can do, but I'm not promising anything.
e What can I do for you?
f I'm sure that isn't so, Madam.
g The matter will be dealt with immediately.

h Well that's what he said, more or less. Repeat each utterance, trying to match the pronunciation on the cassette.

3 Reproduction

Using the flow diagram to help you, act out the dialogues, using the original language where possible and improvising when necessary.

4 Improvisation

Improvise a similar dialogue, following the instructions given. Student A should read on. Students B and C should turn to Study page 165.

Student A

You are a businesswoman. You've left your car at a garage to be repaired, and have had a hard day without it because you need it for work. You don't want to be without it for another day. In your job you often run up against sexist attitudes, which make you very angry. You go to the garage to pick up your car, which you were assured would be ready by the end of the afternoon. You are in a hurry. You drive a silver grey Saab, registration number F123 ABC.

a The customer speaks to the receptionist.
b The customer returns to the receptionist, but nothing has been done.
c The customer speaks to the manager.

Flow diagram for Exercise 3

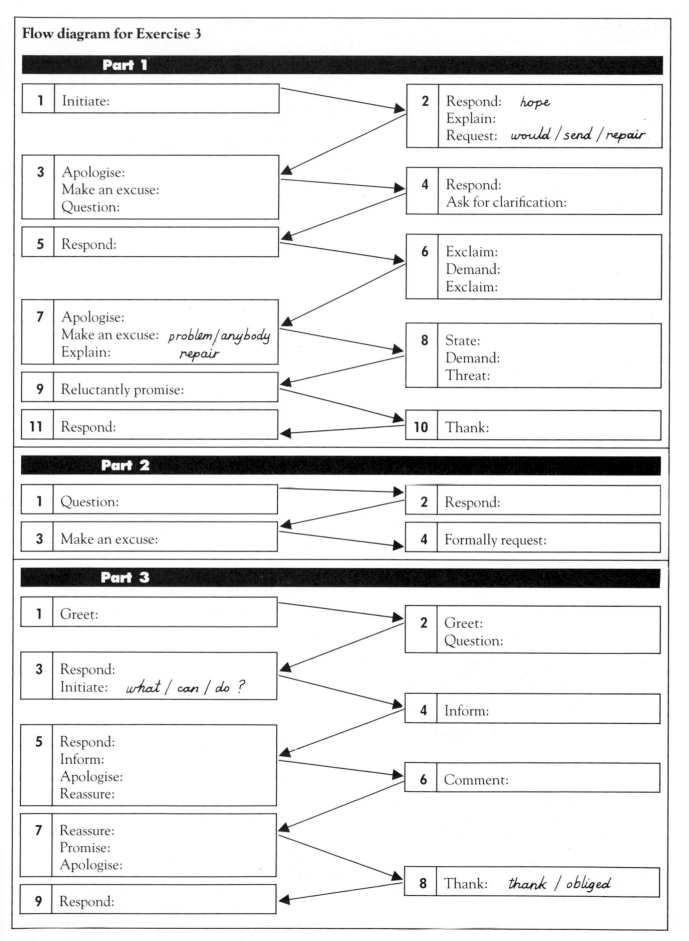

Part 1

1	Initiate:

2	Respond: *hope*
	Explain:
	Request: *would / send / repair*

3	Apologise:
	Make an excuse:
	Question:

4	Respond:
	Ask for clarification:

5	Respond:

6	Exclaim:
	Demand:
	Exclaim:

7	Apologise:
	Make an excuse: *problem / anybody*
	Explain: *repair*

8	State:
	Demand:
	Threat:

9	Reluctantly promise:

11	Respond:

10	Thank:

Part 2

1	Question:

2	Respond:

3	Make an excuse:

4	Formally request:

Part 3

1	Greet:

2	Greet:
	Question:

3	Respond:
	Initiate: *what / can / do ?*

4	Inform:

5	Respond:
	Inform:
	Apologise:
	Reassure:

6	Comment:

7	Reassure:
	Promise:
	Apologise:

8	Thank: *thank / obliged*

9	Respond:

G Vocabulary

Compound Verbs

Compound verbs combine an adverbial particle (often *over* or *out*) with a verb. The particle acts as a prefix, and the root verb carries the stress. There is an example in A Reading 1: 'I thought I would *overtake*'.

The prefixes usually have predictable meanings.

Over

i *Over* is often added to a verb to mean *too much*, with the verb retaining its original meaning, (e.g. *overeat* = eat too much).

ii Many other verbs beginning with *over* share the idea of *defeating* or *dominating*. The root verb usually loses its original meaning, (e.g. *overtake*).

Out

Out adds the meaning of *better*, *longer*, etc. (e.g. *outlive* someone = live longer than someone).

Under

i *Under* usually means *too little*, when added to a verb, i.e. the opposite of *over*, (e.g. *underfeed* = feed too little).

ii In many other verbs, *under* retains much of its original meaning, (e.g. *undercut* someone = reduce his/her business by charging *less* than she does).

1 Using your dictionaries, choose one of the following verbs for each definition below. Give each group member a set of verbs to work on. Not all the verbs will be needed.

oversleep	overthrow	overhear
outnumber	overcrowd	overdress
overflow	overwork	overcharge
outweigh	overrate	overcome
outclass	overpower	underpay

undermine	offset
overbalance	update
overbook	outwit
overlook	overdo
oversimplify	undergo

a have too high an opinion of
b accept too many reservations
c dominate physically, by greater strength
d win against (*problems, difficulties*, etc.)
e be more important than
f lose balance, fall over
g remove from political power

h hear without intending to
i give a view over
j spread beyond the usual area
k make something seem more simple than it is
l (*sport*) defeat by being much better
m deceive/beat by being cleverer
n compensate for
o dress too well for an informal occasion
p experience something unpleasant
q make something up-to-date
r make something or someone weaker, gradually or secretly
s do more than is necessary or correct
t ask for more money than something really costs

2 Put one verb from the list in each gap.
a So many people came to the party that it _____ into the garden.
b My bedroom window _____ the river.
c People arrested by the secret police frequently _____ bad treatment and even torture.
d The thief thought he had _____ the police by using a disguise.
e But he was recognised at the airport by detectives, who _____ him and took him to the police station.
f Popular newspapers do not inform people properly because they _____ the news so that everybody can understand it.
g John _____ and fell off the ladder.
h They had to _____ enormous difficulties to reach the North Pole.
i I think his paintings are _____: I can't see why people think they are so good.
j It's best to get to the airport early in case our flight is _____ .
k Tourists are often _____ by unscrupulous traders.
l The champion completely _____ his challenger, making him look like an amateur.
m The 1789 revolution _____ the monarchy in France.
n It's not a perfect system, but the advantages _____ the disadvantages.
o Foreign security services conspired to _____ the president's position by destabilising the country.
p I didn't know it was an informal party: I felt rather _____ in my dinner jacket.
q He's the sort of player who _____ his lack of skill with 100% physical effort.
r Sorry, but I couldn't help _____; did I hear you mention the name Parkinson?
s We have to _____ our files every three months, or they get out of date.
t All right, all right, I know you're grateful, but stop kissing my shoes; don't you think you're _____ it a little?

UNIT

4 Entertainment, going out

A Reading 1

Discussion

● List in order the three things you most like doing when you go out at night 'on the town'. If you don't like going out, say why this is.

● Why do people go out at night?

● What factors are important in deciding which restaurant, discotheque etc. to go to? Say what matters to you and what matters to most people (in your opinion).

● If you have been to London, what did you do at night while you were there? What recommendations can you make?

● If you have not been to London, is there anything you would like to do or see if you did go?

Reading exercises

1 Read the extract. What do the following words and expressions mean?

a running (para. 1)
b hits (para. 1)
c curtain time (para. 1)
d theatre buffs (para. 2)
e matinee days (para. 2)
f intermissions (para. 2)
g brokers (para. 2)
h subject to availability (para. 3)
i patronises (para. 5)

2 Mark the following statements T (true) or F (false), according to what is said or implied in the extract.

a You can get seats for the most successful plays a few minutes before curtain time.
b You will never need to pay more than £16 to sit near the stage in the best theatres.

c Balcony seats are cheaper than seats at ground level.
d At the Leicester Square Ticket Booth you will be able to buy a cut-price ticket for any London theatre which has tickets available, if you buy on the day of the performance.
e At the Leicester Square Ticket Booth, a £10 ticket would be sold for £4.20.
f Students with identification can get cut-price tickets, if tickets are available, from theatres marked 'S' in ads, if they buy on the day of the performance.
g The writer recommends no rock-clubs because he can't update his information quickly enough.
h Young single people go to the Empire Ballroom in search of romance.
i The music there is live.
j There is a globe made of mirrors on a revolving stage.
k Drinks are free at the Empire Ballroom.
l The Hippodrome is the greatest disco in the world.

3 Decide these questions as a group:

a For whom is the extract intended? Note down the evidence for your answer.
b What is the purpose of the extract? Choose one or more of the following aims.
to entertain   to warn
to inform   to advertise
to complain   to recommend
to express a personal point of view
c Have you found any of the information in the extract useful? What?
d How do you think the author spends most of his time? Would you like to do what he does? Why/Why not?

Evening Entertainment

THE THEATRE: London offers playgoing in its most exciting, comfortable and inexpensive form. At least forty plays or musicals are always running and all but the top two or three hits have available seats up to five minutes of curtain time, which is 7.30 or 8 p.m. in most London theatres. The highest-priced orchestra seats (here they're called 'stalls') in the best theatres rarely cost more than £16 ($25.60), but you needn't pay more than $18 in the 'upper circle' (first balcony); and you can do it for less. 'Slip seats' (side circle) for performances at the new National Theatre on the South Bank can be had for as little as £8. My idea of a London vacation is to see a play a night. They're the city's top attraction, and they can be managed on the tightest budget.

2   In fact, if you are extreme theatre buffs, as Hope and I are, you can hustle to as many as three plays in one day in London. That's because on certain matinee days, some London theatres schedule their afternoon performances for 3 p.m., others for 5.30 or 6 p.m. On one memorable Saturday in London, we saw Alec Guinness in *Ross* at 2 p.m., Ralph Richardson in *The Complacent Lover* at 5 p.m., and Sir John Gielgud in *The Ages of Man* at 8 p.m. We did it by eating sandwiches at numerous intermissions throughout the day and evening (sandwiches and tea are sold in most London theatres), and by then taxi-ing to the next theatre in the five-or-so minutes between performances. I certainly don't recommend this tiring fanaticism, but merely set it forth, as an example of the attraction that London theatre can have ... Try to avoid buying your tickets at brokers. Since nearly all theatres have available seats, there's no need to incur the added commissions.

3   And do use the half-price ticket offerings of the **Leicester Square Theatre Ticket Booth** in a Jack-and-Judy-puppet-show-type structure in the park area of the square. They sell day-of-performance seats at all London theatres (subject to availability) for 50% off plus a 80p fee, from noon to 2 p.m. for matinees, from 2.30 to 6.30 for evening performances, Monday through Saturday. Students and senior citizens with identification can also receive large discounts by presenting themselves half an hour before performance time at the theatres which

identify themselves with a circled 'S' in their ads. That's also subject to availability, of course.

4   **A READER'S COMMENT:** 'Any bright tourist should take advantage of the British theatres — every night! You can appear 10 or 15 minutes before curtain time at any theatre of your choice and you can always find a 'single' priced at just about £9 or often less.' (Anne Fomin, Dearborn Heights, Michigan).

5   **DISCOTHEQUES AND DANCING:** London's inexpensive night life is centered in a number of rock clubs which sprout and die much too rapidly for this once-a-year book to keep up with them. They're listed, though, in a weekly magazine called *Time Out* (80p), to be picked up at any London news-stand ... For disco dancing, you ought definitely to make at least one visit to the phenomenal **Empire Ballroom** on Leicester Square (get off at the Leicester Square or Piccadilly tube station), a gigantic dance hall and legitimate pick-up spot for London's unmarried young people, with space for over 2,000 celebrants. This is one of the top tourist attractions of London: hundreds and hundreds of single men and women (on a Saturday night), flashing colored lights, a famous revolving globe of light-reflecting mirrors, continuous bands on a revolving stage. The action extends from 8 p.m. to 2 a.m., Monday through Thursday (admission is £3 before 10 p.m., £4 thereafter); on Friday and Saturday, from 8 p.m. to 3 a.m. (£5 before 10 p.m., £7 after). Sunday hours are 8 p.m. to 1.30 a.m., with an admission fee of £3.50 for the entire evening. You're under no obligation to pay a single thing more, after you've purchased your entrance. A somewhat older crowd patronizes the **Hippodrome**, corner of Charing Cross Road and Cranbourn Street (nearest tube stop is Leicester Square). The self-styled 'greatest disco in the world,' it boasts seven revolving speakers descending from the ceiling, smoke machines, lasers, a revolving stage, impressive lighting, and admission of £5 (Monday through Thursday), £9 on Friday and Saturday nights. Closed Sunday.

Arthur Frommer's *Frommer's Europe on $30 a day*, © 1988. Prentice Hall

B | Grammar

Verb patterns using the gerund and the infinitive

Review

Look at the following language items, from A Reading 1.

Try to avoid . . .

. . . avoid buying tickets . . .

We did it by eating sandwiches . . .

There's no need to incur the added commissions.

To avoid and *to incur* are the infinitive forms of the verbs. *Buying* and *eating* are gerunds.

Whether to use the gerund or the infinitive of a verb is an area of English where correct use may seem to be arbitrary and follow no rules.

However, there are certain regularities of usage, and knowing these will help you to learn to use the right form at the right time.

Firstly, where a preposition is followed by a verb, it must be by a gerund, not the infinitive. This means that phrasal verbs are also followed by a gerund.

1 Working in pairs, fill the gaps in the following sentences with a phrasal verb or an expression ending in a preposition. For the moment, cover Exercise 2.

a _____ being made redundant, he lost his house, because he couldn't pay the mortgage any more.

b Why don't you do something positive, _____ sitting here complaining?

c Why not apply for the job? All right, you probably won't get it, but _____ trying, is there?

d Oh no, there's Andy! Just _____ walking as if you hadn't seen him.

e She never _____ losing her daughter so tragically.

f _____ being popular with everyone, she still feels insecure.

g You're such a lazy slob, you're always trying to _____ doing any work around the house.

h He hasn't got a job, but he _____ cleaning windows.

i He's _____ jogging recently, in an attempt to get fit.

j _____ getting angry with me, there's nothing I can do about it!

k 'What's that letter?' 'I don't know, it's something _____ stopping a big supermarket being built in the village.'

l You're a friend of his, he'll listen to you. See if you can _____ resigning.

2 Now choose one of the following expressions for each sentence in Exercise 1. Use your dictionaries if necessary.

carry on	talk (someone) out of
there's no point in	take up
as a consequence of	instead of
get out of	there's no harm in
make a living out of	get over
to do with	in spite of

Secondly, verbs which can be followed by a gerund or the infinitive can be divided into the following groups.

1a Verbs followed by a gerund alone
Example: *Do you fancy **going** for a walk?*

1b Verbs followed by a direct object (or not), a preposition, and a gerund
Examples: *Please forgive **me for being** so rude.*
*He apologised **for being** rude.*

2a Verbs followed by the infinitive alone
Example: *I decided **to apply** for the job.*

2b Verbs followed by a direct object and the infinitive
Example: *I order **you to fire**!*

2c Verbs which can be like 2a or 2b
Examples: *You dare **to threaten** me, boy?*
*I dare **you to push** that policeman in the river.*

3 Verbs which can be followed by a gerund or the infinitive
Examples: *It began **raining** at ten.*
*It began **to rain** at ten.*

3 Choose two of the five columns, and place each verb in a group. Use your dictionaries if necessary. For verbs in group 1b, give the preposition. Check your answers on Study page 165.

enable	thank	instruct
practise	threaten	hesitate
prevent	tell	avoid
promise	entitle	persuade
delay	compel	get
encourage	involve	postpone
permit	face	afford
finish	beg	command
bear	stand	risk
empower	cause	succeed
discourage	challenge	tempt
bother	escape	congratulate
learn	tend	persist
resent	appear	arrange
imagine	blame	expect
enjoy	miss	intend
detest	volunteer	consider
hate	prefer	try
remember	forget	

advise	fail
insist	oblige
happen	stop
deny	allow
claim	praise
choose	swear
manage	admit
remind	suggest
long	hope
teach	regret
force	entail
accuse	consent
attempt	mind
refuse	invite
dissuade	pretend
agree	forbid
continue	need
help	mean

4 In each pair, how does the verb change its meaning? In e to h the change is greater.

a i Your hair *needs* cutting.
   ii You *need* to practise more.

b i The amnesia made him *forget* committing the murder.
   ii Don't *forget* to post those letters.

c i I must *remember* to send them a Christmas card.
   ii I *remember* meeting him for the first time, when I was very young.

d i I *regret* to inform you that that will not be possible.
   ii Now I *regret* throwing that old umbrella away.

e i Sorry, I know it's rude, but I can't *help* laughing.
   ii I *helped* him to repair his roof.

f i Finish by tomorrow? That will *mean* working all night!
   ii 'I *mean* to make some important changes,' said the new minister.

g i I'm *considering* leaving the country.
   ii Many critics *consider* his work to be excellent.

h i I'm *trying* to understand, but it's very complicated.
   ii Why don't you *try* advertising in a newspaper.

5 Some of the following sentences are correct and some incorrect. Put the incorrect sentences right.

a I denied to go there.
b This job will entail travelling all over the country.
c He was congratulated for winning the prize.
d I insist in seeing the manager.
e I accuse that you stole the money.
f I challenge you to prove your accusation.

g He threatened me to shoot.

h Practise doing that until you can do it perfectly.
i John avoids to meet Henry, whom he dislikes.

j I suggest you to go to a doctor.
k I expect you to do your duty.
l I can't afford going on holiday this year.
m I resent being spoken about as if I were not present.
n I promised him to do my best.
o My glasses enable that I see properly.
p My student card entitles me to travel cheaply by rail.
q I reminded him of going to the bank.
r It has stopped to rain!
s I forbid you to meet that boy again!
t John volunteered for talking to the boss about pay.

C Reading 2

Discussion

● What do you know, or think you know, about young people in the Soviet Union?
● The article opposite describes an evening in a Russian discotheque. It was taken from the American magazine *Time*. What impression do you think it will give of the discotheque?

Reading exercises

1 Read the article, making a note of anything which gives:

a a depressing impression, or one of poverty and poor quality;

b an impression of governmental repression and suspicion.

2 Answer the following questions in groups.

a Why does the writer say, 'The place is certainly exclusive'? (para. 2)

b 'Once inside, we are not so sure we want to stay.' Why? (para. 2)

c What is the writer's impression of the food?

d Why are the other people so suspicious of the writer?

e What makes censorship of the records by the authorities particularly absurd?

f Why doesn't the disc jockey talk between records?

g Why do you think nobody pays any attention to the news?

h Why do you think the article is called 'Saturday evening fever'?

3 Find words or expressions with the following meanings.

a dull, depressing, boring

b decoration, furnishings etc.

c shine (*like stars*)

d old (*polite word*)

e rude, unfriendly

f talkative

g become expert in/at

h thought long and deeply about

i flow strongly, like a river

j go towards

Scene In Moscow —

The Izmailovo complex, a group of five hotel towers built for the 1980 Olympic Games, rises like a concrete slag heap over a dreary Moscow suburb. Despite its drab appearance, however, Izmailovo has a remarkable attraction: a discotheque reputed to be the best in Moscow.

2 The place is certainly exclusive. After talking our way past a guard at the entrance to Izmailovo's 30-story Building D, we find a darkened doorway tucked into a corner on the ground floor. Over the door are the words in Russian BAR-DISKO. Just inside, three men stand around a small table. 'What do you want?' one asks menacingly. We reply, rather meekly, that we had heard this was a disco. 'You must buy a ticket,' says another, eyeing our western clothes suspiciously. The bouncer at New York's Palladium could not be more forbidding. We pay the requisite five rubles ($7.25) each, but once inside we are not so sure we want to stay. Young people seated at booths around the large room regard us with cold stares.

3 We find a seat at one of the booths and inspect the decor. Four huge black columns stand at the corners of the dance floor. Atop each column is a television set. But instead of a music video on the screens, we see the face of Soviet Leader Mikhail Gorbachev as he gives a speech. Strobe lights flash from the ceiling. At one end of the room a string of Christmas-tree lights twinkle over a curtained stage, from which a young blond-haired disc jockey occasionally emerges.

4 Along one wall is a bar, where people are lined up waiting to be served. We join them, obtaining a plate of snacks. This is not the usual disco fare. We have been issued a sort of pink Napoleon pastry, a scoop of black caviar on

a pastry puff and a glass of chocolate milk. It is all included in the price of the ticket, but five rubles still seems a lot of money for such meager comestibles. Most of the young people in the disco probably earn about 100 rubles a month ($145), so this must be a large chunk out of their paychecks.

5 Meanwhile, the tables are being cleared by a babushka, an elderly woman who is a ubiquitous figure in the Soviet Union, usually seen sweeping streets, guarding doors or watching visitors at museums. This one wears slippers, a baggy dress and dirty apron, and her hair is gathered in a bun. She walks from table to table, asking in a surly voice if she can take the dishes.

6 A voluble young Georgian, who seems to have been drinking, asks if we are speaking English and says he would like to polish his language skills. When we mention that we are American journalists, he stammers, 'This is too dangerous for me,' and leaves our table abruptly.

7 Dozens of fellow patrons are still watching us, so we stare back. Most of them are young and dressed in the latest European fashions. The clothes must have been purchased abroad by travelers and then sold at home for high prices. A nice imported sweater in the Soviet Union can cost as much as a month's salary.

8 We spot a young man whose biceps and shoulders rival those of Sylvester Stallone in *Rambo*, a film much vilified in the Soviet press. This young Rambo wears sweat pants, a headband, strips of leather on both wrists and a cutoff T-shirt that reveals his bulging muscles. We remark to him that it seems as if everyone in the disco knows everyone else. He looks around nervously to see who is watching and replies, 'Yes, it's like our club. We all know each

Saturday evening fever

other, and we get together almost every night.' Then he walks quickly away. Many people in the room seem similarly tense and self-conscious.

9   A young man who works at the disco tells us that at least four plainclothes police circulate through the hall each night, checking to see that people do not drink or 'violate the order'. He says the disco is overseen by four different government and party agencies, and every record played must be approved by each of the four. Some officials, he says, have not mastered English, the universal language of rock. 'Once we played a song that had the word *six* in it. The Ministry of Culture said the song was about sex. We had to make a special appeal before we could play it again.'

10   For much the same reason, the four large TVs no longer show music videos, and the disc jockey no longer delivers a 'rap' between records. He used to, but he was required to type up his patter and submit it to the authorities who would strike out what was unacceptable. They pondered over every word, taking so long that it became impossible to get a new script approved for each night's performance. The disco's management finally decided to silence the disc jockey.

11   We watch the 9 p.m. news program *Vremya* on the TV sets over the dance floor. An announcer reads a government statement about the Chernobyl nuclear reactor, but no one pays attention. Eventually, after the weather and sports reports, a huge digital clock over the bar flashes 10.00, and a woman's voice comes over the loud-speaker, 'Comrades, our evening program is now concluded. We will be closing shortly. Have a safe journey home.' The lights go up, and the men who took our tickets begin urging the crowd to leave. People stream out the door, and we wonder what they will do with the rest of their still young evening; all Moscow establishments that cater to youth are required to close early.

12   As we head for the door, we notice that we are being followed by a rather well-dressed man. He makes no effort to conceal himself. When he sees us climb into our car with foreigners' license plates, he seems satisfied as if he has fulfilled his mission. We drive away feeling relaxed and, for the first time during the entire evening, like dancing.

Nancy Traver *Time* (Copyright 1986 Time Inc.)

43

D | Writing

Guided work: descriptive and narrative/descriptive writing

The aim of a piece of descriptive writing like C Reading 2 is to give the reader a clear impression of a place, including what it feels like to be there. Three important factors in such a piece are organisation, vocabulary, and direct speech.

1 Organisation

The following are two ways of organising a description.

A **sequential** organisation: a place is described as the writer moves through it. Such a description is similar to a narrative essay, and is paragraphed according to the sequence of events. Look again at C Reading 2, noting the stages in the description.

A **spatial** organisation: a place is described from a static point of view, using prepositions of position and expressions like *close by*, *in the distance*. It is usual to describe first the things which strike the writer most strongly. Paragraphing depends on how the writer divides up the scene.

In both, present tenses can be used to give a feeling of being there.

2 Vocabulary

Vocabulary can make a description more vivid, so that the reader imagines clearly how things looked, sounded etc. The writer can also give the impression s/he wishes to convey. Read this new version of the beginning of C Reading 2.

The Izmailovo complex, a group of five hotel towers built for the 1980 Olympic Games, rises like a gleaming fairy-tale palace over a picturesque Moscow suburb. Apart from its stylish appearance, however, Izmailovo has a remarkable attraction: a discotheque reputed to be the best in Moscow.

The place is certainly exclusive. After chatting for a while to a guard at the entrance to Izmailova's 30-storey Building D, we find a discreetly-lit doorway tucked into a corner on the ground-floor. Over the door are the words in Russian BAR-DISKO. Just inside, three men stand around a beautiful antique table. 'What do you want?' one asks cheerfully. We reply confidently that we had heard this was a disco. 'You must buy a ticket,' says another, gazing at our western clothes admiringly. The doorman at New York's Palladium could not be more welcoming.

How has our impression of the discotheque changed?

Reread the article. Which words have been replaced? Such value-loaded words can make a big difference to the impression given of a place.

3 Direct speech

Small incidents make a description more interesting. They can involve the writer or they can simply be observed, as if the writer were a fly on the wall. In either case, direct speech is often used instead of reported speech.

a Read these reports of things said at the disco. What do they lose, compared with the original direct speech?
i He looks around nervously to see who is watching and replies that it is like their club. They all know each other, and they get together almost every night.
ii A woman's voice comes over the loudspeaker, saying that the evening program is now concluded, and that the discotheque will be closing shortly. Then she wishes the patrons a safe journey home.

b The layout of direct speech is important. In A Reading 1, for reasons of space, each utterance is part of a paragraph, but it is more common to begin each utterance on a new line. This gives a story a much more open and readable appearance.

c Punctuation is important. Note the punctuation of the following conversation.
'Hello,' he smiled, standing up. 'I thought you weren't coming.'
'No, I wasn't,' she began, 'but, well . . .'
'Never mind, it's nice to see you. Do you want a drink?'
'Yes, all right, a glass of wine, please.'

d Note also that the verb used is important. The verb phrase can go before, after, or in the middle of the utterance. Look for examples in C Reading 2. Other verbs can be used instead (e.g. *smile*, *began*). The verb phrase may be left out when it is clear who is speaking.

4 Rewrite the following passage, using some of the features of direct speech described above.

She said that she fancied going for a walk, and invited him to come. He yawned, saying that he didn't, really. He felt like just lying around. She insisted, smiling, saying that it would do him good and that it was a lovely day. She was putting on her coat as she said this. He agreed to come, and asked where they should go.

5 Write a true or imaginary description of a night out in about 300 words.

E Listening

Working down the middle

Discussion

● What factors would you say are important in making a successful rock star?

● What would be the good and bad points of being a rock musician?

● You are going to listen to Dave Chumbley, a rock-music agent. His job is to arrange concerts for rock groups who are his clients. What questions would you ask him if you were the interviewer?

Listening exercises

1 Listen to Dave talking about his work, take notes, and answer the following questions as fully as possible.

a What three things have to be considered in choosing places for clients to play?

b What is the most important of these things?

c Which of the following performers is/are big at the time of the interview?
The Style Council   The Cure   Amazulu
T'Pau   Julia Fordham

d Dave talks about difficult aspects of his job. Which of the following does he mention as stressful?
having to work under non-stop pressure
working with unprofessional people
not being ultimately responsible for the quality of the product he sells
What other things cause him stress?

e What are the two problems he's dealing with at the moment? The second is an example of something mentioned in **d**. What?

f What advice or warnings does Dave have for would-be rock stars?

g Which does he feel is the most important?

h Why does he say, 'Be aware of your own limitations'?

2 Listen again, filling in the gaps in these sentences with prepositional expressions. Each line represents a word.

a As an agent, my job is to work ____ ____ ____ a set of clients.

b 'So you decide that certain cities like certain types of music?' ____ ____ ____ , but also, more importantly, if . . .

c Everyone wants you to ____ ____ ____ an answer two minutes ago yesterday.

d We had a problem with her eye, and we thought we could ____ ____ that by wearing dark glasses on the TV.

e . . . and hopefully keep everyone ____ ____ so we can replace it in two or three weeks.

f . . . but ____ ____ ____ ____ , if anyone is aware of what being a middle person is like, you do get the rough end of the stick from both ends.

g You've also got to ____ ____ ____ a huge amount of boredom, of . . .

h . . . flying and ____ ____ airports.

i ____ ____ ____ , you need good advice, honest advice.

j . . . the mistakes you make in the early days usually come back to you ____ ____ ____ ____ .

3 Match these meanings to the expressions above.
i on the other hand
ii as the representative of
iii ultimately
iv available in case of necessity
v waiting with nothing to do
vi find (*a solution, idea, answer*)
vii avoid (*a law, problem etc.*)
viii partly
ix most importantly
x accept, tolerate

4 One problem with listening to people speak freely is that they often invent or modify expressions in personal ways that you have never heard before, nor ever will again. There are two such expressions in Exercise 2. What are they? What do they mean?

F Speaking

Focus on function: inviting; accepting and refusing; responding to acceptance and refusal; making arrangements; asking and talking about prior arrangements

1 Listening comprehension

Listen to five short dialogues, and answer the following questions.

a What is the least and which the most formal of the dialogues?

b In which dialogue is the invitation most insistent? Why is it?

c Two of the dialogues are between the same speakers. Which ones?

d Why can't John come out straight away in Dialogue 2?

e Is Charles or Roger leading the conversation in Dialogue 5?

2 Pronunciation

Listen to the eight utterances below, and mark the syllables which carry the main stress.

a I was wondering if you might like to come out with me.

b We'd like that very much.

c Perhaps you could let me know tomorrow.

d Fancy coming out for a drink?

e Do you want to come round, or shall I see you in the pub?

f I don't really feel like going out tonight actually.

g When did you have in mind?

h Well, I was going to see Perkins.

Repeat each utterance, trying to match the pronunciation on the cassette.

3 Reproduction

Using the flow diagram to help you, act out the dialogues in pairs, using the original language where possible, and improvising when necessary.

4 Improvisation

In pairs, improvise the following dialogues. For instructions, Student A should read on. Student B should turn to Study page 167.

> ### Student A
> It's Saturday afternoon, and the weather's quite nice. You are indoors studying. It seems a pity to waste the nice weather, but you must get some work done. Student B phones. S/he is a new friend whom you like very much, but don't know very well yet. You hate shopping.

> Student B is your immediate superior at work. S/he speaks to you about arranging a meeting. Today is Tuesday. You are busy this afternoon, tomorrow afternoon, and Friday morning. You are going away for the weekend, and would like to get away early on Friday afternoon.

Flow diagrams for Exercise 3

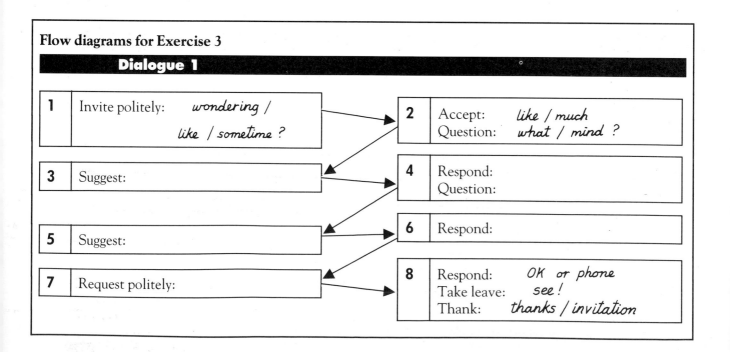

Dialogue 1

1	Invite politely: *wondering / like / sometime ?*	→	2	Accept: *like / much* Question: *what / mind ?*
3	Suggest:		4	Respond: Question:
5	Suggest:		6	Respond:
7	Request politely:		8	Respond: *OK or phone* Take leave: *see !* Thank: *thanks / invitation*

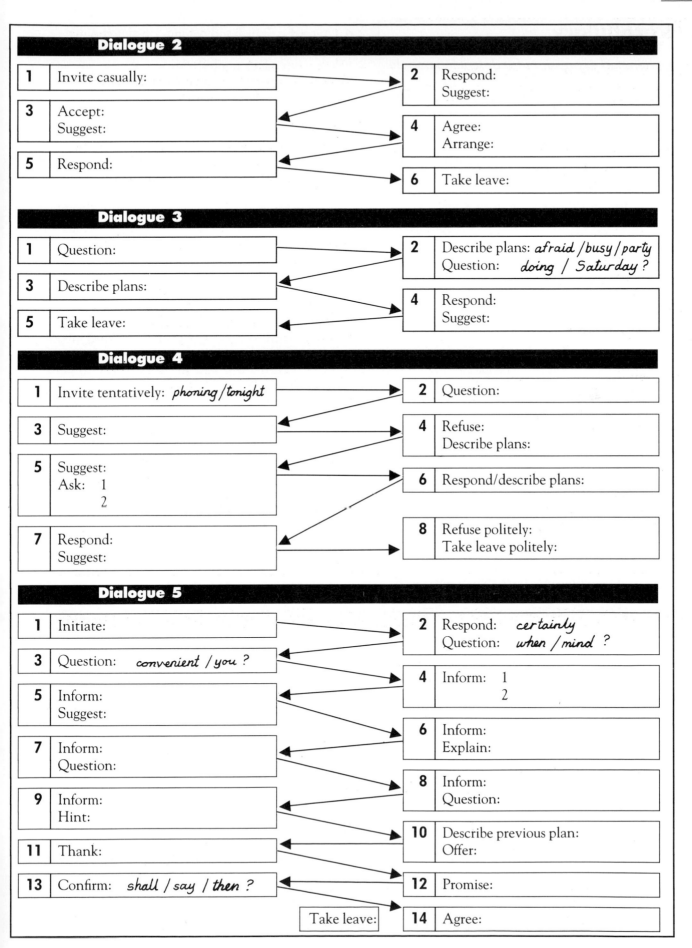

G Vocabulary

Hyphenated expressions for describing people

Look at these descriptions from C Reading 2. Such expressions are very useful in describing people.
i *a young* **blond haired** *disc-jockey*
This is a literal, physical description, consisting of an adjective plus a noun which is a part of the body + *ed*.
ii *a rather* **well-dressed** *man*
This is a literal, non-physical description, consisting of an adverb (usually *well* or *badly*) plus a past participle.

1 Expressions like example i usually concern colour, length (or shortness), and fatness (or thin-ness). What other similar expressions do you know or can you invent?

2 What expressions similar to Example ii could you use to describe the following people.
a He has read a lot of good books.
b She went to good schools, etc.
c He knows a lot about the world.
d She has plenty to eat.
e He earns plenty of money.
f She knows a lot of influential people.
g She is pretty famous.
h He is very polite.
i She is sensible and not neurotic.
j He doesn't behave in a noisy, disruptive way. (*normally used for children*)

3 The opposite of *well-dressed* is *badly-dressed*. Which of the expressions have similar opposites?

4 Equally useful are figurative expressions, consisting of an adjective (usually) plus a noun which is a part of the body plus *-ed* (e.g. *ham-fisted* = very clumsy, like someone whose hands are as big as hams).
On the left of the list below are some expressions of this kind. On the right are their meanings, jumbled up.

a Cover the right-hand column. Study the expressions on the left. Explain any that you know, giving examples.
b Uncover the right-hand column and match each expression with its meaning.

i self-centred	A	unwilling to accept the ideas of others
ii big-headed	B	intent on one purpose, almost fanatical
iii hot-tempered	C	unaware of what is going on around one
iv tight-fisted	D	with a tolerant, liberal mind
v narrow-minded	E	stupidly obstinate, stubborn
vi single-minded	F	selfish, only caring about oneself
vii thin-skinned	G	ungenerous
viii absent-minded	H	over-sensitive
ix long-winded	I	generally in a bad mood
x pig-headed	J	liable to get angry suddenly
xi broad-minded	K	stupid
xii bad-tempered	L	liable to talk too much, not concisely
xiii dim-witted	M	the opposite of modest

c Though the expressions are idiomatic, it is fairly easy to see how the meaning of some derives from the two parts. For example, if someone's mind is narrow, there isn't much room for new ideas. Are the meanings of any other expressions as clear?

5 Listen to the cassette. You will hear thirteen short pieces. Which expression could describe the person (or one of the people) speaking?

6 Write three similar dialogues or speeches, and practise them until you can perform them naturally. Perform your dialogues for another pair. After each dialogue they must say which expression is concerned.

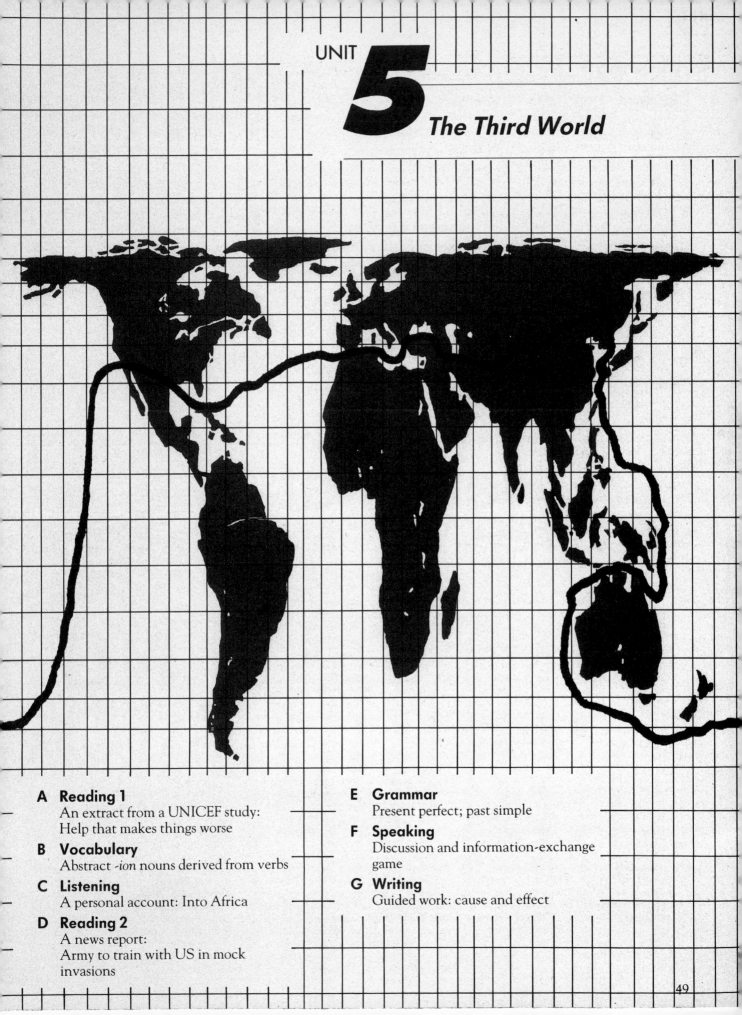

49

A Reading 1

Discussion

● What are the features of a developing or Third World country?
● Would you call yours a developing country? Why/Why not?
● Does your group agree with these statements about developing countries?

a They are poor because they are inefficient.

b Standards of living are slowly improving.

c People should not expect minimum living standards like those in the West.

d Governments should raise living standards, not pay back debts.

e All that will really help the poor is revolution.

Reading exercises

1 Before reading the article extracted from a UNICEF study, make sure you understand the following terms from economics.

a budget deficit
b recession
c export earnings
d demand
e government expenditure
f trade balance
g national resources
h subsidies
i state-owned assets
j to reschedule a debt

Help that

a MALNUTRITION during the 1980s is increasing in many parts of the developing world. Evidence of rising malnutrition exists in ten African countries, Belize, Bolivia, Chile, Jamaica, Uruguay and parts of the Philippines and Sri Lanka.

b Infant mortality has been rising in some areas — including Barbados, Brazil, Ghana and Uruguay — after decades of decline, while the trend towards improvement has been halted in at least twenty-one countries.

c The proportion of low birthweight babies increased in at least ten countries between 1979 and 1982, including Barbados, Cameroon, Guinea-Bissau, Jamaica, Malaysia, Rwanda and Tanzania. Diseases thought to have been eliminated have reappeared — yaws and yellow fever in Ghana, for example, and malaria in Peru ...

d Education has also been affected. In Chile and Ghana, for example, primary-school attendance has been falling and drop-out rates increasing; child labour has become more common. In Bolivia absenteeism from primary schools increased from 2.2 per cent in 1980 to 8.5 per cent in 1983.

e In Sri Lanka there is evidence that literacy and school attendance decreased from 1979 to 1981. In Jamaica the percentage of children passing examinations has dropped sharply. School failures and drop-out rates have been increasing in Sao Paulo, Brazil.

f The health services are acutely short of drugs in most countries; and in many, including Ghana, Jamaica and Sri Lanka, health workers' morale is low because of falling incomes, deteriorating facilities, and lack of money for day-to-day expenses.

g In Ghana attendance at clinics and hospitals fell by a third between 1979 and 1983. In Jamaica charges have been introduced for services which were previously free, while patients in hospitals have to bring their own linen and food to survive.

h These problems are the end product of the most severe economic recession since the 1930s. Developing countries were the victims of the world recession of 1980–83, of an almost unprecedented worsening in their terms of trade (which has not been reversed despite some recovery in the industralised countries), and of an intolerable debt burden.

i These negative trends had a magnified effect on developing economies. Stagnant world trade reduced their trade opportunities and the prices of their exports. Aid flows stagnated, being less in 1985 than in 1980, while net private bank lending, which had provided the major source of development finance in the 1970s fell to almost nothing in the 1980s. By 1985, the only net positive bank lending to developing countries was the lending mandated by international agreements.

2 There are twenty-one paragraphs, which can be divided into five groups. Put these groups in order, saying which paragraphs make up each group.

The effects on the poor of adjustment policies	
The study's recommendations	
The worsening situation	*in paragraphs:*
The form of present adjustment policies	
The causes of the worsening situation	

3 Read the first part of the article, and note down the following:
the four problems concerning ill health;
the problems in the field of education;
the five examples of problems in the health services;
reasons why the morale of health workers is low.

Compare notes with other students.

4 Note the three typical elements of IMF adjustment policies, with the objectives of each and the measures included in each. Clarify your notes by arranging them in a diagram.

5 In what ways do such policies make things even worse for the poor?

6 What are the recommendations of the study?

makes things worse

j   Developing countries also had to contend with the huge debt accumulated in the 1970s which, for the third world as a whole, had grown to $888 billion by the end of 1985, while debt service payments — payments owed on past borrowing — exceeded $130 billion, representing nearly a quarter of their export earnings.

k   The resulting imbalances led to a need for major economic adjustments in many countries — but unfortunately the form of the adjustment policies adopted has frequently contributed to worsening conditions among vulnerable groups, especially in the short run.

l   IMF adjustment policies typically include three elements: first, policies to cut demand, especially government expenditure, so as to lower imports, improve the trade balance, and reduce the budget deficit; secondly, policies to improve the allocation of resources so as to increase the production of exports and of substitutes for imports; and thirdly, policy reforms designed to improve the long-run efficiency of the economy.

m   In the first category, adjustment packages almost invariably include limits on government expenditure, with cuts in subsidies being a priority, and controls over domestic lending.

n   In the second category, policies include exchange rate devaluation and increased producer prices to boost agricultural production.

o   In the third category, a typical adjustment package includes reforming financial markets and increasing interest rates, liberalising imports, and privatising state-owned assets. Restrictions on demand — or deflation — dominate all conventional adjustment packages while the other elements occur in the majority of cases.

p   There are three major mechanisms by which adjustment policies tend to worsen conditions for the most vulnerable, at least in the short run: by reducing employment, and earnings from employment, for low-income households; by increasing the price of basic commodities, especially food; by reducing government expenditure on basic services — especially health, education and sanitation . . .

q   Between 1979 and 1983 expenditure per head on health at constant prices decreased in nearly half the African countries for which data exist, and in 60 per cent of the countries in Latin America. Education expenditure per head declined in a third of African countries and 59 per cent of Latin American countries . . .

r   No adjustment programme is acceptable which allows children to be sacrificed for the sake of financial stability. Yet this has happened, and it need not happen. Alternatives exist. What is needed now is to convince decision makers at all levels — both in national governments and international institutions — to take appropriate action quickly. Many children will die; and many of the survivors suffer permanent damage because of failure to act now.

s   Debts should be rescheduled. Very poor countries need to have at least some of their debt cancelled.

t   Aid flow needs to be more substantial, they should be redirected to measures which benefit those at risk, and they must be guaranteed over the medium term.

u   Almost all developing countries need greater access for their exports to the markets of developed countries.

Adjustment with a human face Volume I edited by G. A. Cornia, Richard Jolly and Frances Stewart, Oxford University Press; adapted for *The Guardian*

B | **Vocabulary**

Abstract -ion nouns derived from verbs

1 Look at these nouns from the article in A Reading 1, all of which end in *-tion*. Write beside each the verb from which it is derived. One has been done for you.

> **a**
> institution *institute*
> education

> **b**
> restriction
> adoption

> **c**
> production
> reduction

In each list the nouns are derived from verbs in similar or identical ways. What are the three derivation patterns?
For example, in list a, nouns are derived by dropping the *e* from the end of the verb, then adding *-ion*. Check your answers on Study page 167.

2 Add to each list any other nouns you know which are derived in the same way, and their verbs.

3 Seven more *-ion* nouns follow. Write beside each the verb from which it is derived.

> **d**
> organisation

> **e**
> persuasion

> **f**
> classification

> **g**
> emission

> **h**
> discussion

> **i**
> description

> **j**
> composition

What are the seven new derivation patterns?
Check your answers on Study page 167.

4 Add to the lists in Exercise 3 any other nouns you know which are derived in the same way, and their verbs.

5 Work in groups. Most of the sixty nouns below belong to the above groups, but twelve are exceptions. Take two of the columns, noting exceptions and grouping the other nouns. Use your dictionaries if necessary.

toleration	subscription
maximisation	destruction
imposition	submission
contraction	commission
decision	imagination
satisfaction	attraction
simplification	impression
suppression	obsession
complication	combination
inscription	permission
intrusion	inclusion
omission	suspicion
minimisation	repression
qualification	seduction
victimisation	invasion
eruption	extension
reduction	consumption
information	intensification
prescription	possession
contribution	exploration
completion	exaggeration
contradiction	admission
specification	supposition
deduction	oppression
depression	exception
opposition	inflation
construction	proposition
realisation	examination
hesitation	reception
prediction	adaptation

Check your answers against Study page 168.

6 Test each other in pairs. Say a noun, your partner must say the verb.

7 For each of the following sentences, write another with the same meaning, using the word in brackets and the right noun or verb in the correct form. Example: Payment will be made on completion of the work. (*when*) *You will be paid when the work is completed.*
Sentences using an abstract noun are more formal than their equivalents using a verb-phrase. Try to make your converted sentences more formal or less formal accordingly, changing other words where necessary.

a Prediction of the future is always difficult. (*It*)
b He didn't hesitate to take the job. (*no*)
c Please forgive the intrusion. (*for*)
d Suppression of individual liberties is common in Third World countries. (*for*)
e This is my proposition. (*what*)
f The Prime Minister's admission that she had been wrong amazed everyone. (*when*)
g The film impressed me very powerfully. (*made*)
h I cannot reveal my decision yet. (*what*)
i Nobody expected the volcano to erupt. (*unexpected*)
j His recent depression led police to believe that he may have committed suicide. (*fact*)
k The doctor's handwriting was so bad that I couldn't read the prescription. (*what*)
l If the economic situation is to improve, there must be a drastic cut in consumption (*cut down*)
m We will have to reduce our prices, if we want to be more competitive. (*be*)
n She contributed significantly to the research programme. (*made*)
o Did they permit him to enter the country? (*was*)
p It made him very satisfied, to see that all his efforts had been rewarded with success. (*great*)

C Listening

Into Africa

Discussion

● You are going to hear an extract from an interview with John Gillow, a collector and trader of Third World textiles. He talks about a long northward journey he made through Africa. In which order do you think he passed through the following countries?

Sudan   Tanzania   Lesotho   South Africa
Ethiopia   Kenya

● Note down anything you know about these countries.

● If the apartheid regime were to be overthrown in South Africa, what do you think would be the result? What do you know of other revolutions in Africa?

Listening exercises

1 As you listen plot his route on your map, filling in the names of the countries listed above.

2 Listen again, take notes, and answer the following questions as fully as possible.
a What difficulties did they have at first in Africa?
b How did it come about that spears were thrown at them in Kenya?
c Explain the reference to Fidel Castro.
d Why were there students in the Ethiopian villages?
e What were their difficulties?
f How did John try to help them?

g What do John's feelings seem to be about the Ethiopian revolution?
h What made the ride into Sudan dangerous?
i What was their initial reaction on arriving in Sudan? What caused it?
j How was their accommodation problem solved in Sudan?
k In what way was Sudan different from all other countries John has been in?
l Which country did John like best and which did he like least?

3 Listen again, filling the gaps in the following. Each line represents a word or contraction.
a ... that was _____ _____ _____ _____ shock to the system.
b ... it took a long time to _____ that _____ .
c ... to get to understand _____ _____ _____ _____ .
d ... the farmers didn't want to _____ _____ _____ _____ _____ .
e ... when we really _____ _____ _____ _____ Africa.
f ... everybody _____ _____ _____ and teach you the words for everything.

4 Match these meanings to four of the expressions above.
i got fully involved with
ii be free of
iii the essential character of people
iv relate to them in any way

D | Reading 2

Discussion

● What countries might be invaded by British or US troops and why?

● Discuss any examples you know of powerful countries invading developing countries.

● What is your opinion of such operations?

Reading exercises

1 As you read the news report opposite, mark the following statements T (true) or F (false) according to what is said or implied in the text.

a Joint British–American military exercises will begin next year.

b The British may not send more than 100 troops.

c Cuban, North Korean or East German troops will also participate in the exercises.

d The Army has said that the main aim of the exercises is to give British troops the chance to work with modern training equipment.

e The writer is sure this is true.

f This will be the first exercise aimed at training British troops for fighting outside NATO.

g The British troops might not be drawn from British intervention forces.

h The exercises will be intended only to prepare troops for intervening in support of Third World governments in trouble.

i In the training, new laser weapons will be tested for use against Third World countries.

2 List the words in the text connected with pretending, or copying reality.

3 Write an essay giving your opinion about powerful countries interfering in developing countries. Alternatively, imagine yourself in a developing country when it is invaded and write a vivid account of your experiences.

Army to train with US in mock invasions

By Mark Urban, Defence Correspondent

THE British Army is planning to send troops to a sophisticated new training base in the United States where they will take part in exercises simulating the invasion of Third World countries.

Exercises by British soldiers, in co-operation with American Rapid Deployment Force units, could begin next year. The Army plans to send the first British unit — a company of about 100 men — in a year's time. It is hoped that regular British participation will be increased to battalions.

They will take part in realistic operations at the Joint Readiness Training Centre at Fort Chaffee, in Arkansas. The centre will feature an imitation capital city in a developing country, including airport and government buildings. It is believed that the realism will extend to the provision of a force of guerrillas to oppose the troops arriving in the mock city. There has apparently been some debate about whether such forces should be outfitted as Cubans, North Koreans or East Germans.

The Army emphasizes that the exercises will allow British soldiers access to the most modern training equipment, rather than prepare them for military operations against specific countries. But the chance to train men at Fort Chaffee coincides with a new emphasis in the British armed forces on training for operations outside the Nato area.

Sources in the Army say that the men who will be sent to Fort Chaffee will almost certainly be drawn from this country's intervention forces, such as the Parachute Regiment. Training for operations beyond the boundaries of Nato — in Africa or the Middle East — has been increased in recent years. Royal Marines will stage an amphibious landing in Scotland this November as part of a continued programme to prepare troops for such operations.

The Joint Readiness Training Centre has been set up to teach American troops the lessons of operations like the interventions in Grenada. Exercises will range from those where American troops have been invited in by a government to simulating opposed landings.

The base in Arkansas will be used by a brigade, about 5,000 men, at a time. These will be drawn from Rapid Deployment Force formations such as the elite 82nd Airborne Division. Units will be airlifted into Arkansas via distant staging posts, to reproduce a complex intervention.

A British delegation will inspect the Fort Chaffee facilities in February. The training will rely on laser technology to simulate fire between combatants.

Mark Urban *The Independent*

E | Grammar

Present perfect; past simple

Review

1 Read the following pairs of sentences. In each pair, only one sentence is correct. Which one? Check your answers on Study page 168.

a i Last year I've been abroad twice.
ii Last year I went abroad twice.

b i You're late! I waited for two hours!
ii You're late! I've been waiting for two hours!

c i I went outside, then I locked the door.
ii I've gone outside, then I've locked the door.

d i I'm sorry, he's gone out; do you want to leave a message?
ii I'm sorry, he went out; do you want to leave a message?

e i I knew Tony since he was a little boy.
ii I've known Tony since he was a little boy.

f i The First World War lasted for four years.
ii The First World War has lasted for four years.

g i Since I came to London I've only been to the theatre twice.
ii Since I came to London I only went to the theatre twice.

h i I haven't been working here long, so my salary is still quite low.
ii I didn't work here very long, so my salary is still quite low.

i i I haven't seen my uncle for years; I can hardly remember his face.
ii I didn't see my uncle for years; I can hardly remember his face.

j i I haven't been to London for the first time until I was 16.
ii I didn't go to London for the first time until I was 16.

k i Switch on the news! The President has been shot!
ii Switch on the news! The President was shot!

l i During recent years she sang in all the major opera houses of Europe.
ii During recent years she has sung in all the major opera houses of Europe.

2 Put each correct sentence in one of the categories from the Language description on Study page 168.

3 For each sentence below, write another with approximately the same meaning, using the present perfect tense.
Example: *I'm afraid they're not in.*
I'm afraid they've gone out.

a Sorry, I can't remember your name.
b Is your hair shorter?
c Hello, reception? My room is still dirty.
d The socialists are now in power.
e Income tax is now higher.
f The children are all adults now . . .
g . . . and they don't live with us any more.
h They're here at last!
i The situation in Ethiopia is worse than it was.
j In Spain things are better than they were.

4 In the following news report there are thirty gaps, each with an infinitive in italics. Convert the infinitives to the correct past or present perfect tense (simple or continuous).

'Good evening. Here is the nine o'clock news. British troops (1) *invade* the small Caribbean island of Negrita. The invasion (2) *take* place before dawn this morning. There (3) *be* little initial resistance to the surprise invasion, but since early morning there (4) *be* intense fighting in the capital, where government troops (5) *establish* themselves in various public buildings. So far few

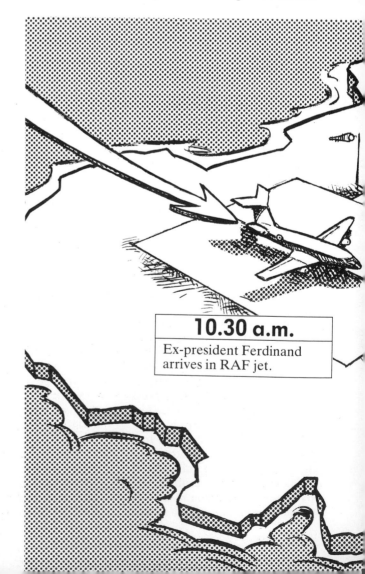

10.30 a.m.
Ex-president Ferdinand arrives in RAF jet.

people (6) *be killed*, but there (7) *be* a number of casualties, among them General Amos Jones, the President of the tiny island republic, who (8) *be* wounded when invading troops (9) *enter* the city and (10) *occupy* the presidential palace during the early part of the morning. General Jones (11) *escape* capture, and (12) *flee* to the main Army barracks; since then he (13) *organise* resistance to the invasion, which so far (14) *be* a great deal more determined than had been expected.

The predicted upsurge of popular support for the invading forces is by no means evident. Most of the island's citizens (15) *keep* out of sight, though some armed civilians (16) *be seen* firing at British troops. This seems to suggest that previous reports of the unpopularity of the government of General Jones (17) *be* greatly exaggerated. In spite of the spirited resistance which (18) *be put* up, a British spokesman (19) *declare* the invasion to be a success. Shortly after midday, a provisional government (20) *be installed*, headed by Mr Marcos Ferdinand, who (21) *be flown* to the island this morning in a Royal Air Force jet. Mr Ferdinand,

who (22) *govern* the island republic for five years until early last year, is felt to be more sympathetic to British and US interests than General Jones, the man who (23) *depose* him in a bloodless *coup d'etat*, and (24) *be deposed* in his turn. Since General Jones took power, Negrita (25) *not pay* the interest on its huge foreign debt, most of which (26) *be incurred* during Mr Ferdinand's presidency. Many industries (27) *be nationalised*, and earlier this year the minimum wage (28) *be increased* by 100%. It is believed that these policies are responsible for today's invasion.

The White House (29) *praise* the British Government's 'decisive action to normalise the Negrita situation'. In Parliament this afternoon, however, the invasion (30) *be criticised* strongly by opposition MPs.'

5 Write ten true sentences about yourself or the world, using past and present perfect tenses.

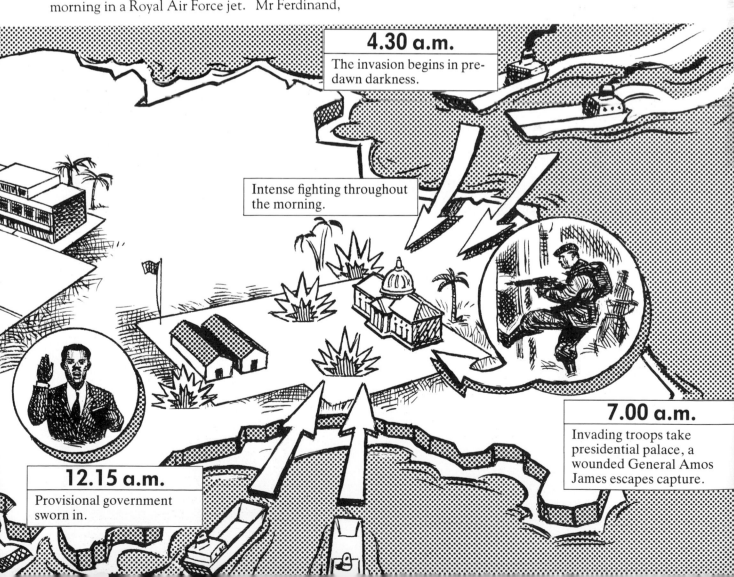

4.30 a.m.
The invasion begins in pre-dawn darkness.

Intense fighting throughout the morning.

7.00 a.m.
Invading troops take presidential palace, a wounded General Amos James escapes capture.

12.15 a.m.
Provisional government sworn in.

F | Speaking

Desert Island

Discussion and information-exchange game

1 Work in groups of four, divided into two pairs, Pair A and Pair B. You have two blank maps of an island. Beneath is a list of things that could be found on the island. Ask your teacher to explain any that you don't understand.

Imagine that some survivors from a shipwreck are on the island. Each pair must draw onto Map 1 certain features from the list. To find out which features, two dice must be thrown.

Sit with partners facing each other. After you have thrown the dice, pass them to your left. Each student throws six times.

For each number on the list there are two items. The first time you throw a number, choose the item you and your partner want. Consider carefully how each might be useful or dangerous. The second time, you must take the other item. If you throw the same number a third time, you can throw again. Note each item you take.

2 Decide privately with your partner where you want your twelve items to be, and draw them clearly onto Map 1. Arrange your items logically. For example, alligators would not be found on high hills.

3 Describe your map to the other pair as exactly as possible. As the others explain their map, fill in Map 2. Do not show your maps yet.

4 Compare maps. How well were they explained?

5 Your group are the castaways. Choose which Map 1 you would prefer to be your island, considering the good and bad points of each. Where/how would you live? To help you all survive, you may decide together on four things which you managed to bring with you from your ship.

Items found on the island
2 a tiger
a crazy old castaway living in a cave
3 an old wrecked ship in shallow water, close to the shore
some wild corn
4 a few banana palms
mosquitos
5 sharks
a large desert
6 alligators
snakes
7 an old ruined temple
cliffs
8 a lake
strong vines and creepers hanging from trees
9 some wild goats
some wild turkeys and rabbits
10 a large swamp
a village inhabited by indians
11 a beach with coconut palms
a stream
12 a bamboo grove
some high hills

Map 1

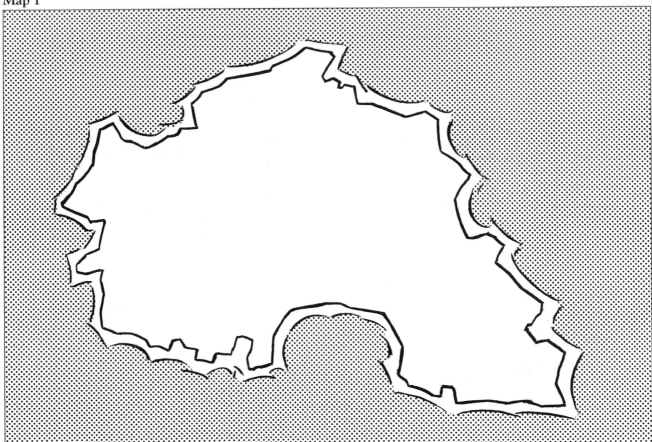

Map 2

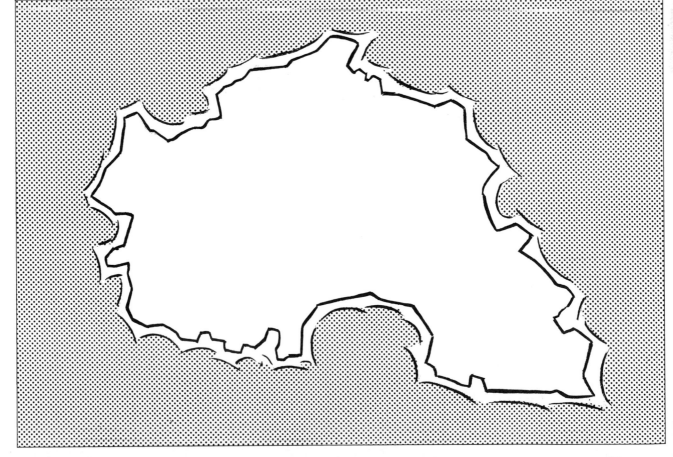

G Writing

Guided work: cause and effect

Causal relationships can be indicated in many ways in English. The word or expression used depends on:
whether one or more sentence(s) are used;
whether the cause or the effect is mentioned first;
whether the cause is expressed in a noun-phrase or a clause;
whether the effect is expressed in a noun-phrase or a clause.

1 Look at these two facts, expressed in noun-phrases and clauses.

Cause		Effect
Noun phrases		
greater demand for accommodation	→	higher rents
Clauses		
demand for accommodation has increased	→	rents have risen

Write six different sentences (or sentence pairs) expressing the causal relationship between the two facts.
The following words might appear in your sentences.
because   led   caused   so   owing   effect   result(ed)   due   reason   therefore   consequently   consequence   by   of   to   as
Compare your sentences with other groups. Check your ideas on Study page 169.

2 Fill in the spaces in the following sentences, all relating these two facts:

Cause	Effect
The government's disastrous economic policies	A drastic decline in the government's popularity

a The government's economic policy has been disastrous. _____ a drastic decline in its popularity.
b _____, the government's popularity has declined drastically.
c _____ has led to _____ .
d _____ the result _____ .
e _____ . _____ , its popularity has declined drastically.
f _____ as a result _____ .
g One consequence _____ .
h _____ because _____ .

3 Write twelve 'cause and effect' sentences, or pairs, about the developing world. A Reading 1 may provide you with facts and ideas.
Note that it is possible to connect more than two facts in a 'cause and effect' chain, using the linking expression *in turn*.
Example: *The government's economic policies caused a decline in its popularity,* and this **in turn** led to the *calling of a general election.*

National Insurance → *N·H·S
= National Health Service
*B·U·P·A Private Health

6

Health and medicine

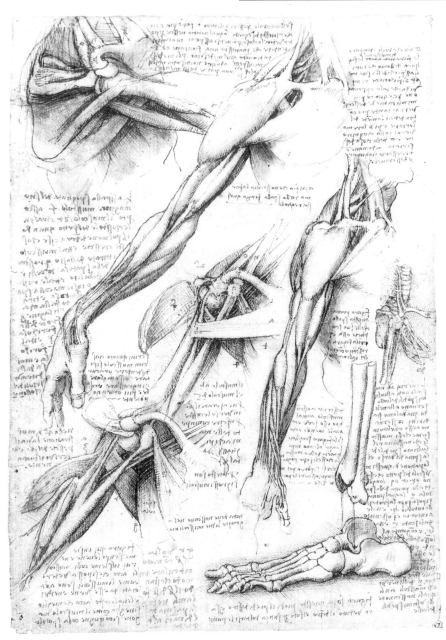

A Reading 1

Discussion

● Write a true sentence connecting the following three things:
primitive peoples (e.g. Indians)
the white man
health

● Think of facts or ideas to support your sentence. Tell your sentence to your group and explain what you mean.

Do you think it's better to keep unpleasant realities like disease and death from children, or is it better to inform them? What arguments could be made for each point of view?

Reading exercises

1 The extract opposite is the greater part (including the end) of a short story by Ernest Hemingway. Read it and answer the following questions, working in groups. In many cases the answer must be inferred.

Indian camp

THEY came around a bend and a dog came out barking. Ahead were the lights of the shanties where the Indian bark-peelers lived. More dogs rushed out at them. The two Indians sent them back to the shanties. In the shanty nearest the road there was a light in the window. An old woman stood in the doorway holding a lamp.

Inside on a wooden bunk lay a young Indian woman. She had been trying to have her baby for two days. All the old women in the camp had been helping her. The men had moved off up the road to sit in the dark and smoke out of range of the noise she made. She screamed just as Nick and the two Indians followed his father and Uncle George into the shanty.

She lay in the lower bunk, very big under a quilt. Her head was turned to one side. In the upper bunk was her husband. He had cut his foot very badly with an axe three days before. He was smoking a pipe. The room smelled very bad.

Nick's father ordered some water to be put on the stove, and while it was heating he spoke to Nick.

'This lady is going to have a baby, Nick,' he said.

'I know,' said Nick.

'You don't know,' said his father. 'Listen to me. What she is going through is called being in labour. The baby wants to be born and she wants it to be born. All her muscles are trying to get the baby born. That is what is happening when she screams.'

'I see,' Nick said.

Just then the woman cried out.

'Oh, Daddy, can't you give her something to make her stop screaming?' asked Nick.

'No. I haven't any anaesthetic,' his father said. 'But her screams are not important. I don't hear them because they are not important.'

The husband in the upper bunk rolled over against the wall.

The woman in the kitchen motioned to the doctor that the water was hot. Nick's father went into the kitchen and poured about half of the water out of the big kettle into a basin. Into the water left in the kettle he put several things he unwrapped from a handkerchief.

'Those must boil,' he said, and began to scrub his hands in the basin of hot water with a cake of soap he had brought from the camp. Nick watched his father's hands scrubbing each other with the soap. While his father washed his hands very carefully and thoroughly, he talked.

'You see, Nick, babies are supposed to be born head first, but sometimes they're not. When they're not they make a lot of trouble for everybody. Maybe I'll have to operate on this lady. We'll know in a little while.'

When he was satisfied with his hands he went in and went to work.

'Pull back that quilt, will you, George?' he said. 'I'd rather not touch it.'

Later when he started to operate Uncle George and three Indian men held the woman still. She bit Uncle George on the arm and Uncle George said, 'Damn squaw bitch!' and the young Indian who had rowed Uncle George over laughed at him. Nick held the basin for his father. It took a long time.

His father picked the baby up and slapped it to make it breathe and handed it to the old woman.

a What is the effect on the focus of the story of referring to the doctor and his brother as 'Nick's father' and 'Uncle George'?

b What exactly is happening to the Indian lady?

c Why does Nick's father say, 'Her screams are not important'?

d How does Nick's father feel after the operation? Why?

e How does Uncle George feel when he says, 'Oh, you're a great man, all right'?

f At what point in the story does the Indian die?

g Why do you think Nick and his father walk back without Uncle George?

h How did they get to the Indian camp in the first place?

i How does Nick feel during the operation? How does he feel after leaving the camp?

j How does Nick's father feel after leaving the camp?

k What do you think Hemingway is saying in the story?

2 Hemingway is known for uncomplicated, realistic, powerful writing, in which words are not wasted. What aspects of this story make it typical of his writing?

'See, it's a boy, Nick,' he said. 'How do you like being an interne?'

Nick said, 'All right.' He was looking away so as not to see what his father was doing.

'There. That gets it,' said his father and put something into the basin.

Nick didn't look at it.

'Now,' his father said, 'there's some stitches to put in. You can watch this or not, Nick, just as you like. I'm going to sew up the incision I made.'

Nick did not watch. His curiosity had been gone for a long time.

His father finished and stood up. Uncle George and the three Indian men stood up. Nick put the basin out in the kitchen.

Uncle George looked at his arm. The young Indian smiled reminiscently.

'I'll put some peroxide on that, George,' the doctor said.

He bent over the Indian woman. She was quiet now and her eyes were closed. She looked very pale. She did not know what had become of the baby or anything.

'I'll be back in the morning,' the doctor said, standing up. 'The nurse should be here from St Ignace by noon and she'll bring everything we need.'

He was feeling exalted and talkative as football players are in the dressing-room after a game.

'That's one for the medical journal, George,' he said. 'Doing a Caesarian with a jack-knife and sewing it up with nine-foot, tapered gut leaders.'

Uncle George was standing against the wall, looking at his arm.

'Oh, you're a great man, all right,' he said.

'Ought to have a look at the proud father. They're usually the worst sufferers in these little affairs,' the doctor said. 'I must say he took it all pretty quietly.'

He pulled back the blanket from the Indian's head. His hand came away wet. He mounted on the edge of the lower bunk with the lamp in one hand and looked in. The Indian lay with his face to the wall. His throat had been cut from ear to ear. The blood had flowed down into a pool where his body sagged the bunk. His head rested on his left arm. The open razor lay, edge up, in the blankets.

'Take Nick out of the shanty, George,' the doctor said.

There was no need for that. Nick, standing in the door of the kitchen, had a good view of the upper bunk when his father, the lamp in one hand, tipped the Indian's head back.

It was just beginning to be daylight when they walked along the logging road back towards the lake.

'I'm terribly sorry I brought you along, Nickie,' said his father, all his post-operative exhilaration gone. 'It was an awful mess to put you through.'

'Do ladies always have such a hard time having babies?' Nick asked.

'No, that was very, very exceptional.'

'Why did he kill himself, Daddy?'

'I don't know, Nick. He couldn't stand things, I guess.'

'Do many men kill themselves, Daddy?'

'Not very many, Nick.'

'Do many women?'

'Hardly ever.'

'Don't they ever?'

'Oh, yes. They do sometimes.'

'Daddy?'

'Yes.'

'Where did Uncle George go?'

'He'll turn up all right.'

'Is dying hard, Daddy?'

'No, I think it's pretty easy, Nick. It all depends.'

They were seated in the boat, Nick in the stern, his father rowing. The sun was coming up over the hills. A bass jumped, making a circle in the water. Nick trailed his hand in the water. It felt warm in the sharp chill of the morning.

In the early morning on the lake sitting in the stern of the boat with his father rowing, he felt quite sure that he would never die.

Ernest Hemingway *Indian Camp*

B Grammar

Making comparative structures more informative

Review

English has two basic comparative structures.

Using -er, more, less, fewer

Examples:

With adjectives

*Generally **older** people have more health problems.*

*Drugs are **more expensive** than they used to be.*

For quantity

*There is **less disease** in Europe than in Africa.*

For number

*There are **fewer hospitals** in Africa than in Europe.*

With adverbs

*I recovered **more quickly** than anyone had expected.*

Using not as … as …

Examples:

With adjectives

*Shortages in our ward **aren't as** bad **as** in others.*

For quantity

*I don't know **as much as** I should about AIDS.*

For number

*She doesn't catch **as many** colds **as** she used to.*

With adverbs

*My grandmother doesn't move **as** quickly **as** she used to.*

1 These constructions could be more informative. For example, we do not know how much more expensive drugs are nowadays, or how many more hospitals there are in Europe. Discuss ways of adding to or modifying the constructions to make them more informative. Consider the use of the following words and expressions.

far   much   a bit   not nearly   even   not quite
a great deal   slightly   twice

Check your ideas on Study page 170.

2 For each sentence, write another with the same meaning, using the words in brackets.

a Learning to ski is much easier than you might think. (*as*)

b He isn't nearly as old as I expected. (*younger*)

c Margarine costs a bit less than butter. (*much*)

d Salaries aren't rising nearly as fast as prices. (*much*)

e Nowadays there aren't nearly as many deaths from typhoid as there used to be. (*fewer*)

f The situation isn't nearly as simple as people think. (*deal*)

g Your house is twice as big as mine. (*size*)

h He earns twice as much as she does. (*half*)

3 In pairs study the tables below, and use comparative sentences to express the statistics they contain. Remember, there is always more than one way to make the comparison.

Example:

In 1980, hospital waiting lists were much longer in NW England than they were in SW Thames.

or

In 1980, people in NW England had to wait far longer for hospital treatment than people in SW Thames.

4 Using these structures, write ten sentences comparing your city or country with others. Consider size, climate, wealth, beauty, interest, principal cities, the people customs etc. Your sentences may be factual or your own opinions.

NATIONAL HEALTH SERVICE?

Regional Health Authority	hospital beds 1980	hospital waiting list 1980	staff & practitioners 1981	midwives, health visitors, home nurses 1981	doctors' practices serving over 3000 people 1981	persons per dentist 1981
		number per 10,000 people			percentage	
Northern	82	117	181	5.5	8	5050
East Anglia	70	143	165	5.3	2	4000
SW Thames	85	119	182	5.4	6	2650
Oxford	58	146	156	5.2	7	3600
S Western	80	141	184	3.9	2	3050
W Midlands	69	156	171	5.3	9	4400
N Western	76	156	193	6.7	8	4250
Wales	84	136	199	7.2	3	4400
Scotland	113	130	248	7.6	3	3900
N Ireland	110	140	256	7.7	5	3850

Source: Regional Trends

HEALTHY AND WEALTHY

occupation of head of household	people with longstanding illness GB 1981 percentages		people consulting doctor in last 2 weeks GB 1981 percentages		death rate of people 15-64 E & W 1978 average = 100		perinatal mortality ◑ E & W 1980 per 1,000 live & still births	infant mortality ● E & W 1980 per 1,000 live births	infants bottle fed E & W 1980 percentages	cigarette smokers GB 1980 percentages	
professional	10	10	8	12	77	82	9.7	8.9	20	21	21
employers & managers	14	15	9	12	81	67	11.1	9.5	12	35	33
other white collar	14	17	10	13	99	92	11.8	10.2	21	35	34
skilled manual	16	17	10	15	106	115	13.0	10.7	21	48	43
semi-skilled manual	20	24	12	15	114	119	15.0	13.5	39	49	33
other manual	19	??	12	15	137	135	17.0	16.0	46	57	41

Sources: Social trends; General Household Survey; Reid
Stephen Fothergill and Jill Vincent *The State of the Nation* Pan Books

◑ still births & deaths in infants under 1 week

● deaths of infants under 1 year

G.P. = General Practitioner → Mostly Free
(Local Doctor)

C Listening

Healthy and wealthy?

Discussion

The British National Health Service (NHS) is famous for providing free, good-quality health care. However, in recent years it has become less effective, causing much political debate. Some people say private, profit-making health organisations should be encouraged. Others propose even greater government investment.
● Describe the health system in your own country. How much care is provided by the public health service, and how much by profit-making organisations?
● What arguments could be put forward for and against private health care?

Listening exercises

1 Dr Hugh King, a British General Practitioner (GP), discusses the questions of private health care. As you listen, tick any of the arguments you noted above which are mentioned by either Dr King or the interviewer. Also note down any other arguments mentioned.

2 Listen again, and mark the following statements T (true) or F (false), according to what is said in the interview.

a In Britain, senior politicians have to use the NHS, like ordinary citizens. F

b A man who is out of work because of a health condition may wait a long time for his operation. T

c Influential people such as politicians can use private health care, so they don't know that there are long waiting lists for operations within the NHS. F

d Doctor King feels that politicians are more likely to do something about a problem if they experience it than if they only know about it. T

e If waiting would make a patient's condition worse, the patient doesn't have to wait. F

f Dr King doesn't agree that private health care takes pressure off the NHS by treating people who would otherwise be NHS patients. T

g What makes waiting lists shorter is hard work from doctors who believe in the NHS, not patients leaving the NHS for private care. T

h Doctors in Britain must either work for the NHS or provide private health care. They cannot do both. F

i If a doctor has a private patient and an NHS patient, and each have exactly the same problem, it is likely that the former will be treated long before the latter.

j Dr King believes it is wrong that patients should be able to have nicer food and a more comfortable room just because they can afford to pay for them. F

3 Listen again, filling the gaps in the following sentences. Each line represents a word or abbreviation.

a I'm very _opposed to_ private medical care.

b ... removed a very important part of the lobby which might _otherwise_ have helped improve health care.

c If these people with influence _had_ to use the National Health Service they _would make sure_ something _was_ done about it.

d I think because this quite powerful section of society can _turn   to_ private health care ...

e The people who've really done well with their waiting lists, _in my experience_ are pretty _committed_ health service doctors.

f The worst examples I know of are of people who deliberately, _as far as I can see_, make a very obvious contrast between the short wait ...

g I mean that's a large part of it, but there are no doubt, there's no doubt that in _the private sector_, some operations would be done ...

h But if money can buy you a bigger car, _why shouldn't_ money buy you better health care?

4 Match these meanings to six of the words or expressions above.

i the part of the economy _private sector_ not run by the government

ii against _opposed to_

iii go to, for help _turn to_

iv serious, dedicated _committed_

v if this were not true _otherwise_

vi it seems to me _as far as I can see_

D | Vocabulary

Idioms based on parts of the body

1 Many English idiomatic expressions are based on parts of the body.
Example: *No one would blink an eyelid.* (Unit 1, D Reading 2)
Note down any other similar expressions you know. The picture may help you.

2 Replace the words in *italics* with expressions using the words in brackets.

a The thieves were *heavily armed*. (*teeth*) ~to the teeth~

b It's a bit risky. Let's just *hope it works out all right*. (*fingers*). ~cross fingers~

c He was really unfriendly to me; I think I must have *annoyed him somehow*. (*back*) ~put his back up~

d It will be strange at first. It might take you some time to *settle down and get used to it*. (*feet*) ~find your feet~

e Are you *joking*? (*leg*) ~pulling my leg~

f Don't *interfere*, it's none of your business. (*nose*) ~Don't put your nose in~

g I understood part of the lecture, but most of it was *too difficult for me to understand*. (*head*) ~over my head~

h They don't seem to *have the same opinion* about anything. (*eye*) ~They don't see eye to eye~

i I gave him *permission to do what he thought best, without consulting anyone*. (*hand*) ~give free hand~

j Of course you should allow children to do what they want, within limits, but sometimes you have to *be firm, and not give in*. (*foot*) ~put your foot down~

k We must act quickly, before the situation gets completely *out of control*. (*hand*) ~out of hand~

l The President has Parliament completely *under his influence and control*. (*thumb*) ~under his thumb~

m Can you *keep watch* on the kids while I get some ice-creams? (*eye*) ~keep an eye on~

n The boss seems to be in a bad mood. He *was very angry and sharp with me* when I asked if I could have tomorrow off. (*head*) ~bite his head off~

o Well, it'll be a difficult game, but I'm going to *take a chance and give my opinion*. I think Italy will win it. (*neck*) ~stick my neck out~

3 Some expressions in Exercise 2 are more idiomatic than others. For example, it is harder to understand how *pull someone's leg* is derived than *keep an eye on*. Can you see how any other expressions are derived?

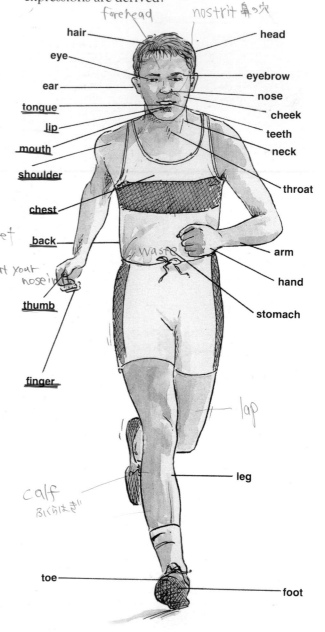

4 Read this letter, putting expressions from Exercise 2 in the gaps. Each line represents a word.

5 With a partner, look up more idioms of this type in your dictionary and choose five which you both like. Write an exercise like Exercise 2, of five sentences. Pass it to another pair. Do the exercise which is passed to you.

Dear John,

The situation in this country is going from bad to worse: there seem to be strikes and demonstrations every day! I must say I don't know what they're all protesting about. I don't understand politics as you know, and all this ideology is a bit ① over my head, but I do know the president doesn't seem to be in control any more. People say the Armed Forces have got him ② under their thumbs and I must say it was a bit of a surprise to see the leader of the Supreme Military Command on TV last month, rather than the President, saying that the protests were threatening democracy, and that the Government would have to ③ put their foot down before the situation got ④ out of hand!

Anyway, since then things have got worse, not better! The security forces used to just ⑤ keep an eye on 'dangerous elements' and 'extremists' (surveillance, they call it), but since all the trouble started they just do whatever they like. They seem to have been given a ⑥ free hand, because people are being arrested and imprisoned all the time, without a trial or anything! (Not to mention that there are soldiers armed ⑦ to the teeth on every street corner.) Well, I suppose the Army know what they're doing.

Of course, the opposition parties in Parliament have protested, but not very loudly. The army have made it pretty clear they don't want any politicians poking ⑧ their noses into matters of internal security, and nobody's brave (or stupid) enough to ⑨ stick his neck out by criticising what's going on. As for united action, well, they can't seem to see ⑩ eye to eye about anything, so how can they be expected to act together on this? It's incredible, if anyone had told me last year that this would happen I'd have thought they were ⑪ pulling my leg, but believe me it's no joke at all. Well, let's just hope for the best and keep ⑫ our fingers crossed!

Regards,
Fred

E Reading 2

Discussion

● Note down anything you know about the causes of disease and poor health in poor countries.
● What is your opinion regarding natural or herbal medicines? Do you know of any herbal preparations which work?
● How far should one trust doctors?

Reading exercises

1 At eight points in the article you are going to read, sentences or fragments have been removed. What was in each gap? Cover the list of sentences and fragments at the end of the article.

2 Study the list under the text, which contains the missing fragments from the article with six additions. Choose the eight correct items. Where do they go in the article? Check with your teacher and fill the gaps in the text.

3 Mark the following statements T (true) or F (false) according to the article.
a Dr Carriconde is working in London to find out if herbal remedies such as lemon grass really do work.
b People living around Kew Gardens know about the healing properties of herbs.

BRAZIL

Herbal Remedy

Anthony Swift on medicine for the people, by the people, in the slums of Recife

For the past two months Dr Celerino Carriconde has been moving between Kew Gardens and Chelsea College, London, identifying plant species in the one and establishing chemical components in the other in order to authenticate the knowledge of the slum dwellers of Recife.

He wants to know, for example, why lemon grass works as an anti-spasmodic, why rue can be used as an antibiotic against uterus infections and (1) _____.
Such herbs and the knowledge local people have of their healing properties have provided Dr Carriconde with a starting point for a health care regime that has aroused the interest of conventional physicians.

Essential to the new medicine — which he believes is being developed in different countries, including America — is that the doctor stops posturing as a provider of health and encourages people to become active in securing their own health and to understand the nature, cures and causes of disease.

It is totally opposed to the pharmaceutical industry, (2) _____

Arbor Camphoræ

Fig. 32.

_____, many of them dangerous and restricted in other countries, and sold 'like bananas' to people ignorant of their side effects.

Dr Carriconde got into the new medicine by a very roundabout route. He was jailed in 1969 while treating striking metal workers, was held for 95 days and tortured. On his release he went into exile, moving from Uruguay, to Chile, to Panama, then Canada.

It has been his choice 'as a Catholic' to work with the poor, and it was in Panama while treating an Indian woman with an infected Caesarean birth wound that he (3) _____
_____.

'Now I know honey has both bactericide and bacteriostatic effects. I began to learn from the Indians about their herbal remedies,' he says.

Unable to work in Canada as a doctor he had to accept the role of hospital orderly and from this unwanted perspective (4) _____
_____.

'I realised I had been completely wrong in my approach. Like them I had regarded my patients as objects I

c Dr Carriconde believes that doctors should stop providing health.

d Dr Carriconde wants people to know more about sickness and what they can do to stay healthy.

e In Brazil, dangerous drugs are sold indiscriminately.

f In Canada, Dr Carriconde took the job of hospital orderly in order to observe the doctors.

g He was positively impressed by the way the Canadian doctors regarded patients.

h He and his wife went back to Recife after elections in Canada.

i An important aspect of Dr Carriconde's scheme is that people should have a sense of community.

j Dr Carriconde just believes in health and has no strong political views.

4 Do you agree that 'the struggle for health leads ultimately to the doors of the rich and powerful'? If not, why not? If so, what can be done about it?

5 One could say that this article and the Hemingway story in Reading 1 contradict each other. How?

6 Summarise the views of Dr Carriconde in seven or eight sentences.

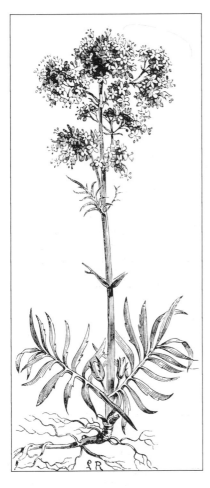

had to heal. It induces people to regard ill-health as something best left to doctors. It induces fatalism.'

A change in government and an amnesty enabled Dr Carriconde and his wife, Diana, to go home. (5) ————

The slum dwellers live in crowded, narrow streets amid stinking fumes from the sewage ducts and uncollected piles of refuse, and having to drink contaminated water.

'They had a half-remembered tradition of herbal remedies, but thought of disease as coming because God willed it. For six months we just learned from them and began to classify their use of herbs and the results. They had empirical knowledge — their herbal cures worked. They didn't know why.'

With the assistance from Unais and Christian Aid, 200 residents have been trained as health workers in a scheme designed to involve the people and increase their confidence in their own resources, and those of their community.

'We would never start by saying bronchitis is a disease of the lungs. We would ask, in their own terminology, how a mother treated her own children for bronchitis.'

(6) ————————.

After the discussion, they are put in a garden and the popular names, uses and preparations are recorded.

'If a person doesn't have the appropriate curative herb in their own garden they are referred to someone else who does. The conversation likely to arise stirs the social memory and helps strengthen the community.'

(7) ————————

—for 'TB or an infant with pneumonia you have to use chemical drugs.' Nor do they challenge the main cause of disease — hunger. The struggle for health leads them ultimately to the well-secured doors of the rich and powerful.

Anthony Swift *The Sunday Times*

a People bring plants to meetings.

b he studies such herbs.

c Because hygiene and natural medicine do not cure all diseases

d which has flooded Brazil with drugs (40,000 different varieties as opposed to 7,000 in the UK)

e why a variety of mint, mixed with honey, eradicates amoebas

f They went to Recife again to put into practice what they had learned from Canadian doctors.

g realised how ignorant primitive people are about sickness

h slum dwellers come to meetings with the health workers.

i he observed his fellow doctors

j how modern drugs can cure their diseases.

k But rubbish removal and herbal remedies do not answer all diseases

l confirmed the curative properties of honey

m the nature, cures, and causes of disease.

n They went to Recife again to work among the poor

tactful

F Speaking

Focus on function: getting information tactfully; giving opinions tactfully; giving advice and making suggestions; accepting and refusing advice; explaining problems; making excuses

1 Listening comprehension

Listen to the dialogue, and answer the following questions.

a What information does Jack get out of Gladys?
b Why is Jack concerned?
c What does Jack suggest or advise?
d How does Gladys react?

2 Pronunciation

Listen to the ten utterances below, and mark the syllables which carry main stress.

a Good Heavens, Gladys, you're getting really fat, you know!
b Yes, perhaps I should.
c Do you mind if I ask how much you weigh these days?
d How old are you, if you don't mind my asking?
e I really think you ought to lose weight.
f Well, I've tried that, but it's no good.
g It's all right for you, you're thin anyway!
h Look, Gladys, if you don't mind my saying so, I think you're being rather negative.
i Have you tried doing exercises?
j You've got a point, I suppose. I'll try again.
Repeat each utterance, trying to match the pronunciation on the cassette.

3 Reproduction

Using the flow diagram to help you, act out the dialogue, using the original language where possible, and improvising when necessary.

4 Improvisation

Improvise similar conversations for the following problems.
A friend who drinks too much.
A friend who smokes too much.
The concerned friend should think first about what advice to give. The person receiving the advice should think about what the advice will be, and think of excuses in advance.

I'LL NEVER HAPPEN TO ME!

sound of eating

sound of drinking

MMMM! YUMMY! CHOMP! SNOOZE! SIP! SIP! GASP! MUNCH! HIC!

BRITISH HEART FOUNDATION
Guide to a healthy heart

Flow diagram for Exercise 3

Dialogue

1 Observe: *really / fat / know !*
Advise: *better / about it*

2 Accept: perhaps / should
really / think / that / bad

3 Question tactfully: *mind / ask /*
weigh / these days ?

4 Answer: know / a bit / more / last year

5 Advise: seriously / laugh / about
Question: How / weigh / in fact

6 Answer: *about 14 stone*

7 Comment: that / an awful
Observe tactfully: hope / dangerously / fat
Question tactfully: *old / mind /*
asking ?

8 Answer: 34
Ask for clarification: what / mean / dangerously

9 Clarify: heart attack / of course
Observe tactfully: hate to / say / a lot / fat / heart / carry
Advise emphatically: think / ought / lose
how / many / a day / eat

10 Accept: Yes / see / your / point
Explain problem: tried / diet / seem / work
Ask advice: you / think / I / ought / do

11 Give opinion tactfully: opinion / complicated / work

12 Answer: hardly / stop / really

13 Suggest: have / tried / eating / less / often
Suggest: why / eat / twice / a day

14 Answer: *tried / no good*
Explain problem: *resist / temptation*

15 Advise forcefully: *way / see /*
you / got to resist

16 Reject 1: easier said / done / isn't it
2: right / you / think / anyway
3: easy / you / talk
Explain: *thing is / so much weight*
hardly worth starting

17 Advise tactfully: you've / got / start / if / might / think

18 Accept: suppose / you / might / better

19 Question: Have / tried / exercising

20 Answer: tried / keep fit / any good

21 Question tactfully: many / tried / don't / mind

22 Answer: often / three or four

23 Exclaim: what / expect / got to / keep
Advise forcefully:

24 Respond negatively: sure / right / what / point

25 Observe tactfully: *don't mind /*
saying / negative
Warn: you / don't / weight / get / problem

26 Accept: got / point / suppose / try

G Writing

Guided work: topic sentences

The first sentence of a paragraph often helps us in our reading by expressing briefly the paragraph's main idea, so that we know what to expect as we read. It is called the topic sentence.

Example: *Poor pay and status, long, hard hours, and lack of support are putting increasing pressure on nurses to leave the NHS.* Take the nursing staff in a psychiatric ward at one North London hospital. They have all considered, or are considering, throwing in three years' training. They find themselves having to do porters' work as well as their own, and take on second jobs to earn extra cash. (*Newspaper report*)

1 Write topic sentences to precede the following short paragraphs, taken from a government booklet on exercise:

a _____ .
A round of golf is a walk of four or five miles in the open air. You'll probably have to walk up and down hills as well, it's not all on the flat. And that's not all. Don't forget that you can't play golf with your bare hands, so you'll be carrying heavy clubs or pulling your trolley every foot of the way.

b _____ .
The simplest is just to add a little walking to your journey to work or to the shops. At weekends, you can explore the parks in your area, and get to know the local streets. If you feel more ambitious, take a car or bus ride out into the country, where you'll find plenty of footpaths. If you prefer walking in company, there are clubs you can join.

c _____ .
Just twenty or thirty minutes, two or three times a week, can keep you fit and active. And no matter how full your day is, the time you spend on exercise will be the best investment you could make.

2 Either write paragraphs for three of the following topic sentences, or choose one of them and use it for the topic sentence of a 300-word composition.
a Smoking really is a stupid thing to do.
b If there's an ideal exercise, it's swimming.
c Walking is the most natural exercise of all.
d Health has become big business.
e The average person in the developing world lives a very unhealthy life.

3 In C Listening, you discussed the rights and wrongs of private health care, and heard Dr King's opinion. Which of the following facts and opinions would appear in:
i a letter to a newspaper arguing for private health care;
ii a letter to a newspaper arguing for an increase in government spending on the health service.
a It is everybody's right to have prompt, adequate health care.
b It is everybody's right to spend their money as they like.
c Private companies help public health services by doing some of their work.
d It is wrong for some people to be healthier than others because they are richer.
e It is nice to have your own room in a hospital.
f If the NHS were only for poor people, with influential people using private plans, the government could never be pressured into improving it.
g Armaments are a waste of money which could be spent on health.
h NHS doctors are dangerously overtired because there aren't enough of them.
i British private clinics do not train nurses, but steal NHS-trained nurses, by offering better pay.
j Visiting hours are freer in private clinics.
k Waiting lists for treatment are very long in NHS hospitals.
l It is wrong to restrict people's choice: patients can go to any private clinic, but only to the NHS hospital to which they are sent.
m Free choice between clinics is only for the rich; other people can't afford any of them.
n Looking after people's health for profit is simply immoral.
Note that some of the facts could be used in both letters. How would they be used?

4 Choose one of the following writing options.
a Write one of the letters, first selecting the opinions and facts you wish to include.
b Write about the health system in your country, and what could be done to improve it.
c Write about what should be done to improve health in poorer countries.
Before you start writing, decide how many paragraphs you are going to use, and what will be said in each paragraph.

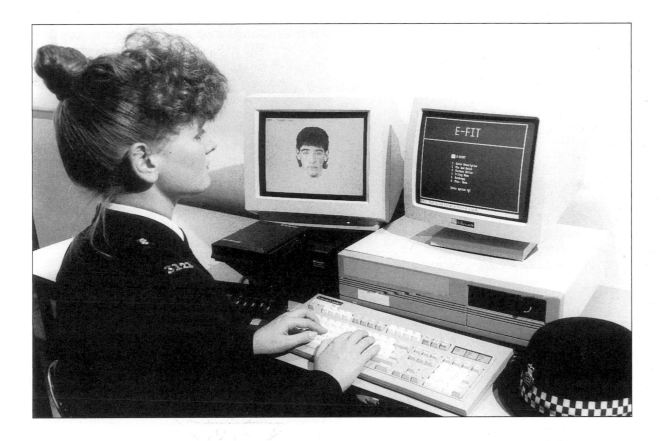

A Vocabulary
Crimes and British legal vocabulary

B Speaking
Story telling, acting: Tell me another one!
Role play: An interview for a job

C Reading 1
A literary extract:
The snatching of Bookie Bob

D Grammar
Ellipsis and substitution

E Reading 2
An advertisement: Brothers-in-law

F Writing
Guided work: tracing the development of an essay; mentioning the opinions of others

G Listening
An account of a crime:
Like going shopping

Lenient 緩やかな   prosecuter

A Vocabulary

Crimes

1

a What is a crime? Work out a definition. Look up the word in your dictionaries. How does the definition compare with yours?

b Make a list of all the types of crime you know of, covering the list at the bottom of the page.

c Check against the list. Look up the meanings of any new words.

d How could this list be divided up into groups of crimes?

e Note down, in order, the three crimes which your group considers to be the most horrible, and the three which it considers to be the least horrible. Provide reasons for your choice.

2 Listen to the cassette, and match the spontaneous definitions that you hear to the crimes on your list.

3 Choose three crimes from your list and define them for your partner (without saying the word). Your partner must say the crime you mean.

4 Listen to the snatches of conversation on the cassette. Which crimes are concerned?
smuggling   treason   espionage   embezzlement
blackmail   bribery   kidnapping   hijacking
mugging   assault   burglary   rape   forgery
murder   manslaughter   arson   terrorism
pickpocketing   fraud   extortion   piracy

British legal vocabulary

5 Read the following, paying particular attention to the words in italics. Discuss the meanings of these in groups, and use your dictionary for any which are still not clear.

When someone is *arrested for committing an offence*, he is taken to the police station for interrogation. If the police decide there is *a case against him*, he is *charged with* the offence, that is to say the police formally accuse him of committing it. After this, the accused *appears before a magistrate*. This is a well-respected member of the public who is empowered to decide, with a lawyer's help, what to do about minor cases. If the magistrate *finds* the accused *guilty*, he will *sentence* him to pay *a fine*, or some other minor punishment.

More serious cases are passed up to the *Crown Court*, where *the accused* is *tried for* the offence by *a judge*, and usually *a jury*. Very serious *cases* are *heard* in the *high courts* in London. The accused may have to wait a long time to *stand trial*. Sometimes he can pay *bail*, as a kind of guarantee, and await the trial in freedom. In other cases, he is *remanded in custody* by the magistrate, and must wait in a cell, in a police station or a remand prison.

At the trial, the accused *pleads guilty* or *not guilty*. If he pleads not guilty, the jury, composed of twelve ordinary citizens, has to decide if he is guilty or not. This decision is called their *verdict*. The judge directs proceedings, and decides what punishment to give, if any. The lawyers who try to persuade the jury are called *barristers*. *In court*, the one on the side of the accused is known as the *Counsel for the Defence*, and the one against him is called the *Counsel for the Prosecution*. Each barrister *calls witnesses* to *give evidence* in support of his case. The witnesses can be *cross-examined* by the other counsel, who tries to persuade the jury that the evidence is untrue or not important.

When all *the evidence* has been *heard*, the judge *sums up the case* and explains legal points for the jury's benefit. He must not try to influence their decision, however. The jury *retire* to another room, where they try to *reach a verdict*. If they find the accused *guilty as charged*, we say he has been *convicted of* the offence. The judge then *passes sentence*. He may *sentence* the guilty person *to pay* a fine, to *a number* of years' *imprisonment*, or to some other punishment. If the verdict is 'not guilty', we say the accused has been *acquitted of* the offence, and he goes free. If the accused feels there was something unfair about the trial, he may *appeal* to the *Appeal Courts*, where three judges decide the case.

6 Cover the text. Which words on the left go with which word or words on the right?

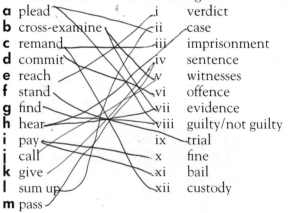

a plead
b cross-examine
c remand
d commit
e reach
f stand
g find
h hear
i pay
j call
k give
l sum up
m pass

i   verdict
ii   case
iii imprisonment
iv   sentence
v   witnesses
vi   offence
vii evidence
viii guilty/not guilty
ix   trial
x   fine
xi   bail
xii custody

7 Which people are connected with which items in Exercise 6. In what way?
the police   the accused   the magistrate
the judge   the jury   the witnesses
the barristers

break into the house
= break in

sleet ミゾレ
slush 雪どけ Melting snow

B Speaking

Story telling

Tell me another one!

1 Work in groups of three or four. Your teacher will give you ten pictures. Together, plan a story concerning a crime, in which the subject of each of these pictures is a key factor.

2 Form new groups, in which there must be at least one person from each original group. Tell each other the stories you made up in your first groups. As you listen, ask questions about anything you do not understand.

3 Get back into your original groups and report back on any changes which you would now like to make in your group's story.

4 Choose one long scene or two short scenes from your story and write a script, as if for a play. Everybody in your group should have a part to play.

5 Rehearse the scenes, and prepare a written synopsis of the story leading up to the scenes, so that they can be understood in their context.

6 Act out your scene(s) for the rest of your class, or find somewhere to work uninterrupted and record the scenes, as if for a radio play.

大恐慌 Depression

Role play

An interview for a job

You are going to do a series of short role plays, each involving a group of three or four students. One student will be a person who wants to join the police force, and is applying for a place on a training course. The other students form an interviewing panel, who must assess the candidate's suitability for a career as a police officer, and accept or refuse the candidate accordingly. Each panel will interview each candidate in rotation. When each candidate has been interviewed, each panel must decide which one was the most suitable and which was the least suitable.

kidnap
abduction
└ 営利目的でない

1 Role play situation
Candidates
All the candidates should form a group and discuss the questions they are likely to be asked by the panel. These will probably include both factual questions and open-ended questions designed to reveal something of the candidate's personality, strengths and weaknesses. Your teacher will help you with ideas. The candidates should first agree who is to be the most suitable candidate and who is to be the least suitable. Together, work out a brief curriculum vitae for each candidate, and plan the sort of answers each candidate will give to open-ended questions. Also consider factors like the tone of voice, posture, and manner of each applicant.

Interviewing panels
The panels should prepare the questions they will ask, and decide which panel member will ask which questions. The questions should include both factual questions and questions designed to reveal something of the candidate's personality, strengths and weaknesses. Prepare a form for noting the answers to the factual questions (one form for each candidate). If necessary, your teacher will help you with ideas for the questions.

2 Acting the role play   *blindfold*
Arrange the classroom suitably for the interviews, preferably with each interviewing panel sitting behind a table, with a chair in front for the candidates. Each interview should last no more than five or ten minutes.

Bail 保釈(金)
Criminal system
police — court —┌ Mental hospital
*   ├ Jail / prison*
*   ├ probation service*
*   └ community service*
┌ neighbourhood watch
└ night watch

Age of ~~agreement~~ consent
*   同意*

potential ?
Latent }

lawyers ┌ Solicitor
*   ├ barrister*
*   ├ prosecution*
*   └ defense*

aquit 放免

ransom 身代金

wound 我ズ

C **Reading 1**

Discussion

● With what motives are people usually kidnapped?
● Do you think kidnappers' demands should be met? Why/Why not? If your answer is, 'It depends', what does it depend on?
● Describe any kidnapping you know about.
● How would you kidnap someone? Consider all the stages. What would be the most dangerous part? How could you make it safer?
● The extract you are going to read is the beginning of a short story by Damon Runyan, an American writer who wrote about the USA of the nineteen-twenties and thirties. Note down anything you know about the USA during that period.

Reading exercises

1 Runyon uses a great many slang expressions from the period, which have since gone out of fashion. Read the extract, and match the slang expressions below with the paraphrases on the right.

a	bust	i	kidnap
b	put the finger on	ii	the police
c	snatch	iii	racket, illegal business
d	mobbed up	iv	a phoney person, story, etc.
e	scratch	v	identify someone to an enemy
f	dodge	vi	go out of business
g	the gendarmes	vii	money
h	chuck a swell	viii	in a gang
i	the phonus bolonus	ix	spend money extravagantly

The snatching of Bookie Bob

lapels 又y

NOW it comes on the spring of 1931, after a long hard winter, and times are very tough indeed, what with the stock market going all to pieces, and banks busting right and left, and the law getting very nasty about this and that, and one thing and another, and many citizens of this town are compelled to do the best they can.

2   There is very little scratch anywhere and along Broadway many citizens are wearing last year's clothes and have practically nothing to bet on the races or anything else, and it is a condition that will touch anybody's heart.

3   So I am not surprised to hear rumours that the snatching of certain parties is going on in spots, because while snatching is by no means a high-class business, and is even considered somewhat illegal, it is something to tide over the hard times.

4   Furthermore, I am not surprised to hear that this snatching is being done by a character by the name of Harry the Horse, who comes from Brooklyn, and who is a character who does not care much what sort of business he is in, and who is mobbed up with other characters from Brooklyn such as Spanish John and Little Isadore, who do not care what sort of business they are in, either.

5   In fact, Harry the Horse and Spanish John and Little Isadore are very hard characters in every respect, and there is considerable indignation expressed around and about when they move over from Brooklyn into Manhattan and start snatching, because the citizens of Manhattan feel that if there is any snatching done in their territory, they are entitled to do it themselves.

6   But Harry the Horse and Spanish John and Little Isadore pay no attention whatever to local sentiment and go on the snatch on a pretty fair scale, and by and by I am hearing rumours of some very nice scores. These scores are not extra large scores, to be sure, but they are enough to keep the wolf from the door, and in fact from three different doors, and before long Harry the Horse and Spanish John and Little Isadore are around the race-tracks betting on the horses, because if there is one thing they are all very fond of, it is betting on the horses.

7   Now many citizens have the wrong idea entirely of the snatching business. Many citizens think that

2 Discuss the following questions in groups.

a What seems to have brought about the increase in kidnapping?

b What kind of people are 'the citizens of Manhattan'? (para. 5)

c 'So of course such a party is no good for snatching.' (para. 9) Who? Why?

d Who is 'the finger guy'? (para. 10)

e What two things must 'the finger guy' know about the person he fingers?

f What reasons are given for people 'settling their bill' (paying the ransom) without making any fuss?

g What percentage of the ransom do the kidnappers get?

h What, it seems, is the most important factor in making a kidnapping safe?

3 One of the things which makes Runyon's writing style so individual and amusing, is the way he puts colourful slang expressions and quite formal English in the same sentence.

Example: . . . *one and all are satisfied and much fresh scratch comes into circulation.*

Find formal words and expressions in the text which mean the following:

a forced

b people

c also

d in every way

e people are angry

f someone like that

g doesn't want to

h to want

i it wouldn't be right

4 Did anything in the extract make you smile? What?

---

all there is to snatching is to round up the party who is to be snatched and then just snatch him, putting him away somewhere until his family or friends dig up enough scratch to pay whatever price the snatchers are asking. Very few citizens understand that the snatching business must be well organized and very systematic.

8   In the first place, if you are going to do any snatching, you cannot snatch just anybody. You must know who you are snatching, because naturally it is no good snatching somebody who does not have any scratch to settle with. And you cannot tell by the way a party looks or how he lives in this town if he has any scratch, because many a party who is around in automobiles, and wearing good clothes, and chucking quite a swell is nothing but the phonus bolonus and does not have any real scratch whatever.

9   So of course such a party is no good for snatching, and of course guys who are on the snatch cannot go around inquiring into bank accounts, or asking how much this and that party has in a safe-deposit vault, because such questions are apt to make citizens wonder why, and it is very dangerous to get citizens to wondering why about anything. So the only way guys who are on the snatch can find out about parties worth snatching is to make a connection with some guy who can put the finger on the right party.

10   The finger guy must know the party he fingers has plenty of ready scratch to begin with, and he must also know that this party is such a party as is not apt to make too much disturbance about being snatched, such as telling the gendarmes. The party may be a legitimate party, such as a business guy, but he will have reasons why he does not wish it to

get out that he is snatched, and the finger must know these reasons. Maybe the party is not leading the right sort of life, such as running around with blondes when he has an ever-loving wife and seven children in Mamaroneck, but does not care to have his habits known, as is apt to happen if he is snatched, especially if he is snatched when he is with a blonde.

11   And sometimes the party is such a party as does not care to have matches run up and down the bottom of his feet, which often happens to parties who are snatched and who do not seem to wish to settle their bill promptly, because many parties are very ticklish on the bottom of the feet, especially if the matches are lit. On the other hand maybe the party is not a legitimate guy, such as a party who is running a crap game or a swell speakeasy, or who has some other dodge he does not care to have come out, and who also does not care about having his feet tickled.

12   Such a party is very good indeed for the snatching business, because he is pretty apt to settle without any argument. And after a party settles one snatching, it will be considered very unethical for anybody else to snatch him again very soon, so he is not likely to make any fuss about the matter. The finger guy gets a commission of twenty-five per cent of the settlement, and one and all are satisfied and much fresh scratch comes into circulation, which is very good for the merchants. And while the party who is snatched may know who snatches him, one thing he never knows is who puts the finger on him, this being considered a trade secret.

Damon Runyan *On Broadway* Picador

D | Grammar

Ellipsis and substitution

When making replies in English, we often use ellipsis or substitution.

Ellipsis means leaving out unnecessary words.
Example:
Is he angry?   Yes he is.
Has she done it?   Yes, she has.
Angry and *done it* are left out.

Substitution usually involves replacing verbs with auxilliary verbs.
Examples:
Did you go?   Yes, I did.
Are you going to the party?   I might do.
Did replaces *went* and *do* replaces *go.*

This section practises advanced ellipsis and substitution.

Neither, so

1 Listen, and write down what the second speaker says in each exchange.
a I don't like this.   *Neither do I* .
b I was there.   *So was I* .
c I wouldn't do it.   *Neither would I* .
d I've done this before.   *So have I* .

Why do we use *neither* and why do we use *so*? *agreement*
How do we know which word to put after *neither* or *so*?
Repeat what the second speaker says each time.   Try to match your pronunciation to the pronunciation on the cassette.

2 Working in pairs, make and respond to the following statements, using *neither* or *so*.   Take turns.
a I wish we were in New York. *So do I* , / *I don't*
b I can speak French. *So can I* . *Neither can I*
c I want to leave. *So do I* / *Neither do I*
d I've finished. *So have I* / *Neither have I*
e I wasn't angry. *So have I* / *Neither have I*
        Neither was I
        / *So was I*

f I wish I hadn't invited him now. *So do I* *I do ~*   *Neither do I*

g If I had the money I'd stop working. *So would I.*
h I haven't seen her recently. *Neither have I*
i I'd never eaten Turkish food before. *Neither had I,*
j I could drive when I was fourteen. *So could I.*

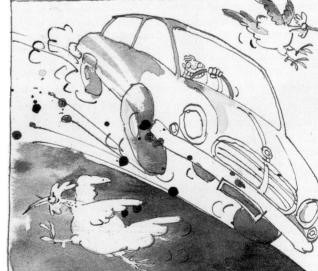

3 If we differ from the speaker, we answer differently.   Listen, and repeat what the second speaker says each time.

4 In pairs, say and respond to the statements in **2** in the same way as the speakers on the cassette.

Agreeing and disagreeing

5 Listen to the following exchanges, and repeat what the second speaker says each time.
a Well that wasn't a very good film.   Yes it was.
b That was a good film.   Yes, it was.
c I wasn't rude!   Yes you were.
d Perhaps I was a bit rude.   Yes, you were.
        What is the effect of stress and intonation on the response in each exchange?

6 Work in pairs. Take turns to be Student A. Read out either the first statement or the second statement for each item. Student B must pronounce the reply according to whether it expresses agreement or disagreement.

Student A	Student B
a At least it's not raining. That's a pity.	Yes it is.
b You wouldn't care if I died. I expect you'd like a rest.	Yes I would.
c You've never even been to Paris. You've been to Rome, haven't you?	Yes I have.
d You're not enjoying this, are you? I can see you're annoyed about something.	No I'm not.
e He should be ashamed of himself. He shouldn't have done that.	No he shouldn't.
f You never do any homework. Do you find this sort of work useful?	Yes I do.

Hope, expect, think

In short affirmative responses, these can all be followed by *so*.
Example:

Are they going to win?	*I hope so.*
	I expect so.
	I think so.
In negative responses, we say:	*I don't think so.*
	I don't expect so.
	I hope not.

7 In pairs, ask and respond to the following questions.

a Is your English going to get better if you keep studying?
b Will it rain tomorrow?
c Will the next American president be a good one?
d Did you lock your car?
e Do you think your country will win the next World Cup?
f Will you go abroad for your next holiday?
g Will you get married in the next five years?
h Will the Socialists win the next general election in your country?
i Are things going to get worse in your country?
j Is this exercise helping your English at all?

Infinitives

In short responses with the infinitive, we only say the *to*.
Example:
Why are you reading this? My teacher asked me to.

8 In pairs, ask the following questions and respond in your own words. Use the clues in brackets if necessary.

a Why did you stop smoking? (*doctor/advise*)
b Are you going on holiday with your parents? (*yes/Dad/persuade*)
c Do you think you'll marry? (*intend*)
d Have you washed the dishes? (*no/but/go*) I'm going to.
e Come on, get this exercise right! (*try*) I'm trying to
f Why didn't you wash the car as well? (*you/not/ask*)
g I can't lend you that money, by the way. (*but/promise*) You promised to.
h Can you drive? (*no/but/learn*) I'm learning to.

Modal verbs

In short answers using modals, we use only the modal, or replace the main verb with *do*.
Examples:
They say he earns a fortune. He must (do).
Will this train leave on time? It should (do)
But who knows?

For the past, we just use *have*, or replace the main verb with *done*.

Examples: *Maybe they've gone out.*	*Yes, they might have (done).*
Well, you could have told me!	*Yes, I should have (done), sorry.*

With *to be*, or progressive verb forms, we include *be* or *been*.

Examples:	
Hard work, by the look of it.	*It must be.*
I wasn't watching.	*Well you should have been!*

All types

9 Work in groups of three. Take turns. One student reads out each sentence and the others respond in turn, agreeing or disagreeing.
Example:

Did she kill him?	*She might have, I suppose.*
	I don't think so.

a Does this train go to Brighton?
b I hate doing exercise.
c It looks as if it's going to rain.
d Life is wonderful.
e I wouldn't like to be rich.
f I didn't do my homework.
g Do you think there will be many people at the party?

E | Reading 2

Discussion

● Write a true sentence beginning: 'The police
…' Read your sentence to your group, and explain
what you mean.
● Note down anything you know or think you
know about the British police.
● What would be the advantages and the
drawbacks of being a policeman, either in the UK
or in your own country?
● What would you put in an advertisement
designed to attract new recruits to the police?

Reading exercises

1 Study the police advertisement, which has been
jumbled. Put the pieces back in the right order,
paying attention to the content of each paragraph
and to words which link paragraphs.
Two pieces have been numbered for you.
When you have finished, turn to Study page 172
and check your ordering against the original text.

2 Discuss the following questions in groups.
a What is the play on words contained in the title of
the advertisement? Why does the picture show a
black man and a white man? What part of the text
expresses the same idea?
b The advertisement arranges sentences as if they
were paragraphs, and short phrases as if they were
sentences. Why?

3 Find words or expressions which mean the
following.
a resolve or clarify ⟨sort out⟩
b disturbance rumpus
c an abusive argument slanging match time & time again
d very often (*usually more than you would like*)
e someone whose job is to help people in difficulties
f nasty sordid/seamy social worker!
g generous, not selfish kind/selfless
h hard, demanding aspects of something
rigour

4 In five or six sentences, explain how the
advertisement tries to make the job of a policeman
sound attractive.

colloquial
乱言葉

a
3 But where some communities may be
divided, the Police are not. And it's not just
the uniforms they wear that unites them.
They share the same basic principles.
Otherwise they would never have wanted to
join in the first place.

b He needs to be something of a social worker
on the one hand.
10

c And it's the experience that makes them
14 mates. Knowing they can rely on each other
in times of crisis.
If you think you are the kind of man or
woman who could cope with the rigours as
well as the rewards, write to: Police Careers

POLICE **OFFICER**

helmet

to evacuate an area
evacuation 立ち退き

admit/confess 白状する
The police extracts the
confessions
with violence.

comradeship
仲間

Brothers-in-law

d
13
When members of the public are helpful, kind and selfless.
The two officers we've pictured here both have a breadth of experience few of us could match.

e
5
And what all Officers have in common is that they are dealing daily with human problems.

f
1
As you can see, the Police have changed in recent years.

g
4
And those are the same principles of law and order that existed twenty years ago and more.
Ask any Policeman or Policewoman why they applied for the job, and you'll get the same answer. 'To get involved with people.' To get involved with the community they patrol. To understand it. Safeguard it. Unarmed, remember.

h
6
With different sorts of people. Who rarely behave predictably.
There are few situations in which an Officer has a textbook solution to the difficulties he faces.

i
12
—Yet he'll also see human nature at its best.

j
7
For example, he's called in to sort out a rumpus on a housing estate.
It has been reported that a man is beating up his neighbour.

k
8
He discovers that there's only been a slanging match. Even so, the peace has been disturbed.
Technically he could arrest either or both of them. But a better solution might well be to talk the problem out.

l
2
—But the way they've changed is simply a reflection of the way Britain itself has changed.
Just as individuals who make up our society come from every imaginable background, from every walk of life, so do our Police Officers.

m
11
Yet, on the other, he is invested with the authority of the law.
He sees the seamy side of life, the sordid and the unpleasant.

n
9
You see, it's a grey area with no easy answer.
And every Officer will tell you that it's like that time and time again.

F Writing

Guided work: tracing the development of an essay; mentioning the opinions of others

1 Consider this essay title: Discuss effective measures for counteracting violence in our cities. Discuss how you would write the essay. What facts or ideas would you include? How would you organise them in paragraphs to make your argument effective?

2 Read the essay. As you read, take notes, putting them in the flow diagram opposite.

The first point that has to be clarified here is the meaning of the word *violence*. There are, after all, many types of violence in our cities, ranging from baby battering to the suppression of political demonstrations by police. For the purposes of this essay I shall limit discussion to the violence which most concerns city dwellers in Britain nowadays: riots, robbery and physical assault on the streets.

What measures can be taken to combat this kind of violence? Well, to begin with, it is often argued that violent crime should be punished more severely. That is to say, more offenders sent to prison, longer prison sentences, and even the reintroduction of the death penalty. The first two ideas seem reasonable, but ignore the problem that our prisons are already full, and also that ex-prisoners are more likely to commit crime than other people. In addition, it is very expensive to keep people in prison. As for the death penalty, there is no hard evidence that it has any effect on the commission of crimes. Punishing crime more severely, then, does not seem to work.

A more effective measure would be to improve the service provided by the police. Many people would say that British policemen should carry guns, but I do not agree, since this would lead to more guns being used by thieves, and consequently more violence, probably involving innocent bystanders. Also, we must remember that not every policeman is psychologically fit to carry a gun. Nevertheless, certain changes can be made. Firstly, the size of the police force could be increased, by improving salaries and conditions. Equally importantly, the police should receive better training, so that they can deal effectively with trouble without becoming unduly violent themselves. Clearly, a large, well-trained police force must be an important factor in any attempt to tackle crime.

However, none of these ideas deals with the root of urban violence, and that is what I shall turn to for the rest of this essay. It has been said that the stress caused by just living in a modern city is an important factor in making people violent. This may be true, but little can be done about it, since we can hardly all return to the countryside. Similarly, it might be argued that people are naturally violent, and that the only solution is to change ourselves from the inside. Religion, meditation, psychoanalysis and so on might be helpful in this respect, but it is difficult to be optimistic.

It seems to me that another idea might offer more hope. I believe that street crime is mainly caused by the predicament of many young people on leaving school: that is to say, unemployed, with no money and with little hope for the future. No amount of punishment and no police force will deter young people from taking to a life of crime when the law-abiding life which is the alternative is empty of hope, interest and achievement. The solution is clear. The government must ensure that jobs are provided for young people. Until young people have work, money and hope, it will be impossible to walk safely in the streets.

3 It is effective in arguing a case to anticipate the arguments of other people and to mention their opinions. If we agree with their opinion, we often introduce it with expressions such as: *Most people would agree that . . .*; *It is well-known that . . .* If we don't agree, we prepare the reader by using different expressions.
Find the ones in the text, and the way in which the writer comments on the ideas that he mentions.

4 Below are four opinions, in note form. State the opinion in full, and then give your objections to it. Use as many sentences as you like.
Example:
Atomic war is inevitable/human nature/violent, competitive, suspicious
It is often said that atomic war is inevitable because of human nature, which has always been violent, competitive and suspicious. This point of view, however, ignores the fact that people are intelligent. When our survival is at stake our ability to think rationally will save us from extinction.
a Marriage/old-fashioned institution/causes more hate than love
b Politics and sport not connected/sport unites people, nations
c Terrorism justified in certain cases/no other way to fight for rights
d Democracy a waste of time, hypocritical/one-party system more efficient, no arguments

5 Reproduce the essay in Exercise 2, based only on your diagram, or write your own essay on the subject, perhaps in the form of a critical reply.

Flow diagram for Exercises 2 and 5

Paragraph 1

Topic sentence for paragraph:	
Amplification:	*many types of violence*
Statement of intent:	

Paragraph 2

Topic sentence for essay:	
Topic sentence for paragraph:	*punish more severely*

Restatement of idea:	Restatement of idea: *longer sentences*	Restatement of idea:

Objection:	Objection:	Objection: *expensive*	Objection:

Conclusion for paragraph:

Paragraph 3

Topic sentence for paragraph:	
Idea mentioned:	

Objection:	Objection:

Change direction: *changes can be made*	
First idea:	How achieved:

Second idea and reason why:
Conclusion for paragraph:

Paragraph 4

Topic sentence for rest of essay:	
Idea mentioned:	Objection:
Idea mentioned:	Objection:

Paragraph 5

Topic sentence for paragraph:	*another idea / hope*
Opinion:	
Restatement:	*unemployed / broke / without hope*
Amplification:	
Recommendation:	
Conclusion for essay:	

G Listening

Like going shopping

Discussion

● Have you ever seen or been involved in a crime? Describe it to your group.
● Decide which was the most frightening or serious crime. Was anybody apart from the criminals to blame in any of the stories?

Listening exercises

1 Listen to Martin describing a crime. As you listen, take notes on the details of the incident.
Afterwards, compare notes with other students and build up the story of the incident.

2 Listen again, and answer the following questions.

a In which city did the crime occur?
b In what sort of area did the story begin?
c What was noticeable about the girl?
d How did the crime begin?
e What seemed to be happening at first?
f When did he realise what was really happening?
g 'Either option seems ridiculous.' What are the options mentioned?

h What else could Martin have done? Why didn't he do it?
i How did the other passengers react during the crime? And afterwards?
j How many criminals were involved?
k How did the girl react after the crime?
l 'It's like shopping.' What does Martin mean by this?
m Why was it lucky that there was no policeman on the bus?

3 Listen again, filling the gaps in the following. Each line represents a word or abbreviation.
a ... it's a pretty ____-____, suspect, grotty neighbourhood.
b ... she was very well-groomed, ____ ____ ____ .
c ... who was a poor-looking sort of chap, a bit ____ , leaned over ...
d ... the basic one being 'What ____ ____ ____ ____ now?
e ... obviously you don't grab the bloke, because the gun will ____ ____ .
f ... my mind was just numb, I couldn't ____ it ____ at all.
g ... I didn't bother, I just ____ ____ , I was very shocked, very shaky.
h ... there would have been a ____-____ .

4 Match these meanings to seven of the expressions above.
i went away (*slang*)
ii dressed in old or untidy clothes
iii comprehend
iv apparently rich
v gun fight
vi unattractive, not cared for
vii be fired by accident

5 Choose one of the following writing options.
a Write the story of the hold-up in your own words.
b Write an account (true or imaginary) of a crime you have witnessed.
c Write one of the stories you heard in your group.

Oh 'aint we a deal better than other people! I guess we're a most a splendid example to them thundering old Monarchies!

LIBERTY, EQUALITY, FRATERNITY,

DEDICATED TO THE SMARTEST NATION IN ALL CREATION.

A Reading 1
A newspaper article:
Albania's dam against time

B Vocabulary
Compound nouns

C Reading 2
A news report:
Modern Tamburlaine gets Soviet
exposure

D Speaking
Role play:
Party political discussion

E Listening
Two views of China

F Grammar
Relative clauses: review and advanced
points

G Writing
Guided work: comparison and contrast;
sentence manipulation

A ⃞ **Reading 1**

Discussion

● What do left wing and right wing mean?

● Which of these ideas are left wing and which right wing?

Private ownership of industry is wrong.

War and killing are never justified.

Women should not go out to work.

To repress a people with security forces is sometimes necessary.

If control of information is necessary for efficient government, there's nothing wrong with it.

Everyone should be healthy, well-educated and have the chance to work. Achieving this aim is more important than non-violence, or freedom of action and expression.

● Has your discussion clarified what left and right mean, or are there contradictions?

● Note down anything you know about Albania, and anything you would like to know.

Reading exercises

1 As you read the article about Albania, take notes on the following:
a what the writer seems to have liked during his stay;
b what he is critical of.

2 'Important dreams are not only visually intense. . . ' (para. 3) There is some good descriptive writing in this article. Which parts are most 'visually intense' for you?

3 Discuss the following questions in groups.
a 'We stared in amazement. . .' (para. 1) What was amazing, and why?
b What aspects of Albanian life seem out of date?
c What indications are there of Albania's isolation, and the way it is being reduced?
d How is Albania similar to Stalin's Russia?
e 'Where is the boundary between consent and coercion?' (para. 10) What did the Scottish lecturer mean?
f Why must Albania 'open to the world'? (para. 13) How does the writer seem to feel about this?
g 'The hedgehog of Europe'. (para. 15) Explain the metaphor.
h 'If the sea became yoghurt, the Albanians would not be given a spoon.' (para. 14) Explain this saying.
i What is the writer's purpose? Choose from the following verbs.
to persuade   to entertain
to inform   to warn
to complain   to recommend
to describe   to criticise
j Which adjectives describe how he feels?
interested   angry   admiring
sad   confused   charmed
enthusiastic   pessimistic
surprised   impressed
amused   open-minded

I T BEGAN to grow light soon after we had left Albania. We had walked through the darkness of no-man's-land, carrying our luggage, to the Yugoslav frontier post. Now, in the dawn, we stared in amazement at the first village in this remote corner of Montenegro. There were neat, newly-plastered cottages, little peasant fields, cars parked and men in jeans getting into them. What world was this?

2 It was like awakening from a strange, brilliant dream. At Titograd, there were traffic and gaudy advertisements; the shininess and haste grew more oppressive at Belgrade. At Heathrow, members of our tour party clung together, reluctant finally to wake up.

3 Important dreams are not only visually intense, but tell of the dreamer's own distant memories and longings. I went on a brief five-day coach tour of Albania, with a party of *Observer* readers. We were bewildered, sometimes repelled, but sometimes strangely moved by what we saw.

4 The coach ground along between white mountains and green, cultivated plains, edged with gold leaves of Mediterranean autumn. In the vast collective fields, flocks of women in white headscarves dug drains or weeded. Sometimes the bus braked to avoid a brigade of girls walking along the road with shouldered spades — figures from an old Maoist poster — or to overtake carts drawn by horses or oxen.

5 In the towns, under the blazing red portraits of the late Enver Hoxha, crowds of young men move at an aimless, sauntering pace up and down the empty streets—no private cars are allowed in Albania. There are thin brown men in polonecked sweaters and thin brown suits, with trousers flared in an almost forgotten mode. They have hawkish faces and a dark

Albania's dam against time

NEAL ASCHERSON

formidable stare. There is no noise of traffic, only the sound of feet.

6 This tiny Balkan nation of three million people is the most isolated and totalitarian state on earth. Enver Hoxha's partisans claim to have liberated themselves from Italian and German occupation (British military aid is written out of history). In 1948, Hoxha broke with Yugoslavia. In 1960, he broke with the Soviet Union. In 1977, he broke with China, whose ageing lorries, locomotives, and bicycles still serve the land. Albania borrows no money, and belongs to almost no international bodies. Last year, a mere 7,500 foreign tourists were admitted to the land.

7 Statues and busts of Joseph Stalin stand in every town. This is the extreme of Stalin's 'socialism in one country', of his total central control of all life by Party and State, of the 'cult of personality' he founded. Enver's face is in every institution, Enver's numerous books on sale in every hotel and museum, Enver's words on every vertical surface, Enver's name carved across mountains.

8 But Enver Hoxha is dead. After consuming all his real or imagined rivals, sent to execution or to labour camps, he died in 1985. And under his successor, Ramiz Alia, there are the first small signs of change. Albania is now joining discussions with its Balkan neighbours. West Germany adopted diplomatic relations a few weeks ago. The 'state of war' with Greece ended in January after 47 years, and our hotel was invaded by a Greek delegation of three Ministers — including Melina Mercouri. There are fewer armed men about. And,

with caution, ordinary Albanians are beginning to talk to foreigners.

9 'We are a serious people,' said one. But they have kept old Mediterranean virtues: hospitality, impulsive generosity (a pot plant, a pen, a round of drinks presented by strangers when the English language was heard), a talent for wild rejoicing seen at a wedding I gatecrashed, the leisurely, garrulous public life of square and street corner. For some of us, it was rural Italy after the war; for others, Serbia in the early 1950s.

10 'Where is the boundary here between consent and coercion?' wondered a Scottish lecturer. After only five days, one cannot begin to know. A few young people cursed the system. Many showed a desperate, hopeless, longing to travel. 'I want to kiss the English earth!' said one. 'Life is short. Here, I am poor boy. There, I am free.' One thing seems clear: out of an illiterate, semi-tribal province, the Hoxha regime has created a highly-educated people (many of the young speak phenomenally good English) whose creative potential is now squeezed agonisingly against the iron limits of the system.

11 Patriotism, if not love of the Party, unites all Albanians. They are astoundingly poor, but at least they are properly fed. Electricity is now everywhere, and the land is full of large, decrepit factories slowly producing the basic needs of life, mines exporting chrome ore and copper, dams exporting hydro-electricity. They are equal: nobody earns more than twice anyone else, although the ruling elite — with its chauffeured Mercedes and Volvos —

is more equal than others.

12 While we were there, Romanians were rioting for bread, Hungarians were storming shops, Yugoslavs were striking against wage cuts and Poles were facing enormous price rises. Albania is insulated against the good things of modern life, but also against some of the bad.

13 How long can Albania hold up its dam against time? Perhaps Ramiz Alia is like King Canute, who did not claim that he could hold back the tide but showed his fanatical courtiers that he could not. A mountainous country not much larger than Wales, whose population has grown from 1.6 million in 1960 to over three million today, will soon be unable to feed itself. That means opening to the world. So does the need to modernise equipment, after ten years of isolation.

14 I think that life for those young figures pacing and drifting in Tirana's Skanderbeg Square — 'like a living Lowry painting' said one of us — will soon be different: less secure, more interesting. Some things, though, won't change. Albania's neighbours, great and small, have always tried to manipulate and dominate her. 'If the sea became yoghurt,' runs a saying, 'the Albanians would not be given a spoon.'

15 The slogans may fade, the pill-boxes crumble — as they are beginning to. But Albanians of all opinions feel that they built their country themselves; foreign helpers always ended by trying to take over. Whatever happens, Albania will remain the hedgehog of Europe.

Neal Ascherson *The Observer*

B Vocabulary

Compound nouns

Many English nouns consist of two parts: an adverbial particle, such as *out* or *up*, followed by a verb, or in some cases a noun.

The basic directional meaning of the adverbial prefix is usually preserved. Words beginning with *out*, for example, often have a sense of outward movement, and words beginning with 'in' often have a sense of inward movement or inner position. For example, an *outcry* is a burst of public protest, and an *inmate* is someone kept in a prison or mental hospital.

In speech, the adverbial prefix is always stressed.

1 List all the words of this type that you know.

2 Work in pairs. Find the twenty compound nouns hidden in the letter box below. They run from left to right or top to bottom. Check on Study page 173.
Examples: *outlet, downfall*

	a	b	c	d	e	f	g	h	i	j	k	l	m	n	o	p	q	r	s	t
1	X	V	O	U	T	L	O	O	K	M	B	S	T	Q	O	O	P	V	W	Q
2	E	O	U	U	V	J	K	U	P	D	O	W	N	P	O	U	R	E	O	H
3	O	U	T	P	A	Q	O	T	L	G	I	N	C	O	M	E	F	X	V	O
4	U	J	C	B	O	F	I	S	N	S	E	T	P	S	W	E	T	M	E	U
5	T	F	A	R	U	O	V	E	R	S	I	G	H	T	A	E	O	G	R	T
6	L	O	S	I	T	F	Z	T	Y	X	O	U	T	P	U	T	U	O	T	S
7	A	U	T	N	C	D	O	W	N	F	A	L	L	A	S	W	T	U	I	K
8	W	T	T	G	O	U	T	B	R	E	A	K	G	Y	S	H	B	T	M	I
9	N	L	D	I	M	P	E	N	O	D	V	L	C	Z	A	J	U	L	E	R
10	T	E	S	N	E	Z	X	V	C	H	P	O	V	E	R	D	R	A	F	T
11	G	T	R	G	M	N	V	J	Q	O	U	T	R	A	G	E	S	Y	Q	S
12	H	A	W	R	J	O	V	E	R	H	E	A	D	S	F	H	T	A	S	L

3 Fill the gaps in the following news report with words from the letter box. Cover the glossary which follows the exercise.

People's protest

There has been intense popular anger about the latest increase in (1) _____ tax. Feelings are running so high that this afternoon there were (2) _____ of looting and rioting in the poorer districts around the (3) _____ of the city, as people found an (4) _____ for their rage and frustration in violence. A factory worker had this to say: 'It's a joke, this! I've already got enough trouble trying to pay off my (5) _____ at the bank, doing (6) _____ every evening to earn a bit more, without having to pay more tax as well!'

The rioting was ended by a sudden (7) _____ of rain, much to the relief of the owner of a small factory damaged in the riots. 'Thank goodness that's over,' he said. 'I've already got enough trouble trying to pay the (8) _____ on my factory and give my children a decent (9) _____, without having the place smashed up by rioters as well! As it is, after all the damage that's been done, production is bound to be hit, which means (10) _____ will be reduced for the next few months. And that's not to mention the financial (11) _____

4 Use the glossary to fill any gaps you still have.

Glossary

outset, start;
outlaw, criminal, bandit;
income, money received (*usually for work*);
outcome, effect or result of an event;
outburst, sudden explosion of anger, energy, etc.;
outbreak (of), sudden beginning of violence, disease, war, etc.;
downfall, fall from power or fortune;
output, what is produced by a factory, etc.;
outlook, what seems likely to happen in the future;
outlet, way of releasing feelings;
outcast, someone outside society, homeless and friendless;
downpour, sudden heavy rain;
oversight, failure to take something important into account;
overtime, extra time worked for extra money;
outrage, an act that shocks public opinion;
outskirts, the outer edges of a city or town;
overdraft, money you owe to your bank over a period of time;
overheads, regular expenses incurred in running a business;
outlay, sum of money which is spent on a specific project;
upbringing, training and education of a child at home.

that's going to be necessary to put the factory back on its feet again!'

In an angry (12) _____ in Parliament, the Opposition Spokesperson for Economic Affairs called the increase an (13) _____. At the (14) _____ of his speech, the Spokesperson reminded MPs of what he referred to as 'the Government's habitual carelessness and bad planning,' going on to say, with heavy irony, 'However, not to consider the disastrous effect which this measure will have on low-paid workers, the unwilling (15) _____ of our society, is an (16) _____ even more disastrous than the others committed so frequently by this Government.' In defence of the rioters, he added: 'It is regrettable that people should show their feelings in such a violent manner. Nevertheless, these people are not (17) _____ but honest citizens provoked beyond endurance by a greedy and insensitive Government.'

It is difficult to predict the (18) _____ of these latest troubles, but the (19) _____ for the government is not bright; it is thought by some observers that this may be the final blunder that will cause its (20) _____.

5 Write a news report with your partner, including as many compound nouns as you can.

Read your report aloud to another pair, taking turns. As the other pair read their report to you, note down every compound noun you hear.

Check with the other pair how many of their words you heard.

C Reading 2

Discussion

- Note down anything you know about how agriculture is organised in the USSR.
- What is the difference between Russia and the USSR?

- Note down anything you know about Tashkent, Tamburlaine, the politburo, Uzbekistan, Literaturnaya Gazeta.
- The following words and phrases are from the news report opposite. What will it be about?

The Soviet press / Akhmadjan Adilov / secret kingdom / 30,000 collective farm workers / private prison camp / prosperous farm complex / forced labour / beatings / people disappeared / underground prison / 50 horses / 15 villas / harem / political influence

Modern Tamburlaine gets

From Martin Walker in Moscow

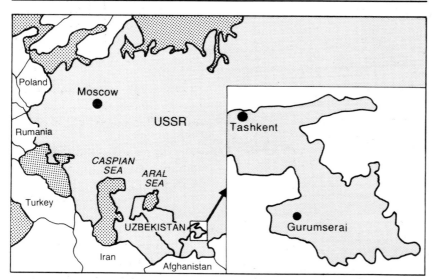

A pocket Stalin who ruled a secret kingdom of over 30,000 collective farmworkers, ran his own private prison camp, and made his subjects kneel in prayer before him, has finally been exposed in the Soviet press — for fear that the charges against him might be quietly dropped.

Akhmadjan Adilov claimed to be a direct descendant from Tamburlaine the Great. Until three years ago he was a Hero of Socialist Labour and the director of (1) _____.
The agro-industrial complex of Gurumserai, in Uzbekistan,

was hailed as the best and most productive of its kind. Loaded with Soviet honours, Adilov's political influence was such that candidates for the job of minister in the Uzbek republic would have to (2) _____

_____,
a process which could take days.
But Adilov was a despot, and his empire was built on terror and slave labour.

Staff who brought his meals late were sentenced to a year's forced labour on the underground bunker and secret prison complex Adilov ordered to be built.

'Adilov (3) _____,
but I refused, because whoever takes material responsibility down here, whether as cashier or foreman, inevitably dies in a few years, from poisoning, a car crash or just disappearing,' claimed one victim, who later escaped.

'In his office, he put a knife to my throat and said he'd cut my head off if I did not obey. Then he and the state farm chief and the personnel director kicked me so hard I blacked out. I woke up a few days later in his underground prison,' the account went on.

Workers who questioned his word would be beaten or slashed with a knife, and even pregnant women were thrashed by whips at his personal open-air court.

This was held on a granite podium by a fountain under a giant statue of Lenin, who seemed to stretch out his hand in blessing above Adilov's chair.

Once he beat a farm worker so hard with a paper weight that the man suffered brain damage.

Strangers who found their way past the police checkpoint and walls around this kingdom would be (4) _____.
Some of the farm workers

Reading exercises

1 At ten points in the report fragments have been removed. What was in each gap? Cover the list of fragments underneath the article.

2 Study the list underneath the article, which contains the fragments from the article with five additions. Choose the ten correct items and match them to the correct gaps in the article. Check with your teacher and fill the gaps in the article. Check against your answers to Exercise 1.

3 Discuss the following questions in groups.

a Why has the newspaper finally decided to publicise the story?

b How do you explain the fact that such a newsworthy story has gone unreported for so long?

c Do you think such a state of affairs could exist in a non-communist country?

d Do you think such things will be allowed to continue in the USSR?

Soviet exposure

who tried to expose Adilov's pocket empire simply disappeared after being thrown into the underground cells, and are presumed to have been murdered.

He lived in lavish luxury, with (5) _____.
He kept a personal stable of 50 thoroughbreds, each worth tens of thousands of rubles. Even outside his private kingdom, he had 15 private villas.

The palace he built for his own family at Gurumserai contained dozens of rooms, and he had other residential blocks built for his harem of mistresses and the compliant husbands to whom he married them. Whenever he travelled outside the farm, a bus went with him containing (6) _____.

He liked to spend his evenings (7) _____.
The lifestyle of the old Central Asian khans apparently flourishing in the modern Soviet Union goes far beyond the wildest satires of dissident writers like Veinovich or Zinoviev.

And such is the nature of political influence in the Soviet Union that (8) _____.
'The constant rumours that Adilov is going to be released without charges convinces us that we (9) _____.

Each day of procrastination might cost lives,' commented Literaturnaya Gazeta yesterday, in the first major expose of the Adilov empire, complete with photographs of the underground bunker.

Adilov was arrested three years ago in the massive campaign to clean up the Muslim republic of Uzbekistan after the death of its party chief, Sharaf Rashidov.

Rashidov himself had lived in similar luxury, based on a vast lie, a regular yearly falsification of the figures for the republic's main crop of cotton. Rashidov claimed it grew each year, regularly praising the contribution of Adilov's farm complex when in fact (10) _____

_____.

When the fraud was discovered, Rashidov's body was hauled from the pompous mausoleum he had built in Tashkent and sent back to his native village in disgrace.

But even though he has lost Rashidov's Politburo-level protection, Adilov still wields enough influence to have stalled the police investigation into his frauds and alleged murders for the past three years.

Martin Walker The Guardian

a his mobile kitchen, cooks, and personal staff, and a live baby lamb for his lunch

b sentenced at Adilov's personal court to penal labour in the fields

c the agro-industrial complex of Gerumserai, in Uzbekistan

d asked me to clean out filthy toilets

e one of the most prosperous and admired farm complexes in the Soviet Union

f ordered me to become a brigade leader

g Literaturnaya Gazeta fears that Adilov's empire may not be finished yet

h lots of strange and expensive animals in his house

i Adilov has been arrested.

j it was declining

k present themselves at his court and await his approval

l sitting in the vast courtyards of his stables sipping imported Napoleon brandy

m should delay reporting this case no longer.

n a personal menagerie of peacocks, lions and exotic fish

o production was increasing year by year.

D Speaking

Role play

This activity is designed to get you using your English by arguing about an imaginary western developed country, described below. Working in large groups, you are going to imagine that you are opposed political parties in this country. You will choose certain ideas and policies to support, and argue against those of the other party. First, read the description of the country, called Rutland. Although it is an imaginary country, think of it as existing in the real world.

1 Role play situation

Rutland is declining industrially, particularly in certain areas, where there is severe unemployment. In other areas, where people earn well, there are shortages of skilled workers. Industrial output is continually hit by strikes against redundancies. More and more people without jobs are flooding to the big cities, overburdening services, living rough and becoming involved in crime and in angry protest, which are increasing alarmingly across the country, along with drunkenness and violence. There are the beginnings of a permanently unemployed, unhealthy, uneducated, antisocial lower class. The maintenance of the poor and unemployed by Government expenditure is bankrupting the country. Social, education and health services do not function well because the Government does not pay nurses, doctors and teachers enough to attract people to the professions, and does not invest sufficiently in equipment and facilities. The natural environment is gradually being destroyed by pollution.

Divide into groups of six or eight students. Each group should split into two political parties, the Liberals (left wing) and the Conservatives (right wing).

Study the lists of general ideas and proposed legislation and choose items which your party supports.

General ideas

- An end to all censorship of the media.
- An end to state ownership of industry.
- An end to financial aid for the poor and unemployed.
- A vast increase in the police force.
- Expensive tax relief for industry in depressed regions, stimulating investment and employment there.
- Drastic reduction of the armed forces.
- Improvement of the public health services.
- A vast and expensive increase in prison building, and recruitment of guards.
- Tax relief for private health organisations, to stimulate their growth.
- An intensive campaign against drinking, like that against smoking. A ban on advertising alcohol and drinking in unlicensed public places.
- An end to very expensive food subsidies.
- Complete nuclear disarmament.
- Salary increases for state-school teachers. A campaign to recruit more. More money available for equipment, books, etc.
- Tax relief on school fees to stimulate private education.
- Income tax increases for the wealthy.

Proposed legislation

- Laws to give Trades Unions the right to represent the work force on the boards of companies and to give the work force a share in profits.
- Laws to force companies to introduce very expensive technology to reduce industrial pollution.
- Strikes about redundancies to be made illegal.
- The introduction of the death penalty for murder, armed robbery and terrorism.
- Heavier prison sentences for theft, assault and the destruction of property.
- Increased powers for the government to censor TV material which is obscene, violent or 'against the national interest'.

2 Choose four or five points and prepare to present these policies and defend your platform with arguments. The platform may be fairly general, but must at some point be relevant to the country's problems.

3 Acting the role play

Each party should put forward its platform in turn, defending it against the other party.

E | Listening

Two views of China

Discussion

● Note down anything you know about China, particularly its recent history.
● Is democracy, as practised in some non-communist countries, any better than a one-party system? Why/Why not? Can you think of any advantages of a one-party system?

Listening exercises

You are going to hear extracts from two interviews with people who have had recent first-hand experience of China, Martin and John (whom you heard speaking in Unit 5).

1 As you listen to Martin in Interview 1, take notes on:
a the bad points of democracies;
b the good points of the Chinese one-party system.

2 As you listen to John, takes notes on:

a What he finds good or praiseworthy in China;
b What he finds bad in China.

3 Listen again, and discuss the following questions in groups.
a What sort of countries does Martin compare China with? Why?
b In what way does Martin think the West misunderstands the one-party system?
c In John's interview, why did the bus seem strange? What cheered everyone up?
d What reason does John give for the Chinese government's policy regarding families?
e According to John, why do poor people in countries like India have so many children?
f What does John think has caused the increase in cheating in China?
g If you had the chance, are there any questions or comments you would like to make to either Martin or John?

4 Listen once more, and fill in the gaps in the following. Each line represents a word or a contraction.
a Communism seems to have done a lot for China, ____ ____ ____ ____ everybody has a bare minimum standard of living.
b . . . the young people we met were very nice, very interesting, but ____ ____ Western ____ rather naive.
c . . . they've been placed in a job where their English is ____ ____ ____ to them ____.
d . . . you know, I'd done many many Asian bus-rides. And ____ ____ ____ ____ I realised that there were hardly any children . . .
e . . . whom nobody much cares for, they've got to ____ ____ ____, there's no social policy to help them.
f 'Was it a safe country to move around in?' 'Yes, ____ ____ ____.'

5 Match the meanings below to four of the words and expressions in Exercise 4.
   i   totally useless
   ii   definitely, absolutely
   iii in our opinion
   iv   manage to survive without help

6 Write a summary of either John's or Martin's views. If you wish, add a paragraph giving your own view or comments.

F | Grammar

Relative clauses

Review and advanced points

The following extracts are from A Reading 1 and C Reading 2. The clauses in **bold type** are relative clauses.

The following are **identifying (or defining) relative clauses**.

Workers **who questioned his word** *would be beaten . . .*

The palace **he built for his own family** *contained dozens of rooms . . .*

. . . his mistresses and the compliant husbands **to whom he married them.**

They **identify** their antecedents, saying which workers, which palace, and which husbands are being referred to.

The following are **non-identifying (or non-defining)** relative clauses.

Perhaps Ramiz Alia is like King Canute, **who did not claim that he could hold back the tides . . .**

China **whose ageing lorries still serve the land.**

They **add information or comment** about their antecedents (China and King Canute), which are already identified sufficiently by their names.

For further information about relative clauses, read on.

Punctuation

Identifying clauses are not preceded by a comma. **Non-identifying clauses** normally are, and are preceded by a slight pause when used in speech.

Relative pronouns

Who is normally used with human antecedents.
Whom can be used when a human antecedent is the object of the verb in the relative clause.
Examples:
That's the man **whom I was telling you about.** (Identifying)
Mrs Smith's brother, **whom I had the pleasure to meet recently** *works as a doctor in London.* (Non-identifying)

Which and *that* are normally used with non-human antecedents.
When and *where* are used for times and places.
Whose is for possessions, for human and non-human antecedents.
Examples:
Children **whose parents get divorced** *suffer a lot.* (Identifying)

They used a stolen Mercedes, **whose owner has not yet been found.** (Non-identifying).

That is used instead of *which* after superlatives, *only, every, no,* etc.
Examples:
It was the longest film **that had ever been made.**
The only thing **that matters is . . .**

That is often used instead of *who* in conversational English:
Example:
Why is it always me **that does the washing up?**
In such sentences the verb (*does*) is third person singular, though the antecedent (*me*) is not.

Contact Clauses

In **identifying clauses** only, the relative pronoun is omitted with object antecedents.
Example:
That's the man **I was telling you about.**
Which can also be left out.
Example:
This is the room **you'll be sleeping in.**
Such clauses are known as contact clauses.

The position of prepositions

In informal English prepositions tend to come at the end of the clause.
Examples:
She's the one I voted for. (Identifying)
Anyway, I found out that this picture, which I'd already paid for, was stolen property. (Non-identifying)

In formal English prepositions tend to come at the beginning of the clause.
Examples:
The employee **to whom you refer** *has now left the company.* (Identifying)
The new deal, **under which wage rises are linked to productivity,** *has been accepted by the union.* (Non-identifying)

However with phrasal verbs, the preposition always stays with the verb.
Examples:
The word **which you looked up . . .** (Identifying)
This letter, **which I came across by chance,** *was important.* (Non-identifying)

Other prepositional expressions also cannot be broken up:
Example:
The recession has reduced demand, **as a result of which many companies have gone out of business.**
Other such expressions are *because of, instead of, according to, the majority of, all of,* etc.

Ellipsis with the passive

In A Reading 1 these items appeared:
. . . *to overtake carts* **drawn by horses or oxen**.
. . . *a talent for wild rejoicing* **seen at a wedding**.
These are hidden relative clauses.   They could
instead be written: *which were drawn by . . .* and
which was seen at . . .

Non-identifying clauses can also be shortened in
this way.
Example:
This government, **elected last year**, *has already
forgotten its promises.*

1 Read this dialogue. Each line in the gaps represents
  a missing word. What words could go in the gaps?
  A   What's a wardrobe?
  B   It's a big cupboard you hang things up in. What
  are drawing pins?
  A   I've no idea. What are they?
  B   They're those things you use to pin things
  up on notice-boards.
  A   Oh yes, that's right. What's a lighter?
  B   That's easy. It's that thing you light
  cigarettes with.

2 Listen to the dialogue on the cassette, and fill in
  the words you hear. Check against your answers for
  Exercise 2.

3 Improvise similar dialogues in pairs. Use the word
  lists on Study pages 173 (for Student A), and 174
  (for Student B).

4 Look at this sentence: which
  *The book the teacher we had the other day brought in
  was really good.*   who

  Apparently nonsensical sentences like this are
  the result of using two contact clauses. They are
  easier to understand if one or both of the relative
  pronouns are put back in:
  *The book (which) the teacher (that) we had the other
  day brought in was really good.*
  Now it can be seen that:
  We had a teacher the other day.
  The teacher brought a book in.
  The book was really good.
  All of the following sentences may seem to be
  nonsense at first, but only two really are. Which
  ones?

a The man the dog I was given attacked was taken to
  hospital.
b The dog the woman we spoke to earlier bit has
  been shot.

c The car the man I didn't like was driving was a
  Mercedes.
d The people that couple we met last week brought
  to the party were awful.
e The flat that estate agent you recommended
  showed us was rather rude to us.

5 Write three similar sentences, including one or
  more which are nonsense. Hand them to another
  pair. Which of the sentences handed to you are
  nonsense?

6 Complete these sentences as you like, using
  defining relative clauses.
a People whose _____.
b Men _____ really annoy me.
c Women _____ really get on my nerves.
d I always get on with people _____.
e _____ bore me to tears.
f _____ is waiting in queues.
g _____ should be shot.
h I don't like food _____.
i I like places _____.
j It was one of those days _____.
k Anybody _____.
l The only political system _____.

7 Combine the following pairs or groups of
  sentences, using non-defining relative clauses.
a The findings of the Wilson report were ignored by
  the Government. The report had been drawn up by
  a committee of experts.
b Mr Smith and Mr Brown quickly became involved
  in a bitter argument. There is a great deal of bad
  feeling between them. In the argument, personal
  insults were freely exchanged.
c Professor Jones' theory has been ridiculed
  throughout the scientific community. According to
  this theory, the universe will end with a big bang.
d British Coal Ltd has started to make a profit. It was
  privatised last year.
e At election time a great deal of political
  propaganda is directed at the electorate. The
  majority of the electorate understand less than half
  of it.
f This project has now been abandoned. The
  Government invested billions of dollars in the
  project.
g The Government was pressed by its foreign advisers
  to make political concessions. Instead of this it has
  banned all political activity.
h Racism is now a more explosive issue than ever.
  There has always been a great deal of controversy
  about racism.

B Vocabulary

Verbs of movement and posture

... *swinging* in endless indolent curves, ...
... They would even *float* in circles ...
... up he *flaps*, slow and awkward, ...
... the vermin *dancing* all over his stinking brown feathers.

These verbs of movement are chosen carefully by the writer to give the impression he wants. Such verbs can be useful in making your own English more vivid and effective.

1 List all the verbs of movement or posture that you know.

2 Work in pairs. Find the twenty-seven verbs of movement or posture hidden in the letter box below. They run from left to right or top to bottom. Check on Study page 174 and do the accompanying exercise.
Examples: *shuffle; crawl.*

	a	b	c	d	e	f	g	h	i	j	k	l	m	n	o	p	q	r	s	t
1	W	P	T	H	U	N	C	H	S	W	A	E	T	K	L	P	O	U	N	W
2	C	S	O	O	S	T	R	O	L	L	S	T	R	I	D	E	T	O	P	A
3	R	T	I	P	T	O	E	C	L	A	L	O	I	N	A	R	D	O	T	N
4	A	A	B	S	O	R	E	C	G	H	I	C	P	O	S	C	I	A	L	D
5	W	G	Q	U	P	T	P	A	B	D	P	L	O	D	H	H	A	T	R	E
6	L	G	O	A	P	N	O	C	K	L	E	A	G	E	N	C	E	U	P	R
7	T	E	A	L	L	O	U	N	G	E	R	M	U	N	K	L	E	M	S	T
8	P	R	I	N	E	G	A	S	T	U	M	B	L	E	R	U	M	B	E	R
9	S	P	R	I	N	T	O	P	O	L	E	E	S	H	U	F	F	L	E	K
10	W	I	A	K	L	P	R	E	W	N	D	R	E	L	E	A	W	E	J	X
11	L	I	M	P	F	J	K	L	E	A	P	W	R	I	G	G	L	E	O	P
12	S	T	R	A	N	T	S	T	R	U	T	R	I	P	P	L	A	N	G	E

3 Fill the gaps with words from your list. More than one word may be the correct one.

a The people in the queue _____ along slowly, each one just behind the other.

b The Hell's Angels _____ into the bar arrogantly, obviously looking for trouble.

c Sit up straight, stop _____ around like that. Aren't you interested in the lesson?

d He _____ around the park every day for exercise. His doctor says he's too old to run.

e The children have ruined the sofa by _____ all over it every day, pretending it's a castle.

f Although his hands and feet were tied, he managed to _____ to the telephone.

g She _____ on her father's knee, as he talked to his friends.

h Her back ached from _____ over a typewriter all day.

i The poor old fellow broke his leg when he _____ down the stairs one day.

j The baby stared up at his father, _____ over him.

k The runner _____, but recovered and managed not to fall.

l It's incredible the way monkeys can _____ from one tree to another.

m The old people _____ peacefully round the park, chatting quietly.

n I left the shop and _____ to the car carrying the heavy box.

o He hurt his leg and _____ all the way home.

p When it was shot the elephant _____ over and hit the ground with a crash.

q The excited dogs _____ around all over the place, getting in everybody's way.

r He didn't see the step, _____ over it, and fell on his face.

s Don't try to run too fast, just _____ along and take it easy.

t The lost child _____ along the beach, crying for her mother.

4 Group the words from the letter box into sets according to meaning. Suggested groups are:
words connected with falling;
words describing ways of sitting;
words describing moving with difficulty;
words connected with moving secretively;
words describing energetic ways of moving;
words describing moving in a casual or directionless way;
words describing ways of jumping.
Not all the words can be put in these groups, and some may appear in more than one group.

C Listening

Snake

Discussion

Match the animals on the left with their appropriate characteristics on the right.

ants	emotional coldness
foxes	mischievousness
cats	hard work
monkey	treacherousness
dogs	timidity
donkeys	overeating
sheep	cleverness
pigs	elegance
mice	stubbornness
rats	courage
peacocks	lack of initiative
lions	faithfulness
fish	vanity
eagles	majesty
snakes	detachment
	stupidity
	rudeness

Are the creatures seen the same way by everyone (including your teacher)? Are the differences cultural or personal?

Listening exercises

You are going to hear a reading of a poem called *Snake*, by the English novelist and poet D.H. Lawrence.

1 Listen to the poem. What actually happens? What parts of the scene do you see or feel most clearly? Share your impressions with your group.

2 Listen again, and discuss the following questions in groups.
 a What sort of day was it?
 b Why did the snake come?
 c What feelings did Lawrence have on first seeing the snake?
 d What was his inner conflict?
 e What did he do as the snake went away? Why?
 f How did he feel then? Why?
 g What, if anything, does the poem have in common with A Reading 1?

3 Turn to Study page 175. Study the poem, and answer any outstanding questions.

D | Reading 2

[handwritten: Eyes reflect light]

Discussion

[handwritten: Nocturnal 夜行性]

● Note down anything you know about these creatures.
owls   baboons   camels
wolves   giraffes   bats
dolphins   eagles   sharks
vultures
Use your dictionaries if necessary.

Reading exercises

1 Read the text below and decide which of the above creatures are described in these five short extracts from the Encyclopaedia Britannica. There are gaps in the text where the creatures' names have been deleted.

2 According to the extracts, which creature(s):

[handwritten top: Vultures, baboons   baboons, dolphines]

a prefer(s) dry country; *[handwritten: camels, baboons]*
b eat(s) many different things;
c are similar (in any way) to humans;
d are (is) more dangerous; *[handwritten: sharks, wolves, baboons, camels]*
e live(s) inside rather than outside. *[handwritten: bats]*

3 How much do you know about tigers? Discuss the following questions, then check against the long extract.

[handwritten: omnivorous]

Creatures in the wild

1   Almost all _____ are nocturnal and live in groups; some live in colonies that may include millions of individuals. Species native to temperate regions migrate south in winter or hibernate. BATS roost in such shelters as caves, trees, tree hollows and buildings. Most species breed once yearly and bear a single young. The gestation period, for those in which it is known, ranges from about two to six months. _____ that hibernate mate in autumn, but fertilization of the egg or development of the embryo or both may not occur until spring.

2   Mainly found in drier savanna and rocky districts, *[handwritten: baboons]* move about both on the ground and in the trees. They feed on a variety of plants and animals, including occasional small mammals, birds, and birds' eggs. They are very destructive to crops and, because of their enormous canines and powerful limbs, are dangerous adversaries, especially *[handwritten: enemys]*

since they generally associate in large troops. Members of a troop form a cohesive society *[handwritten: very close]* and are led and guarded by one or more dominant males. Females as well as males rank within social hierarchies. _____ are noisy animals and have a number of calls with definite meanings. Alarm is given by a doglike bark. Individuals also communicate by posturing and tail signalling. _____ are considered highly intelligent and educable.

3   *[handwritten: Dolphins]* _____ are popularly noted for grace, intelligence, playfulness, and friendliness to man. The most widely recognized species are the common and bottle-nosed _____; both are widely distributed in warm and temperate seas. These are probably the species of _____ mentioned in the works of Aristotle, Aesop, Herodotus, the Plinys, and other early writers, often as a child's mount or the rescuer of someone lost in the sea.

4   *[handwritten: Vultures]* _____ are widely distributed in temperate and tropical regions but absent from Australia and most oceanic islands. Most _____ have broad food habits, consuming carrion, garbage, and excrement, but rarely live *[handwritten: dead flesh]*

animals. A few occasionally take helpless live prey (as lambs and tortoises). _____ may remain aloft for hours, soaring gracefully on long, broad wings. When one _____ finds a dead or dying animal, others fly in from miles away. Feeding _____ maintain a strict social order, by species, based on body size and strength of beak. They all give way, however, to mammalian competitors (as jackals and hyenas).

5   *[handwritten: Camels]* _____ are docile when properly trained and handled, but, especially in the rutting season, are liable to fits of rage. They spit when annoyed and can bite and kick dangerously.

   If necessary, _____ can subsist on coarse, sparse food such as thorny plants and dried grasses. They store fat in their humps, drawing on the reserves in adverse conditions. They do not store water in the misnamed 'water cells' of the stomach, but they can fast and go without drinking for several days. _____ lose their body water slowly and can regain lost weight in ten minutes by drinking as many as 25 gallons of water.

Encyclopaedia Britannica

a In which parts of the world are tigers found?
b Where are the biggest tigers found?
c In which places are you more likely to find a tiger?
a forest   a swamp   in a river, swimming around for fun
up a tree
in a hole in the ground   on a mountain peak
in a ruined building

d What colours can tigers' coats be?
e Do tigers spend their time in groups or alone?
f Do tigers hunt by night or by day?
g Do tigers ever attack elephants?
h Do tigers ever mate with lions to produce mixed young?
i Why would a tiger attack a human?
j Are tigers bigger or smaller than

lions? How big is a large tiger?
k How long do tigers live?

4 Guess the meanings of the following words from their context.
a mane (para. 4)
b preys (para. 5)
c cubs (para. 5)
d litter (para. 6)
e breed (para. 6)
f hybridises (para. 7)
g offspring (para. 7)

The tiger

tiger (*Leo tigris*), great cat of Asia, is the largest member of the cat family (*Felidae*). Like the lion, leopard, and others, the tiger is one of the big, or roaring cats; it is rivalled only by the lion in strength and ferocity.

2   The tiger is thought to have originated in northern Eurasia and to have moved southward; its present range extends from Siberia and Turkistan south to Djawa and Sumatra. There are about seven generally accepted races of tiger. Of these, the following tigers are listed as definitely endangered in the *Red Data Book*: Siberian, Caspian, Javan, and Bali.

3   The size and the characteristic colour and striped markings of the tiger vary according to locality and race. Tigers of the south are smaller and more brightly coloured than those of the north. The Bengal tiger and those of the islands of Southeast Asia, for example, are bright

reddish tan, beautifully marked with dark, almost black, transverse stripes; the underparts, inner sides of the limbs, the cheeks, and a large spot over each eye are whitish. The very large and very rare Siberian tiger of northern China and the USSR, however, has longer, softer, and paler fur. There are a few black and white tigers, and one pure white tiger has been recorded.

4   The tiger has no mane, but in old males the hair on the cheeks is rather long and spreading. The male tiger is larger than the female and may attain a shoulder height of about 1 m (3.3 ft); a length of about 2.2 m (7 ft), excluding a tail of about 1 m; and a weight of about 160–230 kg (350–500 lb), or a maximum of about 290 kg (640 lb).

5   The tiger inhabits grassy and swampy districts and forests; it also haunts the ruins of buildings such as courts and temples. A powerful, generally solitary cat, it swims well and appears to enjoy bathing. Under stress, it may climb trees. The tiger hunts by night and preys on a variety of animals, including deer, wild hog, and peafowl. Healthy large mammals are generally avoided, although there are records of the

tiger having attacked elephants and adult buffalo. Cattle are sometimes taken from human habitations. An old or disabled tiger or a tigress with cubs may find human beings an easier prey and become a man-eater.

6   In warm regions the tiger produces young at any time of year; in cold regions it bears its cubs in spring. Litter size is usually two or three, exceptionally five or six, and gestation averages 113 days. The cubs are striped and remain with the mother until about the second year, when they are nearly adult and are able to kill prey for themselves. The tigress does not breed again until her cubs are independent. The average life-span of a tiger is about 11 years.

7   Under certain conditions, as in enforced confinement in zoos, the tiger occasionally hybridises with the lion; the offspring of such matings are called tigons when the father is a tiger, and ligers when the father is a lion.

Encyclopaedia Britannica 5th edition, © 1974 by Encyclopaedia Britannica, Inc.

E | Speaking

Focus on function: asking for permission; giving and refusing permission; making requests; agreeing to and refusing requests; apologising; reacting to negative responses; thanking

1 Listening comprehension

Listen to six short dialogues and answer the following questions.

a For which of the dialogues can you imagine a physical setting? What setting do you imagine?

b In which dialogues does a speaker make a request, and in which does a speaker ask for permission?

c Which is the least tentative request?

d Which are the two most formal dialogues?

e In which dialogue does one person have power over the other? Why is the powerful person tentative?

f In which dialogues is the request, or the request for permission, unsuccessful?

g In Dialogue 3, is the relationship between the student and the teacher formal or informal? Why does the student use careful language?

2 Pronunciation

Listen to the twelve utterances below and mark the syllables which carry main stress.

a Do you think you could lend me ten pounds, Sue?

b I can't actually.

c Sorry about that.

d Sure, I'd be glad to.

e Would it be all right if I left the lesson early today?

f I was wondering if you would mind working late tonight.

g I'm afraid that's rather difficult, Mr Thompson.

h I don't suppose you could pick them up for me, could you?

i You couldn't pick them up afterwards, I suppose?

j Sorry to bother you.

k Would it be possible for me to leave my bags here?

l It's all right, I quite understand.
Repeat each utterance, trying to match the pronunciation on the cassette.

3 Reproduction

Using the flow diagram to help you, act out the dialogues, using the original language where possible, and improvising when necessary.

4 Improvisation

Improvise dialogues for the following situations. Agree, refuse, explain, insist, etc., as appropriate. Bear in mind formality and tactfulness.

a You are in a restaurant. You want the wine list.

b The chair of the person behind you is squeezing you against your table. In the first situation it is a well-dressed old lady. In the second it is a young man who looks friendly.

c You are feeling ill, at a dinner party given by some people you don't know very well. You want to lie down for a while.

d You need to have a day off work tomorrow. Ask your boss and explain why.

e You want a friend to lend you £25.

f Someone's car is blocking the exit from your garage. It is a policeman's car.

g It seems that you and your friend cannot sit together at the cinema, because there is someone sitting between two empty seats. Ask the person to move. He is a middle-aged gentleman.

h You must use a telephone, but yours is out-of-order. Your neighbours have one. In the first situation, you don't know your neighbours at all. In the second, you get on well with them.

i You need someone to babysit tonight. Ask a friend.

j You are going to a party at a friend's house later this evening. Two old friends of yours have suddenly turned up. You would like to be able to take them along too. Phone your friend and ask if it's all right.

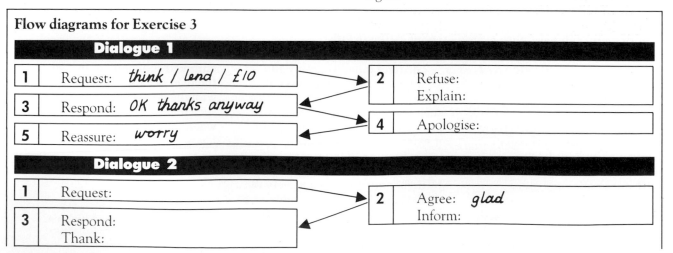

Flow diagrams for Exercise 3

Dialogue 1

1	Request: *think / lend / £10*	→	2	Refuse: Explain:
3	Respond: *OK thanks anyway*		4	Apologise:
5	Reassure: *worry*			

Dialogue 2

| 1 | Request: | → | 2 | Agree: *glad*
Inform: |
| 3 | Respond:
Thank: | | | |

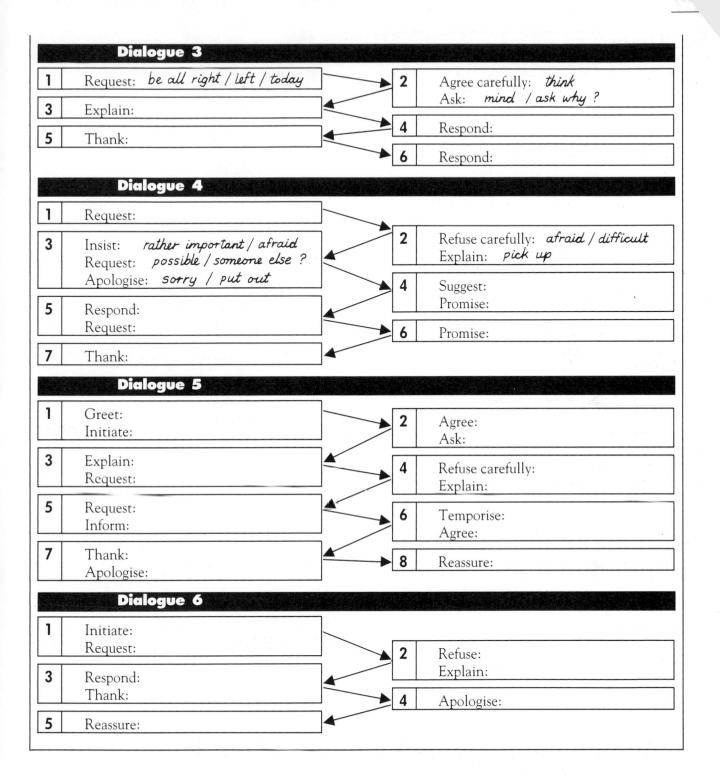

writing

Guided work: connecting words and expressions

1 Discuss in groups how you would write the following essay: 'Is it wrong to eat meat?' Consider what facts you would include and how you would order and organise them.

2 Read this attempt at the essay. You may disagree with the ideas, but it is a useful example of organised writing in support of an opinion. Notice the connecting words and expressions in italics, most of which you have studied in other writing sections. As you read, take notes, putting them in the box diagram opposite. Some notes have been taken for you.

Is it wrong to eat meat?

It is hard to see how any reasonable person can object to the eating of meat. *In fact*, the vast majority of the world's population, who are too poor to do so, would all eat meat from morning till night, if they only had the chance. The reasons for this are obvious.

Firstly, meat is by far the most nutritious food available to us: it contains more protein than anything else, and *thus* gives our bodies more strength. It is hard to imagine an Olympic athlete, *for example*, feeding his body with yoghurt and cabbage. *Apart from* that, meat is tasty, and satisfying to eat. *Indeed*, most people don't feel they're eating a proper meal unless what they are eating contains meat. *That is why*, even in poor countries, meat is the only socially acceptable food to offer guests on ceremonial occasions. *Take the case of* Christmas Dinner in England: it wouldn't seem very special without the turkey!

To turn to the ethical question, *it is often claimed* by vegetarians that it is cruel to kill animals for food; these same people, *however*, don't complain when carnivorous animals do the same thing. *It is difficult to understand* why it is acceptable for animals to kill for food, but wrong for humans to do

so. *After all*, we are carnivores as well, and have been so ever since we realised killing animals was an easier way of staying alive than eating roots and berries. It's a question of intelligence.

One could perhaps understand objections to meat-eating *if* it endangered the species which are eaten. *However*, this is not the case, since every animal slaughtered for its meat only exists in the first place because the farmer intends to have it killed. If we didn't eat pork, *for instance*, pigs would have died out long ago. *Thus* we are taking nothing from meat-producing animals by killing them.

There are, *in fact*, no reasonable arguments against meat; what is really appalling is the fact that so few people in the world have the chance to eat this tasty and nutritious food.

3 Choose one of the following writing tasks.
a Reproduce the essay, using only your box diagram.
b Write a reply to the essay, disagreeing with it.
c Write an essay describing and defending or criticising one or more of the other ways in which humans use (or abuse) animals.
Consider beforehand all the points you wish to make. Decide how many paragraphs you will need, and what you will say in each.

Flow diagram for Exercises 2 and 3a

Paragraph 1

Topic sentence:	*hard / see / object / meat*
Amplification:	
Prepare for paragraph 2:	

Paragraph 2

First reason:	
Amplification:	
Example:	*Olympic athlete*
Second reason:	
Amplification:	
Result:	
Example:	

Paragraph 3

Transition (argument against):	*turn / 'ethical question' / claimed / cruel*
Rejection:	
Amplification:	
Amplification:	
Comment:	

Paragraph 4

Second argument against:	
Rejection:	
Reason:	
Example:	*if not eat / pigs died out*
Conclusion:	

Paragraph 5

Summary + conclusion:	

G | Grammar

Passive voice

Review of simple variations

1 Discuss the following questions in groups.
a How is the passive voice in English formed?
b When is it used instead of the active voice?
c What constructions could replace the passive voice in the following?
My car is going to be serviced this afternoon.
My car needs to be serviced
Check your ideas on Study page 177.

2 Listen. Write down the two dialogues you hear. Use the prompts to help you remember.
Dialogue 1
John's hair is getting long.

_____

_____

Dialogue 2
The windows are dirty.

_____

_____

3 Make similar dialogues using the prompts and the verbs in brackets.
a The grass is getting rather long. (*mow*)
b The TV keeps going wrong. (*look at*)
c We haven't checked the oil for ages. (*check*)
d The time has come for an oil-change. (*change*)
e The carpet is dirty. (*clean*)
f The flat is looking awful. (*redecorate*)

Advanced variations

4 For each sentence, there are two passive-voice variations, using the words given. Write the alternative sentences. Check your answers on Study page 177. Study the Language description.
a People think he is living in Leningrad.
It _____ .
He _____ .
b Many think that Steven Spielberg is an underrated director.

It _____ .
Steven Spielberg _____ .
c Nowadays, people agree that Galileo was a genius.
Nowadays, it _____ .
Nowadays, Galileo _____ .
d In his lifetime, people thought that Galileo was evil.
In his lifetime, it _____ .
In his lifetime, he _____ .
e People suspected that he had sold his soul to the devil.
It _____ .
He _____ .

5 Using both of the above constructions, convert each of the following sentences twice.
a Unfortunately, most people feel that environmental preservation is of secondary importance.
b Witnesses allege that the police used excessive force in the arrest.
c People suspect that stress is a cause of cancer.
d Many people consider that Picasso was the greatest artist of this century.
e Brazilians claim that Pele was the greatest footballer of all time.
f Some people still believe that the world was made in seven days.
g Supporters of apartheid claim it is good for South African Blacks.
h We found that pesticides were present in all the foods tested.
i People report that troops are massing on the Sino–Soviet frontier.
j In the mid-eighties the White House claimed that the Nicaraguan Contras were freedom fighters.

6 Make sentences of either type about the following:
dolphins	Mikhail Gorbachev
pair-work	the pyramids
cigarettes	vitamin C
John F. Kennedy	jogging
AIDS	Margaret Thatcher

UNIT 10 *Unusual beliefs, the occult*

A | Reading 1

Discussion

- The Moonies, or the Unification Church, are a powerful religious cult. Note down anything you know about them or other cults.
- Why are such cults so often criticised?
- Why do you think young people join cults?
- Why are so many cults based in the USA?

Reading exercises

Here is an extract from *Escape from the Moonies*, a book by a girl called Susan Swatland who joined the cult for eight months, before being rescued (against her will, at the time) by an anti-cult organisation.

1 As you read, note down:
a the ways in which the 'battle for her mind' was won;
b good things about the experience.
c Compare notes with other students afterwards.

2 Decide on answers to these questions as a group.
a Why is a feeling of guilt 'much-desired'? (para. 6)
b Why are 'Cereal Drama' and 'Love Bombing' so called? (paras. 5 and 14)
c Why does Susan comment, 'Surprise, surprise'? (para. 8)
d Why is everyone so happy?
e What would be a good title for the extract?

3 Find words and expressions with the following meanings.
a walked unsteadily
b someone who has just arrived
c chewing energetically
d revealed (*information*)
e cheerfully
f regard, consider
g bad, wong, immoral
h interesting, making one curious
i wander, lose concentration
j a manoeuvre to gain an advantage

4 Summarise in seven or eight sentences the ways in which the Moonies brainwash recruits.

Escape from

I stumbled yawning into the sunlight where we all joined hands and sang 'Oh, What a Beautiful Morning'; and indeed it was. There wasn't a cloud in the sky. The rising sun had formed a halo over the trees of the forest. And the hills had been painted gold by the shrubs of summer. We did exercises for half-an-hour, press-ups, stride jumps, Jumping Jacks; and although some of the older Moonies lost their smiles, I was enjoying myself in the morning air. We finished with a choo-choo and then Jacob, an amiable Welsh-man who tipped the scales at just over 200 pounds, stepped out in front of us and said, 'We have a rule at Boonville, no smoking, no drinking and no drugs, because we believe in attaining a natural high. And we would be grateful if you would follow this for the next two days. I can promise you that you'll find it a worthwhile experience.'

2 We were then divided up into groups of eight, I went in Bethie's group and Diana into Jacob's, sup-posedly because she was Welsh. But this is stan-dard Moonie policy to separate friends.

3 They also discourage newcomers from talking to other newcomers. It encourages negativity, they say.

4 We had breakfast of cereals and fruit under a tree and it gave me my first chance to study these people

the Moonies

who had come so suddenly into my life. The boys were clean-cut and wholesome, college-style, with unfashionably short haircuts. The fixity of their smiles and something about their eyes worried me vaguely, but I was becoming accustomed to it. Some of the girls looked very old fashioned in their long dresses, a bit like 'The Little House on The Prairie'; still there wasn't much time for independent thinking at Boonville.

5 While we were still munching our cornflakes Bethie was explaining, 'At breakfast we have a custom called Cereal Drama, this means sharing something with each other, some experience that has made us happy or troubled us. This will help us to get to know each other better and so bring us closer together.'

6 Sharing is another word for confessing and as such an important weapon in the brainwashing armoury of the Moonies. Once a newcomer had divulged some secret sin, this would be later magnified and used to home in on our weak spots, thus creating the much desired feeling of guilt.

7 'Well, who's going to be the first to share?' asked Bethie brightly and immediately five hands were raised. Mine stayed down. I had been assuming that everyone in Bethie's group had been newcomers, but this wasn't so. There were five old Moonies and only two newcomers, besides myself ... a Swiss girl called Vrenni and a husky fair-haired boy with mischievous eyes called Barney.

8 And surprise, surprise, it was the five old Moonies who had their hands raised. That was part of the act. They would confess to the same things over and over again. Each told us a relatively minor thing about his past. Then Bethie turned to me and said, 'Come on, Sue, please tell us something about yourself. We would all love to hear.'

9 So I told them that I lived on a farm in the south of England, had two younger brothers called Mark and Chris, and spent a term as an exchange student at Brockfort just outside New York and still had a year of my course to complete before I could qualify as a physical education teacher. At this, the Moonies clapped and Bethie gave us her motherly smile.

10 'I know it isn't easy to share with others just because they want you to; or to sing because it makes others happy. And it's never easy to be a totally unselfish person, to start thinking about the happiness of others before you think of your own.

11 'But this is what we're doing at Boonville. We are trying to set up a model community where people learn to truly care about one another. Look upon it as a two-day experiment in a different way of living.

Some of the things you see here may seem strange to you. But please open your minds and give yourself the chance to understand. You have all known fleeting moments of ecstasy. Well, stay with us for a while. We can give you eternal ecstasy.'

12 It was heady stuff. We were being shown the gateway to paradise; and if all those smiles truly reflected inner joy, then maybe it wasn't entirely a dream.

13 Boonville was proving to be a merry-go-round that might slow down from time to time to let people climb on, but never ever stopped. We moved from one activity to the next without pause. There always seemed to be someone holding my hand, talking to me or smiling deep into my eyes. Breakfast was followed by a lecture on evolution which was followed by more sharing; which in turn was followed by a truck ride out into the fields. Encouraged by Bethie, we sang all the way...

14 I had never known so much loving *sans* sex. There always seemed to be somebody holding my hand, hugging me or rubbing the back of my shoulders to keep me awake during lectures. It was what the Moonies call Love Bombing and is a vital part of their Mind Control techniques. So too is the constant singing and chanting which disorientates you from the big, wide, wicked world that lies somewhere out there beyond the barbed wire of Boonville. Mostly I was enjoying myself. I liked the land and the country air. I was touched by the friendliness of the people. I had enjoyed working in the fields, swimming and the exercises. And as a student I found the lectures intriguing.

15 But I desperately needed to do a little independent thinking and this was seemingly impossible. That is unless you have the ability to think while you're singing or chanting, doing Jumping Jacks or a choo-choo, looking into an everlasting line of smiling eyes or sharing. You couldn't even cheat during the lectures and let the mind ramble. There was always Bethie, Carol or one of the older girls alongside to make sure my eyes didn't wander even for an instant. At the slightest hint of this there would be a gentle prod and a pleading voice saying 'Sue, try to listen. This next bit is fascinating. It would be such a shame to miss it.'...

16 Just before midnight we boarded a Moonie bus and arrived at Camp K (K for Korea) in the early hours. These late-night journeys are part of a deliberate ploy intended to increase the newcomer's sense of disorientation. I felt as though I was in the middle of nowhere. I presumed we were still in the state of California, but wasn't sure. I didn't even know which was north and which was south.

Susan and Anne Swatland *Escape from the Moonies*
New English Library

B Speaking

Story telling

Tell me another one!

1 Work in groups of three or four. Your teacher will give you ten pictures. Together, plan a story concerning one of the following topics.
Faith of some kind, e.g. cults, voodoo, religion
Astrology, fortune telling, reading palms, etc.
The supernatural, ghosts, etc.
Some related topic
Use the subject of each of the pictures you are given as a key factor in your story. Take notes for the story.

2 Form new groups, in which there must be at least one person from each original group. Tell each other the stories you made up in your first group. As you listen, ask questions about anything that you do not understand.

3 Go back into your original groups and report back on any changes which you would now like to make in your group's story.

4 Choose one long scene or two short scenes from your story and write a script, as if for a play.
Everybody in your group should have a part to play.

5 Rehearse the scenes. One of you should prepare to explain the story leading up to the scenes, so that they can be understood in their context.

6 Act out your scenes for the rest of your class, or find somewhere to work uninterrupted and record the scenes, as if for a radio play.

Miming game

The fortune teller

The setting for this game is the tent of a gypsy fortune teller. She can tell fortunes by reading palms or by looking into her crystal ball. The problem today is that she has a very sore throat and is unable to speak. However, she has decided to go on working. Instead of using her voice to tell fortunes, she will mime what she wants to say.
Work in groups of four students. Half of each group is Pair A, and the other half is Pair B. Each pair has two messages to mime, one a prediction of the future and one a vision seen in the crystal ball. Pairs should take it in turns to mime their messages, word by word and sentence by sentence. As one pair mimes a message, the other pair must guess what the message is. The aim of the activity is to communicate the message as accurately as possible. This means not just the meaning, but also as many of the original words as possible.
The messages are not all the same length, and do not all contain the same number of sentences. As a group, work out a way in which pairs will be able to show how many sentences there are, where a sentence ends, and which sentence is going to be mimed next. You might also like to work out a few simple signs for words like 'and' and 'but'.
Pairs should study their messages very carefully before they begin, exchanging ideas for mimes and deciding which member is going to mime which sentence.
Pair A turn to Study page 178. Pair B turn to Study page 179.

C Listening

Tales of the unexpected

Discussion

● Do you believe in ghosts, or poltergeists, or other supernatural phenomena of this type? Why/Why not? If ghosts don't exist, how do you explain the fact that so many people claim to have seen them?
● Tell your group any spooky experiences you've had, or any ghost story you know.

Listening exercises

You are going to hear two ghost stories. The first is told by Psyche, and the second is told by Malcolm. In some ways they are similar, and in some ways they are different.

1 For the first listening, work in two groups. One group should listen to Interview 1 while the other listens to Interview 2.
As you listen, take careful notes about any important points, including the following facts.
a the place
b any other people involved
c the details of the experience
d what the story-teller found out afterwards
e the reaction of the story-teller, and her/his attitude to the story now
f anything that makes you think there really was/wasn't a ghost
When you have finished, compare notes as a group.

2 Now work in pairs, containing one member from each of the two groups who did Exercise 1. Tell your stories to each other. As you listen to the other story, ask questions to make sure you understand everything. When both stories have been told, make a list together of differences between the stories.

3 Listen again, this time to both stories. As you listen to the story you are hearing for the first time, check that your partner told you all the important details. Add to your list of differences if you can.

4 Listen once more, filling the gaps in the following. Each line represents a word or an abbreviation

Interview 1: *Psyche's story*
a ... the whole ____-____ was really strange ...
b ...it had water and electricity, but it used to ____ ____ in electrical storms.
c ... ____ ____ ____ ____ ____ it would ever blow open in the wind.
d ... the door opened ____ ____ ____.
e ... there was nothing there at all, and I just ____ ____ straight out of there.
f ... yes well, ____ that part of the wing was, that wing of the castle was haunted, ____.

Interview 2: *Malcolm's story*
g ... to push the spider away from me, and at that point I was ____ awake.
h ... yes, I was sitting ____ ____ in the bed.
i ... there were lights on in the campus of the university, ____ ____ you could actually see in the room.
j ... he wasn't exactly transparent, but he didn't look whole, if you ____ ____ ____ ____.
k ... this story to some friends, it ____ ____ ____ the ladies who cleaned the rooms.

5 Match the meanings to the expressions above.
i I was told, I learnt
ii completely
iii arrangement, way the place was organised
iv exactly then
v straight up, not bent over at all
vi was heard by, eventually (like gossip, or a secret)
vii it was not possible that
viii went very quickly
ix stop working
x and because of this
xi understand what I'm trying to say

D | Grammar

Conditionals

False conditionals

1 Listen. Write down the two short dialogues you hear.

Dialogue 1

_____

_____

Dialogue 2

_____

_____

Both the responses resemble conditional sentences, but neither of them is a true conditional sentence. The speaker does not doubt that the *if* clause is true, but draws a logical conclusion from it or makes a comment. The logical connection between the two parts of each sentence could also be expressed by the connecting words *since* or *as*. Such sentences have been called false conditionals. They are extremely common in spoken English, especially when we wish to comment on something that seems to make no sense, like the second speaker in Dialogue 2. Unlike true conditional sentences, false conditionals are not governed by special rules about which tense or verb form to use in each half of the sentence. We use the one which is best for the situation.

2 For each sentence, improvise a dialogue in pairs. Take turns. Student A makes an observation containing a false conditional. Student B responds.

Example: A friend of yours has spent the last half-hour telling you how fed up with her boyfriend she is.
Student A *If you're so fed up with him, why don't you say goodbye?*
Student B *I just don't seem to have the energy to make the break.*

a Someone tells you s/he is allergic to animals, and is thinking of buying a dog.

b Someone asks for your opinion about something, then starts talking about another subject while you are still speaking.

c You are a teacher. A student says she didn't do her homework because she didn't understand your explanation in class.

d Somebody asks you what a friend's astrological sign is, telling you he was born on 5 September.

e Your sister is looking for her umbrella, but she has already said she is sure she left it at work.

f A friend of yours asks you to repair his motorbike, then stands looking over your shoulder, giving advice.

g You were at university from 1983 to 1986. Someone says she was at the same university from 1985 to 1988.

h Because of a quarrel, your brother is not going to a friend's party. You are loyal to your brother.

i You are an English teacher, interviewing someone who wants lessons. He says he never needs to speak English.

3 Working in pairs, write two dialogues of two or three lines each, containing false conditionals. Choose the one you like best and learn it by heart. Perform it for your class, first explaining the situation.

Variations on *if* clauses of conditional sentences

4 In Unit 2, you reviewed the four main types of conditional sentence. Now work in groups and note down the variations which are possible on the *if* clauses of the first, second and third conditionals, and discuss their effect on meaning. The following list of words may help you.
provided   condition   as long as   should   happen ~~by~~ *chance   if...   for   but for* the rain yesterday, I would have visited my friend.
Check your ideas on Study page 178.

If it hadn't been for the rain

5 Complete the following sentences, using clauses containing *provided* or *as long as*.
a _____, the match will go ahead as planned.
b _____ you keep your eyes open and don't take silly risks.
c All right, you can go out and play in the snow, _____.
d I have no objection to your joining the army, _____.
e _____, the strike will be called off today.
f _____, the police will not interfere in the demonstration.

6 Carrying on from the sentence stems, write sentences using *should, happen to* or *by any chance*.
a I'm sure he won't arrive before I get back, but....
b I don't think there'll be any trouble about your visa, but....
c I'm sure the car won't go wrong again, but....
d I'm sure I won't be late home, Mum, but....
e I'm sure you won't need any help, but....
f You probably won't go near the Post Office, but....

7 Complete the following sentences, using *But for* or *If it weren't/hadn't been for*
a _____, England wouldn't be a bad place to live.
b _____, (*your own country*) would be a great place to live.

c _____, unemployed people would starve.
d _____, many developing countries would be better places.
e _____, Argentina wouldn't have won the 1986 World Cup.
f _____, a lot of Holland would be covered with water.
g _____, I would leave home for good and live on my own.
h _____, my English would be almost perfect.
i _____, the Earth would still be a beautiful planet.
j _____, nuclear power would be a sensible solution to our energy problems.

8 Using *were to* in second-conditional sentences, make suggestions for the following situations, based on the prompt-sentences which are given. The prompt-sentences are rather direct, but your suggestions should be very careful and polite.
Example:
Someone never has a girlfriend: 'Why don't you dress better!'
If you were to dress a little better, you might have more luck with girls.
a Someone always does badly at job interviews: 'Have your hair cut!'
b Someone can't seem to lose weight: 'Eat a bit less!'
c Advice to a driver: 'Talk less when you drive!'
d Teacher to a student: 'Listen more carefully to instructions!'
e Student to a teacher: 'Explain more clearly!'
f A friend has had a row with her boyfriend: 'Call him and explain!'

9 Working in pairs, write three short dialogues, using *if* clause variations. Use your teacher as a consultant. Practise your dialogues until you can perform them naturally. Perform your dialogues for another pair, and listen to their dialogues. Are they using the language correctly?

E Reading 2

Discussion

- Note down anything you know about ways in which people claim to be able to predict the future.
- Would you ever consult an astrologer? Why/Why not?
- Some kind of divination has existed in all cultures. How do you explain this?
- Among other things, astrologers claim to be able to predict a person's future profession, and important events such as marriage, etc. Can you think of any way in which such claims could be tested scientifically?

Reading exercises

1 At eight points in the extract opposite, sentences or fragments have been removed. In pairs, decide what was in each gap. Cover the list of sentences and fragments underneath the extract.

2 Study the list, which contains the fragments from the extract with four additions. Choose the eight correct items. Where do they go in the extract? Check with your teacher and fill the gaps. Check against your answers to Exercise 1.

3 Working in pairs, mark the following statements T (true) or F (false) according to what is said in the text.

a Nearly all the doctors whom Gauquelin studied were born when Mars and Saturn had just risen, or were at their highest points.

b In Gauquelin's experiments, people doing the same profession tended to 'avoid' or to be closely linked with the same planets, whereas groups of people chosen at random were not especially linked with any planet.

c In Clark's first test, twenty astrologers were given the horoscopes of ten people, and a separate list of their professions, and seventeen astrologers managed to match all the horoscopes with the right jobs.

d In Clark's second test, the twenty astrologers were given lists of important dates from the lives of ten people, and a pair of horoscopes for each list, one the real horoscope for the person, the other a false one.

e In Clark's second experiment, seventeen of the astrologers scored slightly better than a chance score, but three chose the right horoscope for all ten pairs.

4 In groups, discuss whether the text has changed your mind about astrology? Why/Why not?

Astrology

not just a meaningless jumble?

In 1950 Gauquelin became interested in planetary rhythms and looked for possible correlations on earth....

He selected 576 members of the French Academy of Medicine and found, to his astonishment, that an unusually large number of them were born when Mars and Saturn had just risen or reached their highest point in the sky. To check these findings, he took another sample of 508 famous physicians and got the same results (120). There was a strong statistical correlation between the rise of these two planets at a child's moment of birth and his future success as a doctor.

Taken together, the two tests produce odds of ten million to one against this happening just by chance. For the first time in history a scientist had produced evidence that the (1)_____ on our lives. This gives science a point of vital contact with the old beliefs of astrology.

Having extended his studies to other professions and collected all the birthdates of famous

Frenchmen he could find, Gauquelin was forced to do similar work in Italy, Germany, Holland, and Belgium until, three years later, he had twenty-five thousand records.... Once again (2)_____. Scientists and doctors were positively linked with Mars and Saturn; soldiers, politicians, and team athletes with Jupiter. Writers', painters', and musicians' births were not linked to the presence of any planet, but clearly avoided Mars and Saturn, while scientists and doctors were negative on Jupiter. Solo performers such as writers and long-distance runners were much more markedly linked to the moon than to any of the planets. A control experiment was performed on people selected at random, which (3)_____.

Clark's first test was to examine the astrologer's claim to be able to predict future talents and capabilities directly from a birth chart. He collected horoscopes from ten people who had been working for some time in a clearly defined profession. These included a musician, a librarian, a veterinarian, an art critic, a prostitute, a bookkeeper, a herpetologist, an art teacher, a puppeteer, and a pediatrician. Half were men and half women, all were born in the United States, and all were between forty-five and sixty years old. (4)_____, together with a separate list of the professions, and they were asked to match them up. The same information was given to another group of twenty people—psychologists and social workers—who knew nothing about astrology. (5)_____. The control group returned only a chance score, but seventeen out of the twenty astrologers performed far better, with results that were a hundred to one against chance. This shows that people's characters do seem to be influenced by cosmic patterns and that an astrologer can distinguish the nature of the influence just by looking at the horoscope, which is a traditional, ritualised picture of the cosmic pattern.

Clark then went on to test the astrologers' ability not only to distinguish between patterns but to predict the effect of a pattern. He gave the same astrologers ten pairs of horoscopes; attached to each pair was a list of dates showing important events such as marriage, children, new jobs, and death that had (6)_____. The astrologers had to decide which horoscope predicted such events. The test was made more difficult by the fact that the two charts in each pair belonged to people of the same sex who lived in the same area and were born in the same year. Three of the astrologers got all ten right, and the rest again scored better than a hundred to one against chance. This shows that an astrologer can tell, from the birth data alone, whether an accident or a marriage belongs to a particular horoscope. Which means that (7)_____ before they happened. Clark concluded that astrologers, working with material which can be derived from birth data alone, can successfully distinguish between individuals. In fact these tests, in which the astrologer works blind, without seeing his subject, are like a physician diagnosing a disease without seeing his patient. To me, as a scientist, they provide impressive evidence that the astrological tradition is not just a meaningless jumble of superstitions, but a real instrument that can (8)_____ than any other tool at our disposal.

Lyall Watson *Supernature* Coronet

a yielded results strictly according to the rules of chance

b be used to extract more information from a simple map of the heavens

c there was an impressive correlation between the planets and professions

d he found that people in the medical profession were linked strongly with two planets

e somehow, the twenty astrologers knew about these events

f taken place in the life of the person who belonged to one of the two charts

g he could, in theory, have predicted these events

h The results were conclusive

i planets actually influence, or indicate an influence

j work we choose to do has an influence

k tell us a great deal about ourselves and our possibilities

l These horoscopes were given to twenty astrologers

F | Vocabulary

Noun-preposition collocations

The following items are from A Reading 1 and E Reading 2.

At this, the moonies clapped...

... more sharing, which in turn was followed by a truck ride.

... he could, in theory, have predicted these events.

The noun-preposition collocations in **bold type** are so called because they are composed of words which are often placed (or **located**) together. Some regularities (with exceptions) can be observed in their use.

Collocations which describe feelings

With tends to be used when one **expresses** a feeling through an action, facial expression, etc.
Examples: *He screamed **with** pain; She gasped **with** horror.*
An exception is *He jumped **for** joy.*
In tends to be used to refer simply to the state, when it is not **expressed** by a verb. It can also be used when the verb is a way of looking.
Examples: *He's **in** terrible pain; She stared **in** horror.*
To is used in the following way.
Example: ***To** my amazement, John won the race easily.*

1 Working in pairs, fill the gaps in the sentences with noun-preposition collocations containing the words listed below. Use your dictionaries if necessary.

excitement   horror   impatience   desperation delight   disbelief   rage   irritation   a state disappointment   terror   disgust   boredom

a He beamed _____ at the compliment.
b They stared _____ at the extraordinary sight.
c He roared _____.
d She frowned _____ at the interruption.

e We grimaced _____ at the smell.

f Everyone was yawning _____.
g _____ our _____, the bill came to over £100.
h I've never seen him so upset. He's really _____.
i _____ the audience's _____, the group didn't come back on stage to play an *encore*.
j The spectators fidgeted _____ at the long delay.
k Everybody screamed _____ as the monster approached.

l _____, she called Alcoholics Anonymous.
m The children chattered _____ as they waited for the clowns to appear.

Collocations concerning time
These are nearly all formed with *in* or *at*.

2 Working in pairs, fill the gaps with noun-preposition collocations. Cover the list at the end of the exercise. When you have filled all the gaps you can, check against the list.

a _____, I'm living in London, but _____ I hope to be able to move to the country.

b I was quite well-off _____ because I had a really good job.

c What are you doing _____? Do you fancy spending it in Paris with me?

d _____, I wonder why I do this job.

e _____, there is no indication that the conflict will escalate into full-scale war.

f _____, all furniture was made by hand.
*at the weekend   at the moment (**informal**)   at present (**formal**)   in the future/past   at times   at that time*

3 Most collocations must be learnt by heart or picked up gradually. The most common are formed with *in*, *on*, *under* and *at*.
All the nouns listed below collocate with prepositions. Discuss:
the preposition(s), or adverbial particle(s), which can go with each;
the meanings of the resulting collocations.
Use your dictionaries if necessary.
trouble   return   condition   theory   practice   guarantee   mind   fact   an/no obligation   an attempt   a/no hurry   no circumstances   order to   behalf of   power   agreement with   stake   the whole   average   strike   attack   love   work   loan   order   zero (*temperature*)   age   fire   arrival   TV   the coast   consequence   belief   all   suspicion   second thoughts   war   peace   the question   doubt

4 For each sentence, write another with approximately the same meaning, using the word in brackets to form a noun-preposition collocation.

a The watch will be repaired for free. (*under*)

b Theoretically it's easy, but there are practical difficulties. (*in*)

c The hostages will die if we attack! (*at*)

d Generally speaking, I like my job. (*on*)

e He helped me, so I paid him. (*in*)

f I agree with his ideas completely. (*in*)

g An agent works for his clients. (*on*)

h Trying to take the thief's gun, he shot him. (*in*)

i The General has been governing for seventeen years. (*in*)

j I'm unemployed. (*out*)

k I'll have a lemonade, no, make it an orange juice. (*on*).

l It's freezing outside. (*below*)

m It's absolutely incredible. (*beyond*)

n He is certainly the finest pianist in the world today. (*without*)

o The Board of Directors is obliged to explain its actions to a meeting of shareholders every year. (*under*)

p They live in a small house by the seaside. (*on*)

q Five plus five make ten, plus another eight makes eighteen altogether. (*in*)

r I can't sell you alcohol because I'd be breaking the law. You're too young. (*under*)

s The Government is being criticised vigorously because of its immigration policy. (*under*)

t I'm afraid I cannot consent to such a request. It's quite impossible. (*out*)

5 In pairs, write an exercise (like **1**, **2** or **4**) for five collocations. Pass your exercise to another pair, and do the exercise passed to you.

G Writing

Guided work: manipulation exercises; topic sentences

1 Working alone or in pairs, put each of the following fragments into three different contexts, using three of the connecting words and expressions listed beneath it. The connecting expression may appear before, after, or in the middle of the fragment. The fragment may become a whole sentence, or part of a sentence, depending on the connecting expression you use, and you may change the wording of the fragment slightly if necessary. You may add as many words or sentences as you like.

Example: *. . . the cult prevents contact between new converts and people in the outside world . . .*
moreover

The cult prevents contact between new converts and people in the outside world. **Moreover,** *they are kept so busy and exhausted that they don't have the time or energy to sit and think on their own. In the end they became completely disoriented and easier to manipulate.*

a . . . the cult prevents contact between new converts and people in the outside world . . .
as a result   in order to   although   because   such as   however   so that

b . . . Christianity has always placed great emphasis on non-violence, and love for one's fellow man . . .
although   in spite of this   take, for example   it's true that   as a result   not only . . . but also   whereas

2 Combine the sentences below to form one sentence, using the words and expressions which are given, in the order in which they are given.
Professor Smithers didn't believe in ghosts.
Professor Smithers didn't believe in other supposedly 'supernatural' phenomena.
All of them were the result of hallucinations or outright trickery.
That was his opinion.
He did not hesitate.
He was challenged to spend the night alone in a graveyard.
He was challenged by a friend.
The churchyard had the reputation of being haunted.
Since   nor   which   in his opinion   when   by which   reputed   haunted

3 Combine the following two groups of sentences in the same way to continue the story.

a Professor Smithers took up the challenge for a reason.
He wanted to prove that the fear was just nonsense and superstition.
He wanted to prove this to his friend.
His friend was not entirely convinced by the professor's rational approach.
The fear was inspired by the graveyard.
in order to   who   that   superstition

b However, there was a discovery the following morning.
It was his dead body, outside the door of the church.
The discovery seemed rather to contradict this theory.
It contradicted it especially when it was found that the Professor had died of a heart-attack.
It was also found that his hair had turned completely white during the night.
His hair had been dark brown when he entered the graveyard.
However   especially when   not only that   but also that   which   night

4 Provide the topic, second and fifth sentences of this paragraph. Afterwards compare your sentences with those of another student.

_____.

_____.

I fail to see how an inspection of somebody's hand can tell us anything about that person's future. Astrology is another example.

_____.

There is simply no rational basis for beliefs and practices of this kind.

5 Choose two of the following topic sentences, and develop each into a short piece of one or two paragraphs (80–100 words), or choose one sentence and develop it into a full essay.

a People are superstitious about a lot different things.
b I'm not entirely convinced that astrology is all nonsense.
c Islam is the most energetic religion of today.
d I've never been able to believe in any religion.
e There is only one true religion.
f The increase in the number and power of religious cults over the last decade or two is a very worrying trend.
g Parents who worry about their children becoming interested in religious cults should perhaps ask themselves why this happens.

11 *Environmental problems*

A | Speaking

A presentation

Green issues

1 Working in small groups, note down all the issues your group knows of which are of concern to people worried about the environment. When you have completed your list, share your ideas with other groups and your teacher.

2 In the next stage of this activity, your group will give a short, informal presentation to the class about one of the issues. As a group, choose the issue you would like to talk about.
Discuss this issue in greater depth, and plan what you are going to say about it. Make notes to help you as you speak later, but do not write out exactly what you are going to say. This is a speaking activity, not a writing activity.
Your presentation need not be formal or very professional, but should be as well-organised and clear as you can make it. It will be helpful to consider the problem along the following lines.

The nature of the problem (i.e. what it is, why it is considered a problem).

Examples of the problem (with informative details if possible).

The cause(s) of the problem. (Ideally, these would include immediate causes and underlying causes.)
Possible solutions to the problem (perhaps including your recommendations).

Possible problems in the implementation of these solutions. (Problems can be of many types, ranging from the political to the practical.)

Naturally, you may not be very well-informed about all of these aspects. If that is the case, there is no harm in saying so during your presentation, when other members of the class may be able to fill in the gaps.
More than one group member should speak in the presentation to the class. Decide now which member is going to talk about which aspect.
Remember that a presentation is far more effective if it contains a visual element, such as a diagram, or even a simple list of headings. An overhead

projector is ideal for this. If one is available, prepare transparencies as you work. If only the blackboard is available to you, plan now how your group will use it during your presentation.
Much of the functional language presented in writing sections earlier in the course will be useful to you in giving your presentation. Bear in mind expressions for exemplifying, adding and listing, talking about cause and effect, talking about purpose, introducing unexpected information, contrasting and recommending.

3 Each group should present its short presentation in turn. Other groups may not interrupt, but at the end of each talk questions may be asked, and further ideas put forward. Your teacher will be the chairperson.

B Listening

Friends of the Earth

Discussion

● Note down anything you know about:
the dangers of using nuclear power to generate electricity;
the environmental problems caused by traditional sources of energy;
less harmful sources of energy.

● You are going to listen to Jan McCarry, Information Officer for Friends of the Earth, talking about these questions. What do you know about 'Friends of the Earth'?

Listening exercises

1 As you listen, fill in the flow diagram with notes. Three have been done for you. Check with another student.

2 Listen again, adding more detail to your notes.
Also answer the following questions in groups.
a The following figures are mentioned (in the same order) by Jan McCarry. To what do they refer?
90%   75%   12 years   20%   40%
b Why is the 'Greenhouse Effect' so called?
c In what connection are the following places mentioned?
Germany   Czechoslovakia   Holland   London   Norway   California
d How, briefly, is energy extracted from waves?
e What are the objections to wind power? How can these be overcome?
f What is the big problem with renewable energy sources?

3 Do you know of any useful information to contradict or add to what Jan says? What is the environmental policy in your own country? Are you in favour of it? Why/Why not?

4 Use the notes you think in Exercise 1 to write an essay entitled: 'Nuclear Energy. Is there an alternative?' Use 300 to 400 words.

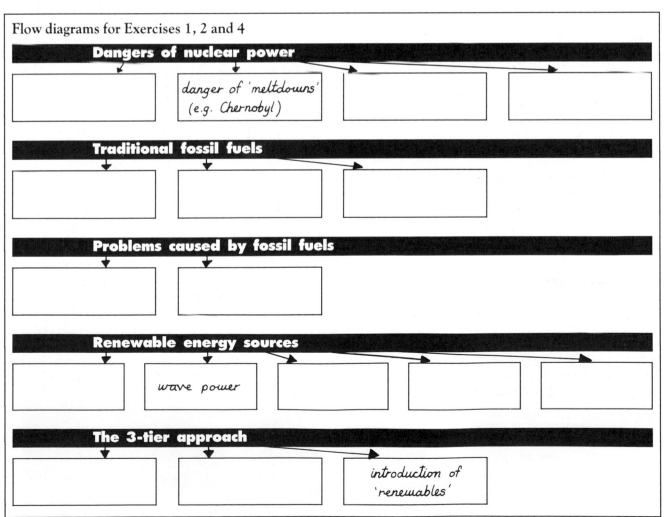

Flow diagrams for Exercises 1, 2 and 4

Dangers of nuclear power

| | danger of 'meltdowns' (e.g. Chernobyl) | | |

Traditional fossil fuels

Problems caused by fossil fuels

Renewable energy sources

| | wave power | | | |

The 3-tier approach

| | | introduction of 'renewables' |

C Reading 1

Discussion

● Note down any endangered species you know about, and the reasons why they are endangered.
● How important is the destruction of wildlife, compared with other world problems?
● Can poor people be blamed for poaching (hunting illegally)?
● Note down any ideas you have, or have heard, about how to save the world's wildlife.

Reading exercises

1 Read the article on rhinos and answer the following questions in groups.

a How did the rangers find the poachers?
b Why didn't the poachers hear the rangers' approach? (Two reasons.)
c Why are rhinos hunted?
d What is special about Zimbabwe's approach to wildlife protection?
e What tells us that Zambia is not as energetic as Zimbabwe in fighting the poachers?
f 'They caught us with our pants down!' What does this mean?
g Why don't the rangers try to arrest the poachers?
h Why aren't there enough rangers or vehicles? What is being done about this?
i Why do you suppose poachers commit such an arduous and dangerous crime?
j How do you feel about men being killed in cold blood to save the lives of animals?
k Can you think of other ways to save the rhino?

2 Find words or phrases with the following meanings.

a broken violently
b move heavily and slowly
c walk quietly, so as not to be heard
d attracted irresistibly
e intense attack
f go (or come) secretively
g not sorry (formal language)
h in my opinion
i approved, given support to
j gave, as an act of charity

WORLD AFFAIRS

A Battle Without End

Stalking a bloody trail

The midmorning stillness of the double-canopy forest was shattered by a fusillade of shots. Two park rangers staking out a dirty watering hole quickly picked up the bloody trail of a dying rhinoceros and the footprints of two tracking poachers. The stricken animal lumbered into a thicket of 14-foot-high combretum bush, where the poachers felled it with two final shots and began hacking at the prized horns. The thud of knives against

horn masked the approach of the rangers, who tiptoed over a carpet of dry leaves to within 15 yards of the unsuspecting hunters and, without warning, opened fire. One poacher fell dead. The second scuttled behind the rhino and emptied a 30-clip magazine from his AK-47 assault rifle. The bullets flew harmlessly overhead, shredding the bushes. The rangers circled the clearing and shot the second poacher dead through the splayed legs of the fallen animal. 'They are the enemy,' recalled scout David Chipesi proudly, 'and we destroyed them.'

The shootout in the Zambezi River valley two months ago was the most encouraging success Zimbabwe's rangers have enjoyed in their shoot-on-sight battle against invading gangs of poachers from neighbouring Zambia. At stake is the survival of the world's last great herd of black rhino. In just six years, two-thirds of Africa's black rhino population has been destroyed. Lured by the soaring prices offered for rhino horn, poachers infiltrated every known rhino habitat. Today, fewer than 5,000 black rhinos have escaped the onslaught. In many parts of Africa the survivors are being herded behind electrified fences for their own protection. But the Zimbabwe Department of National Parks and Wildlife wants to defend a herd of some 750 to 1,000 animals on their own turf, in the wild. In early 1985 Operation Stronghold was launched.

'Make no mistake: we are fighting a very nasty bush war here, with no quarter given,' says Glenn Tatham, the chief warden of the region. He was speaking over the crackle of a battered radio, in the cluttered operations room of the Kapirinhengu ranger base camp, set in a clearing on the banks of the Zambezi. Across the several hundred yards of crocodile-infested river lay Zambia, sanctuary for the poachers who slip almost daily across the current in sleek banana boats and fade into the bush in search of instant fortunes.

Shoot on sight Poaching in the region began in earnest two years ago. Gangs numbering as many as 16 men and armed with the latest automatic weapons have killed 100 rhino since then. 'They caught us with our pants down,' admits 28-year-old Blodie Leathem, a senior ranger in the Operation Stronghold force. But now the rangers' alert presence is paying off. Since Stronghold's start, rangers have killed 13 poachers; 11 others have been captured. Tatham is unrepentant about his controversial shoot-on-sight policy. 'It's very difficult to arrest someone with a rifle who is prepared to shoot you,' he said. 'Unless they throw their guns up in the air and raise the white flag there is no chance we are going to try to reason with them and arrest them. We shoot first to protect our men. It is a sensitive subject—killing a man for killing an animal. Many people don't agree with this policy. But as far as I'm concerned, killing an animal is no different than robbing a Barclays bank.'

Prime Minister Robert Mugabe has personally endorsed the harsh penalties for poaching, but he has not been able to spare much money for the operation. At any one time Tatham has fewer than 50 rangers in the field. Two-man patrols are often away from base camp for a month, covering as much as 15 miles on foot each day. Only five official vehicles patrol more than 3,800 square miles. But the anti-poaching effort has won valuable support from outside the country. The Foundation to Save African Endangered Wildlife (SAVE), a US-based volunteer organization, donated two bright red Yamaha dirt bikes, two single-engine airplanes, a tractor-trailer, tents and more than $100,000 worth of desperately needed radio equipment. Says SAVE president Ingrid Schroeder, 'The Zimbabweans deserve all the help they can get.'

> The black rhino (the white rhino is distinguished by its long head and square muzzle), a lumbering, prehistoric tank that has survived for more than 70 million years, is already extinct in most parts of Africa. As late as 1970 there was a healthy population of 65,000 rhinos scattered throughout east, central and southern Africa. Today only 4,500 remain, living in tiny groups that could die or be poached out unless they are immediately protected. 'It must surely represent the most appalling example of the destruction of a large mammal in the history of man,' says Peter Jenkins, a senior game warden in Kenya. The only major herd of black rhinos left in the world—the several hundred animals living in Zimbabwe's Zambezi valley—is now struggling against a similar fate.

Ray Wilkinson and Marilyn Achiron
Newsweek

[handwritten notes at top:]
plip-plop - 雨音
clip-clop - Horse walking
moo - cow
bow-wow / woof - dog
miaowe - cat
oink - pig
quack - duck
neigh - horse
smash - ガラスの割れる音
choo-choo train
hiss - snake

D | Vocabulary

Sound-words

1 Look at these two extracts from C Reading 1.
*The **thud** of knives against horn masked the approach of the rangers. . .*
*He was speaking, over the **crackle** of a battered radio. . .*
Thud and crackle are **onomatopoeic** words: to the ear of an English-speaker they actually sound like the noises they describe. Many English words describing sounds are onomatopoeic.
Which of the following noises could be described by *thud* and which by *crackle*? Note that *thud* is a single sound, and *crackle* is a continuous sound.

a a sweet being unwrapped from its cellophane wrapping *CRACKLE*
b a knocked-out boxer hitting the floor of the boxing ring *THUD*
c an axe chopping into a big tree *THUD*
d a dry bush, burning in a forest fire *CRACKLE*

2 In groups, list all the sound-words that you know, together with the thing or animal which might make them.

3 Work in pairs. Find the twenty-five sound-words hidden in the letter box below. They run from left to right or top to bottom. Check and do the exercise on Study page 179.
Examples: gurgle; lap.

	a	b	c	d	e	f	g	h	i	j	k	l	m	n	o	p	q	r
1	P	T	G	U	R	G	L	E	S	W	A	N	V	O	C	K	L	V
2	A	G	R	O	A	N	P	T	C	O	B	C	O	D	R	I	P	T
3	V	S	O	H	T	L	M	B	R	L	D	R	T	S	A	W	R	O
4	H	O	W	L	T	Z	F	E	E	T	S	U	I	S	S	X	V	S
5	I	R	L	A	L	S	W	Q	E	U	S	N	N	T	H	C	M	A
6	S	N	L	P	E	C	H	O	C	L	I	C	K	R	J	R	B	A
7	S	Q	U	A	N	T	I	D	H	I	G	H	L	P	S	A	L	R
8	S	C	L	A	N	G	N	R	U	S	T	L	E	W	Q	C	E	A
9	A	O	K	U	C	R	E	A	K	X	A	Q	U	E	U	K	R	N
10	P	S	Q	U	E	L	C	H	A	B	P	D	G	R	E	C	M	C
11	M	O	A	R	L	S	W	I	N	T	O	E	R	O	A	R	N	E
12	B	A	R	K	F	R	O	B	L	A	R	E	N	S	K	R	O	T

4 Discuss in groups
a Which words are connected with wetness or water?
b Which words are associated with the following animals?

a lion   a wolf   a parrot   a mouse   a dog
[monkey]
a snake   a mosquito

5 Discuss in groups the sounds which might be made by the following things.
a a strong wind on a hilltop
b a sergeant in the army (*figurative use*)
c a lot of car horns at the same time
d a lorry pulling away from traffic lights
e someone's stomach when it is empty
f dry leaves
g a wooden ship
h someone eating a raw carrot or biscuits   *crunch*
i someone hitting metal with a hammer   *clang*
j tyres on the road when a car brakes very suddenly   *screech*
k small waves, breaking gently on a beach   *lap*
l huge waves, breaking violently on a beach   *crash*
m a camera taking a picture   *click*
n pills in a box, when you shake it   *rattle*
o a heavy lorry going fast over a metal bridge   *rumble*
p a tree branch suddenly breaking in the wind   *crack*
q walking in mud   *squelch*
r pressurised air escaping through a small hole   *hiss*
s a broken wine glass being swept up   ~~rattle~~ *tinkle*
t someone knocking gently on the door   *tap*

Most of these words can be used in three ways.
Examples:
Noun
The piano fell over with a deafening **crash**.
I heard the **click** *of the key turning.*
There's a **rattle** *somewhere in the engine. I hope it's nothing serious.*
Verb
The car **screeched** *to a halt.*
-ing form
We listened to the thunder **rumbling** *in the distance.*
We listened to the **rumbling** *of the thunder in the distance.*

6 Listen to the cassette and write down the sounds you hear.

7 In groups, list the sounds you might expect to hear while walking in: a tropical forest; a busy street.

8 Write a description of such a walk, using as many of these words as you can.

(My stomach is rumbling)

E Reading 2

Discussion

● In what ways are the tropical forests important?

● What do you know about the connection between tropical forests and 'the Greenhouse Effect' mentioned by Jan McCarry in B Listening?

Reading exercises

Before reading the article about tropical forests, check that you know the meanings of the following words.

nutrients   to harvest
extinction   a warehouse
a species   a strain (*of a species*)
to squander   sustenance   the wild

1 At four points in the article, topic sentences have been removed. In pairs, decide what was in each gap. Cover the list of sentences under the text.

2 Study the list, which contains the topic sentences with four additions. Choose the four correct items. Where does each go in the article? Check with your teacher and fill the gaps in the article. Check against your answers to Exercise 1.

3 Discuss the following questions in groups.

a Why is it more destructive to cut down trees in the tropical forests than it was in temperate forests?

b According to estimates, approximately how many tropical forest species have not yet been identified?
Between 28·4 and 30 million
1·6 million
15 million
Between 13·4 and 15 million

c Why is it important to preserve wild strains of rice, wheat and corn, when what we eat are the cultivated strains?

4 Fill in the boxes in this diagram for a cause and effect chain representing the argument of the text. Some have been filled in already.

Diagram for Exercise 4

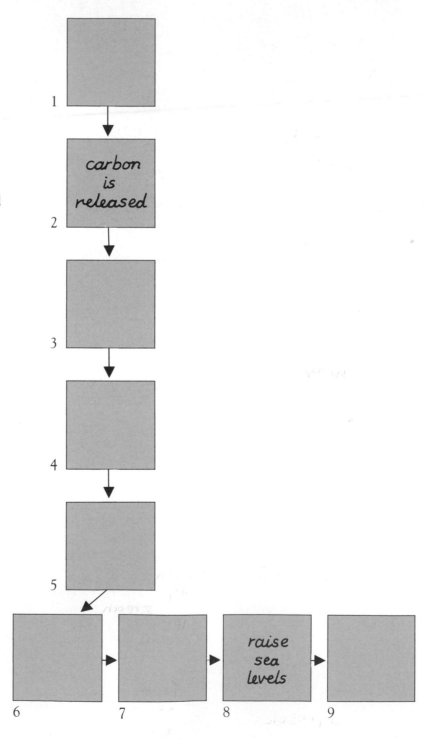

5 Which of these effects are already fact, and which are possible?

6 What do you think the 'short-term economic benefits' of destroying the forests are?

Time is Running Short For the Tropical Forests

By Roger D. Stone

WASHINGTON — (1)_____.
In Europe and the United States, they say, deforestation was the inevitable and desirable consequence of economic progress; why should it be any different in the largely underdeveloped nations where the world's tropical forests are found?

It **is** different. The rich soils and relative biological simplicity of the temperate world enhances forest conversion and eventual reforestation. But in the tropical forest regions, soils tend to be poor. Life-supporting nutrients are stored not in soils but in the trees. Remove them and the whole fragile system collapses.

(2)_____. Such forests supply the world with goods—hardwoods, rubber, fruits and nuts, drugs and medicines and fragrances and spices—that often cannot be raised in any but natural conditions. Harvesting beyond sustainable limits has already brought some of the tropical forests best hardwoods—Brazilian rosewood for example—near extinction.

(3)_____. Estimates of the total number of species on the planet range up to 30 million, of which only 1.6 million have been identified. It is further estimated that tropical forests, while occupying only 7 per cent of the Earth's surface, may contain half of all life forms. Thus, relatively few tropical forest species have been studied. Concerned biologists view the heedless squandering of the tropical forests' resources as a tragedy.

Similarly, we depend on a small group of plants—corn, rice, wheat—for

a large part of our sustenance. From time to time, plant pathologists have found, the commonly used strains of these plants requires genetic fortification from the wild to protect them from blight and disease. Since many such plants originated in tropical areas and only later were cultivated elsewhere, the primeval forests of the tropics represent a vast genetic storehouse of great potential value.

(4)_____. But when the forests are burned, the carbon released plays an important role in the build-up of atmospheric gases producing the 'greenhouse effect,' which is causing a warming trend on the planet.

This could turn America's Corn Belt into a subtropical region. And the melting of polar ice could raise sea levels and lead to drastic losses of coastal land.

Unfortunately, the present defoliation, motivated by short-term economic benefit, probably will continue unless a revolution in public and official attitudes comes to the rescue at the eleventh hour.

The writer is a conservation fellow at the World Wildlife Fund and author of a book about the Brazilian Amazon.

Roger D. Stone *International Herald Tribune*

a Many Americans feel that saving the world's tropical forests warrants little serious concern

b Most species from the 'biological warehouse' of the tropical forests can also be kept and observed in zoos

c It is true that the tropical forests have little economic importance

d People and nature both lose when the tropical forest is clumsily invaded

e Many Americans are rightly concerned at the destruction of the tropical forests

f Moreover, destroying tropical forests can destabilise the world's climate

g Left untouched, tropical forests also contribute to the stability of the world's climate

h The tropical forest is also a biological warehouse

F | Grammar

Future arrangements and intentions; predictions

1 Below are fifteen situations and language contexts. Beneath each are three sentences. Tick the most appropriate sentence. Discuss your answers and check on Study page 180.

a Someone asks me to give John a message. I hadn't intended to see him, but I promise to do so. I say:
  i I'll be seeing him later; I'll tell him then.
  ii I'll see him later and tell him.
  iii I'm going to see him later; I'll tell him then.

b Someone asks me to give John a letter. By chance I've already made a firm arrangement to see John. I say:
  i I'll see him later and give it to him.
  ii I'm seeing him later; I'll give it to him then.
  iii I am to see him later; I'll give it to him then.

c Someone asks me to give Mike a message. Mike is someone I assume that I will see later, because I normally do. I say:
  i I'm seeing him later;
  ii I'll be seeing him later; } I'll tell him then.
  iii I'm going to see him later;

d Someone asks me to give Mike a letter. There is no previous arrangement to see Mike, nor do I normally see him today. However, I have already decided to drop in on him later. I say:
  i I'm dropping in on him later, } so I'll give
  ii I'm going to drop in on him later, } it to him then.
  iii I'll drop in later and give it to him.

e Late at night, you decide to go to bed. You stand up, then say:
  i I'll get some sleep.
  ii I'm getting some sleep. } See you tomorrow.
  iii I'm going to get some sleep.

f A friend wants to meet you after work on Friday. You always have a drink in The Crown after work on Friday. You say:
  i I'll be having a drink in The Crown.
  ii I'm having a drink in The Crown. } How about meeting there?
  iii I'll have a drink in The Crown.

g A Buckingham Palace announcement:
  i The Queen is visiting
  ii The Queen is going to visit } Japan in early October.
  iii The Queen is to visit

h A courteous clerk at a hotel reception desk:
  i How long are you staying?
  ii How long are you going to stay?
  iii How long will you be staying?

i Italy are going to play Malta at football. You are sure about the result. You say:
  i Italy will win that one.
  ii Italy are going to win that one.
  iii Italy will be winning that one.

j The teams are playing. It's 0–0 in the second half, and Malta are playing better. You say:
  i } Malta are going to win.
  ii I think } Malta will win.
  iii } Malta are winning.

k You look up and see thick black clouds. You say:
  i } It's going to pour with rain.
  ii Look at that! } It'll pour with rain.
  iii } It'll be pouring with rain.

l Someone asks about your plans for Saturday night. You have no special plans. You say:
  i } I suppose we'll eat out or something.
  ii Oh, I don't know } I suppose we're eating out or something.
  iii } I suppose we're to eat out or something.

2 Reread the sentences in Exercise 1. In groups try to formulate some rules about which tenses we use to express:
a arrangements and intentions;
b predictions
   Check your ideas on Study page 180.

3 Work in pairs. Student A should read on. Student B should turn to page 180.
   Student A
a Opposite is a page of your appointments book for the next week. Fill it in as you like, with things you intend to do and things you have definitely arranged to do.

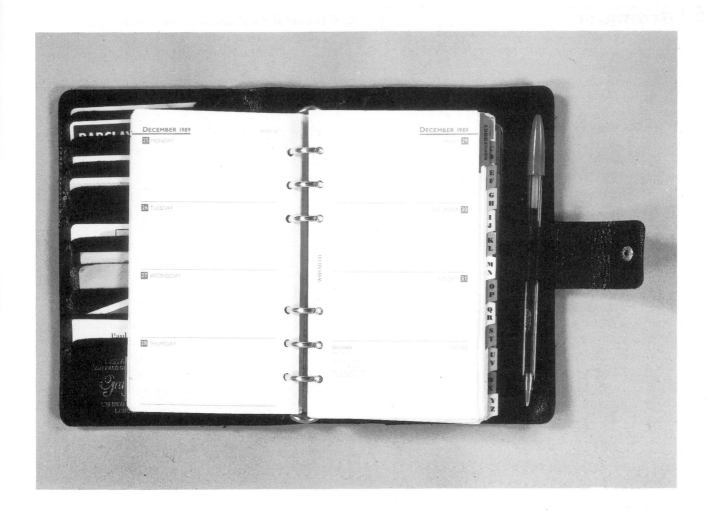

b It is Sunday evening when you call Student B. Improvise a telephone conversation with your partner, bearing in mind the following information.

> You work with **Alan**, a friend of yours and Student B's, and see him every day.
> You and Student B both know **Anne**, who lives close to you. You haven't got her telephone number.
> You have a letter for **Betty**, another mutual friend. She used to live at your house, and you still get mail addressed to her. She now lives round the corner from Student B, who could give it to her perhaps.
> You've lost **Boris's** telephone number. Maybe Student B has it, or can get it for you.
> You want to invite Student B to accompany you on one of the things you intend or have arranged to do this week.

4 Imagine the world in twenty-five years' time. In groups, make a list of important changes there will be in the way we live, work, play, fight, study, etc. (See the list below if you need some ideas for discussion.) Decide on the three most important changes, and tell your class and teacher about them.

5 Choose two topics and write a paragraph of about 100 words on each, containing your predictions for the next year, or any other period you wish. If you prefer, write about some other topic.
The Middle East
Politics in your own country
Islamic fundamentalism
Environmental problems
Sport
The economic situation in your country
Exploration of space
Computers
Pop music
The weather where you are
The Soviet Union
Your own future

G Writing

Guided work: manipulation exercises

1 Combine these sentences about wildlife conservation to form one sentence, using the words and expressions which are given, in the order in which they are given.
Publicity is given to the continuing slaughter of African wildlife.
Little is being done to stop it.
The Governments of the countries concerned simply don't have the resources.
In some cases they don't have the will.
The resources and the will are needed to act effectively.
In spite of because or which

2 Which of the following two sentences would begin a letter to a newspaper, looking at poaching and wildlife conservation from the point of view of poor Africans?
a Sir,
One can appreciate the concern felt by well-fed citizens from rich countries regarding the imminent extinction of African species.
b Sir,
One can understand the horror felt by concerned nature-lovers at the imminent extinction of innumerable African species.

3 In groups, discuss how the letter might continue. Continue the letter to the end, using four or five sentences, or write a letter beginning with sentence b.

4 Combine these sentences about deforestation to form the topic sentence of a paragraph, using the words and expressions which are given, in the order in which they are given, and making any changes to the wording of the sentences which become necessary.
Some of the disadvantages of destroying the tropical forests are obvious.
One example of these disadvantages is the loss of valuable commercial resources.

Another example is the loss of an area of great biological importance.
But there are also the effects on the world's climate.
These are only now beginning to be understood.
Apart from such as and also which

5 Combine the following two groups of sentences in the same way to continue the paragraph.
a One of these effects is the Greenhouse Effect.
The Greenhouse Effect is the result of changes in the Earth's atmosphere.
The changes in the atmosphere are partly the result of the burning of trees.
One caused which due
b One inevitable effect of this phenomenon is hotter weather worldwide.
This may have the effect of melting the polar ice-caps.
A rise in sea-level would be the result of the melting of the polar ice-caps.
The consequence of a rise in sea-level would be the loss of much coastal land.
This phenomenon lead and the possible in turn result in and the consequent

6 Working alone or in pairs, put each of the following fragments about pollution into three different contexts, using three of the words and expressions listed beneath it. The connecting expression may appear before, after, or in the middle of the fragment. The fragment may be a whole sentence, or part of a sentence, depending on the connecting expression you use, and you may change the wording of the fragment slightly if necessary. You may add as many words or sentences as you like.
a . . . it is almost impossible to dispose of nuclear waste safely . . .
whereas moreover for example because in spite of as a result it is often thought
b . . . nowadays, Western European governments are beginning to take measures to protect the natural environmental . . .
however unlike for example because owing to whereas on the other hand nevertheless consequently

A [Reading 1]

Discussion

● What are the good and bad things about the following?
owning a car
driving
being a car passenger

● Would you enjoy a motoring holiday? Why/Why not?

● You are going to read an account by an Englishman of a US motoring holiday, spent in a Recreational Vehicle (a huge camper van for eight or ten people) similar to the one in the picture. Imagine that you are considering going on such a holiday yourself. Note down information you would like to learn from the account.

Reading exercises

1 At ten points in the text sentences have been removed. In pairs, decide what was in each gap. Cover the list of sentences under the text.

2 Study the list, which contains the sentences from the text with five additions. Where does each go in the article? Check with your teacher and fill the gaps in the article.
Check against your answers for Exercise 1.

3 Discuss the following questions in groups.

a Find three verbs which emphasise an RV's size and power on the road.
b Find three expressions which mean *to cost*.
c What does the writer mean when he says the following things?
an introduction session (para. 1)
A seedy sort of ramshackle site (para. 7)
the curious American fear that, if you can't hear recorded music, you must be dead. (para. 9)
rock-bottom (para. 11)
a mini-Beast (para. 12)

4 Discuss in groups whether you would like to try an RV holiday, saying why or why not.

THE BEAST

WE CALLED IT 'THE BEAST' and we picked it up in Denver, Colorado. I phoned the Cruise America people from the airport and they sent round a van to take us to their office for an indoctrination session. We needed it. The Beast was 31 ft long. (1)_____. It looked terrifying.

2 Our party was eight: me, my wife and our baby, and my sister with her husband and three children. A camper van had seemed a good idea, since it would let us travel a long way for less money than a combination of motels and rented cars. Confronting the behemoth, we were less sure.

3 Inside it looked cosier, like the cocktail lounge of a Holiday Inn, all plush drapes and tassels. (2)_____. Down the left side there was a sofa which did the same. The driver's and front passenger's seats were massively upholstered buckets which swung round, so that these two people could join the rest of the party while the Beast was at rest, though from an elevated position, like a king and queen. Above those seats was another double bed which pulled down from the roof. (3)_____. Behind that was the bathroom, which had a toilet, sink and shower-cum-tub. In the rear was the second bedroom with two single beds — also comfy

if you wanted a nap on the move.

4 The Beast was a Winnebago, the best known of the many brands of the camper vans — also known as R.V.s or recreational vehicles — in which Americans like to hurtle along their highways. They are not for people who want your basic, primitive, outdoor life. (4)_____. So ours was fitted with electricity, gas and water and, when stationary, could be linked up to mains sewage. There was air conditioning, full interior lighting (plus bedside lamps) and a stereo tape deck.

5 By mid-afternoon we were on the open highway, storming west along Inter-state freeway O-70. Here we learnt two valuable lessons. First, you have an in-built tendency to steer to the right. There are two ways of realising you've gone wrong: either you look into the left-hand mirror, where you can see your wheels next to the lane markings, or you wait till your right tyres start bumping over the dead animals on the hard shoulder. The second lesson was better: they are more scared of you than you are of them. A Winnebago steaming along at 60 m.p.h. is an awesome sight. (5)_____. Instead they treat you with the respect you always crave and rarely get.

6 (6)_____. The Beast had a tank holding 60 U.S. gallons, which seemed to need topping up most days. Luckily it ran on the cheapest leaded petrol, which you can generally find for less than a dollar a gallon. That was just under one penny per person per mile — some consolation at the end of 20 minutes as the pump meter ground up towards 50 dollars.

7 Campsites vary almost as much as hotels do. (A word about terms: to most Americans, 'camping' means huge vans like ours. What boy scouts do is 'tenting'.) A seedy sort of ramshackle site with few amenities and distractions can cost as little as 12 dollars a night, though there's usually an extra charge for

additional people. (7)_____ _____. Travelling with kids, we found it best to pay the extra few dollars for their amusement, though cooking the evening meal was often interrupted by requests for quarters to put in the video games. I thought they were great, too.

8 (8)_____. If you have 'full hook-up' as we usually did, you drive into your site, then attach the electric cable to the nearby power outlet, plug the hose into the mains tap, and push the flexible drainpipe thing into the sewage outlet. The last is only a minor convenience, since all sites have a place where you can drive to dump your waste. You can get running water from the tank on board, provided you've remembered to fill it. Electricity is the most useful hook-up, since it lets you have the van blazing with light while you cook with the oven and listen to the stereo in air-conditioned comfort.

9 Almost all the sites we visited were wonderfully quiet, and free from the curious American fear that, if you can't hear recorded music you must be dead. (9)_____. If you are travelling at a busier time, it's worth booking ahead. Nearly all sites will take your credit card number. (Visa and MasterCard, i.e. Access are the most useful.) . . .

10 It was an unforgettable trip, as much a voyage as a vacation. But was the Winnebago the best way to make it? Without an R.V., a party of eight would need to rent a very big station wagon, or two smaller cars. Even with a deal which includes air fares, that can work out at hundreds of dollars a week. On top of that you'll need accommodation.

11 The rock-bottom cheapest hotel rooms (you generally pay by the room, not the person) cost about 20 dollars. Fifty dollars will buy you a big comfy room in a motel with a pool. Meals are also dearer than cooking for yourself.

12 On the other hand, with a van, campsites are between 12 and 24

dollars a night and petrol costs more. There are also unavoidable charges above the basic rental: add 12 dollars a day per R.V. for 'Vacation Interruption Protection', which pays for your hotels and food if the van breaks down. (10)_____. You have precious little privacy. That matters less with family, but it might be worrying with friends. The greatest advantage was a satisfying sense of freedom. Of our many British friends in the U.S. who've also tried R.V.s, all would willingly do it again. We certainly would, and to prove it my wife and I took the baby off to California this autumn in a mini Beast. But that's another tale.

Simon Hoggart *The Observer Colour Supplement*

a The campsite which has everything, including free outdoor movies, can run to twice that.

b Ours was extremely comfortable.

c It was 11 ft high and had an overhang at the back longer than some cars.

d Owners of Cadillacs and Mercedes don't think, 'Ha, I'll bet there's some terrified Brit driving that thing.'

e A table with benches on either side converted into a double bed

f We found this a very reasonable charge.

g There are other disadvantages.

h Other drivers tend to keep out of your way.

i Most sites also charge you extra for hook-ups.

j At the back of this room was a well-equipped kitchen.

k The theory is you can have all the conveniences of home wherever you are.

l Down the right side was a large table, with benches on either side.

m But we were there in late April and early May.

n They do use lots of fuel.

o It was white, with long windows down each side.

B | Grammar

Modal auxiliaries used for logical deductions:
must; might; might not; can't

1 Look at the following sentence pairs. In groups, discuss the difference between the sentences in each pair. Check your ideas on Study page 181.

a i That car is expensive.
　ii That car must be expensive.

b i He isn't in.
　ii He can't be in.

c i They might be having dinner.
　ii They must be having dinner.

d i He can't have heard the doorbell.
　ii He might not have heard the doorbell.

e i You must be tired.
　ii You must have been tired.

f i They must be very well-off.
　ii They can't be very well-off.

g i They were going too fast.
　ii They must have been going too fast.

h i She might have been telling the truth.
　ii She can't have been telling the truth.

2 Listen. You will hear twelve sentences. Write them in the spaces below. Parts of some sentences are written in for you. When you have finished, check with another student.

a _____ must 　　be exhausted!
b _____ might 　　be in the garden.
c They 　_____ be _____.
d _____.
e _____.
f _____.
g _____.
h _____.
i _____.
j _____.
k _____.
l _____.

3 Working in groups, imagine a situation for each of the sentences in Exercise 2.
Example:
You must be exhausted!
You've been watching someone dig the garden. Now s/he stops for a moment.

4 Study the two pictures below. Each presents a situation. Referring to the prompt-words for picture **a** and the dialogue for picture **b**, try to find out what has happened in each case, using the language in focus.

a Seat-belt　drink　skid　fast　argue　icy

b 'Yes, Chief Inspector, it's most mysterious. When I arrived this morning the door was locked as usual, but when I got inside I found that the safe, which weighs nearly half a ton, was gone. For once, that safe had a great deal of money in it. Now the odd thing is that the alarm is connected to the police station, but no alarm was heard all night. But the alarm is not easy to find, and it's not a simple matter to switch it off. It's really most upsetting. Everything seemed to be going so well! I took my grandchildren to the circus last night, you know. And now this!'
'Yes, sir. Well, if we can return to the robbery, sir. Now, what about that window up there?'
'Well, yes, also most perplexing, you see, bent bars, but such a small gap, no adult could get through, and those bars are colossally strong. That's why we didn't bother to have the window alarmed like the door and the other windows. And no ladder lying nearby, you see.'
'Yes sir, I see what you mean. Now sir, you say you're quite sure no-one was in the building when you left last night and turned the alarm on. Hmm. Well don't worry sir, we'll soon get to the bottom of this.'

5 Statements made with *must* and *can't* are often backed up by conditional sentences. *Might* is often used to suggest other possibilities. Listen to the following exchanges, bearing in mind the particular situations.

Exchange 1
She never writes to me.
Speaker 1 Do you think she's missing me?
Speaker 2 No, she can't be. If she was, she'd write to you.
Speaker 3 Not necessarily. She might have lost his address.
Speaker 2 Yes, I suppose she might have.

Exchange 2
The burglars took the picture my aunt painted and left the Picasso.
Speaker 1 Do you think they know much about art?
Speaker 2 They can't do. If they did they would have taken the Picasso.
Speaker 3 Yes, I agree.
In **Exchange 1** Speaker 2 leaves out *missing you* twice, and then *lost his address*. What is the name of this language feature?
In **Exchange 2** Speaker 2 says *do* instead of *know much about art*, and *did* instead of *knew much about art*. What is this feature called?

6 Taking turns to begin, improvise similar 3 or 4-line dialogues from the following prompts, trying to use ellipsis and substitution. The first question is suggested by the words in brackets.
a She was thrown straight through the windscreen. (*seat belt*)
b It's 4 a.m. and Mary still isn't home. (*kidnapped*)
c Jimmy keeps trying to run away from home. (*happy*)
d They're already two hours late for the dinner party. (*lost*)
e My grandfather had fifteen dogs. (*liked animals*)
f Fred drives a limousine. (*rich*)

g We've interrogated him for a week, and he hasn't told us anything. (*knows anything*)
h No one's answering the phone. (*out*)

7 We often use *must* or *can't* sympathetically or politely when listening to someone. Listen to the following dialogues. What is the difference between the stress and intonation patterns of the *must* response and the *can't* response?
Dialogue 1
I've been working for twelve hours without a break.
Really! You must be exhausted!
Dialogue 2
I had to go to the morgue to identify the body.
Ugh! That can't have been very nice.

8 Practise similar dialogues based on the following sentences and the words in brackets.
a I haven't eaten all day. (*starving*)
b I smashed up my Dad's car. (*furious*)
c Then the man pulled out an enormous knife. (*terrified*)
d There were people dying and screaming everywhere. (*awful*)
e So I had to try to persuade the bank to lend me £10,000 (*not easy*)
f Then her grandad told us all about his roses. (*not interesting*)
g So there we were, stuck in a sports car in the middle of a snowstorm. (*freezing*)
h I had to sleep in an armchair. (*not comfortable*)

i It's made of three kinds of fruit and topped with cream. (*delicious*)
j Alan's car can hold six people with their luggage. (*enormous*)

C Vocabulary

American and British equivalents

In A Reading 1, the writer explains:
A word about terms: to most Americans, 'camping' means huge vans like ours. What boy scouts do is 'tenting'.
Although American (US) and British (GB) English are very similar, there are a number of differences of vocabulary.
Different words may be used to express the same idea, e.g. US *faucet* = GB *tap*.
The same word may express different ideas, e.g. In Great Britain, *a vest* is something worn under the shirt for warmth, whereas in the USA it is a small sleeveless jacket, worn under the outer jacket of a three-piece suit.
Although the British are using more and more US English nowadays, many differences still exist.

1 One vocabulary area rich in differences between US and GB English is motoring. In A Reading 1, the writer uses the US words *highway* and *freeway* (*main road* and *motorway* in GB English) and the GB words *windscreen* and *camper van* (*windshield* and *camper* or RV in US English).
Look at the matching columns of GB English and US English words below.

a In groups, discuss the meanings of those words and not phrases not already mentioned. Use your dictionaries, if necessary.

b For each word, fill in the space in the opposite column.

GB English	US English
VEHICLES	
a car	_____
_____	a trailer
a taxi	
_____	a truck

GB English	US English
PARTS OF VEHICLES	
_____	the fender
the bonnet	_____
the windscreen	the windshield
	the motor
the gear lever	_____
ROADS	
a motorway	a freeway
a main road	a highway
	an intersection
_____	
a flyover	_____
the verge	_____
_____	a traffic circle
MISCELLANEOUS	
a spanner	_____
_____	a flashlight
petrol	_____
a crash	_____
a puncture	_____

2 Choose one of these vocabulary areas, and write a dialogue in which each of the GB words is used.

a Practise your dialogue until you can perform it without reading it, then perform it for another pair.

b As the other pair perform their dialogue, note down all the words you hear from the list.

c Write a sentence or short paragraph using the US equivalents.

3 Other vocabulary areas contain many differences between US and GB English. Note down any pairs you know in the following areas:
buildings, houses, and their contents;
shops and the street;
clothes, etc.;
travelling;
food.

4 The following rather alarming letter, written by a
student to his mother, contains forty choices
between GB and US words or phrases. Decide
whether you want the letter to sound more British
or more American, and delete accordingly.

Dear Mom (US) / Mum (GB),
I thought I'd write and let you know how I'm ① doing / getting
on since I moved. My ② flat / apartment is pretty well located—
it's near a ③ tube / subway station, and there are a lot of
④ stores / shops nearby, too. There's a ⑤ drug store / chemist
on the corner, and ⑥ an off-licence / a liquor store next door
to that, where I buy beer. I don't drink in the ⑦ pubs / bars
nearby, because it's a ⑧ mean / tough ⑨ area / neighbourhood,
and I don't want any trouble. Only last week a ⑩ guy / bloke
got beaten up ⑪ just / right outside where I live. A lot of
my ⑫ mates / buddies think I'm ⑬ crazy / mad to live where
I do, but ⑭ like / as I said, it's convenient in many ways.
Apart from the other things I mentioned, it's near the ⑮ center of
town / town centre , and that's good because I go to the ⑯
movies / cinema a lot; I probably see two or three ⑰ films /
pictures a week.
    The ⑱ block of flats / apartment building where I live doesn't
look ⑲ too good / very nice from the outside, ⑳ I've got to /
I must admit. There's always a lot of overflowing ㉑ dustbins /
garbage cans outside, and there's usually a lot of ㉒ trash /
rubbish lying around because the ㉓ dustmen / gurbage collectors
aren't very careful about keeping the ㉔ sidewalk / pavement clean.
There's no ㉕ lift / elevator, either, and mothers have a lot of
㉖ trouble / bother getting ㉗ baby carriages / prams up and
down the stairs. Fortunately I live on the ㉘ first / ground floor,
so I never have to use the stairs anyway.
    My place is all right for me. There aren't many ㉙ closets /
cupboards, but that's all right because all they contain is a
few pairs of ㉚ trousers / pants, one or two shirts, and a
couple of pairs of ㉛ sneakers / tennis shoes. The ㉜ cooker /
stove is no good, either, and the landlord is too ㉝ stingy / I
mean to pay for a new one, but I don't cook much anyway. I
usually eat ㉞ take-away / take-out meals, with ㉟ candy /
sweets or ㊱ biscuits / cookies for ㊲ pudding / dessert, and
when I do cook, it's usually ㊳ French fries / chips , with
something out of a ㊴ tin / can.
    Well that's all from me. I'm going to put this in the ㊵
mail / post now, so you should be getting it soon.

                    Love,
                    Dave

D Reading 2

Discussion

● If you are buying a car, what factors should be borne in mind?
● How important are advertisements in making you decide to buy one car rather than another? What other things could make up your mind?
● In what ways do advertisements try to interest people in cars?

Reading exercises

1 Read the advertisements opposite. Which car(s) offer, or make a point of the following features?
a passenger safety in case of accident
b cheapness
c status, luxury
d internal space
e rapid acceleration from a standstill
f reliability starting in cold weather
g low fuel consumption
h specific warranties (guarantees)
i resistance to rust
j special financing arrangements for buying on credit
k roadholding in all weather conditions
l styling and appearance
m comfort

2 Discuss the following questions in groups:
a Which advertisement is the most informative and fact-filled?
b Which offers least information?
c Which seems the silliest to you?
d Which advertisement seems aimed most at men?
e Which seems aimed most at women?
f Why does the Subaru advertisement speak so much of marriage?

3 Some of the advertisements aim to be clever with language. Discuss these extracts from this point of view.
a The Polo:
A car, then, whose beauty is many skins deep.
Aerodynamically, it certainly puts the wind up many of its rivals.
. . . it's safe to say you won't be sorry.
b The Subaru:
. . . How to keep your marriage on the road.
Gripping stuff, Subaru four-wheel drive.

1 Croma

F·374 MLF

The Fiat Croma Turbo i.e. is a rare combination of power and luxury. Not a conventional two-litre executive car, by any means. But we think you'll appreciate the difference.

The power is provided by a Garrett T3 intercooled turbo-charger.

The result is an impressive 155 brake horsepower that will whisk you from nought to sixty in less than eight seconds.

Effortless Power. And effortless braking too, thanks to the Bosch Electronic ABS.

Whilst the power steering means you never have to strain to stay in control. In fact, you never have to strain to do anything. Perish the thought.

Windows, mirrors and front seats are all operated electronically. The heating system is fully programmable and can be controlled to the degree.

Thoughtful little details for such a big spacious car. (There's enough room for five adults all sitting comfortably.)

Equally thoughtful is our Gold Cover free warranty and free servicing for a full three years. The Croma Turbo i.e. really is the civilised way to travel. But then so too is the Croma CHT, the Croma i.e. Super, and the Croma i.e. SX.

2 Suzuki

Mud, snow & ice are all part of a day's work to a Suzuki SJ.

When the weather goes from bad to worse simply flick from 2-wheel to 4-wheel drive.

Now you have a choice of high or low ratio gears to get a grip while all around are losing theirs.

So you've got total mobility throughout the length and breadth of the British Isles, whatever the weathermen say.

The weather-beating SJ range starts from £5,599.

3   Subaru

The Subaru of his and hers. Or how to keep your marriage on the road.

Faithfully through the rough and the smooth. Through stormy weather and the big freeze.

Gripping stuff, Subaru four-wheel drive.

The world and his wife's favourite in fact. With 1½ million four-wheel drives to prove it.

Mind you, it only takes two to make a perfect marriage.

The Justy for one. The world's first 1.2 4WD supermini.

A poetic little mover. 3 valves per cylinder. 5-speed box. 3 or 5 doors.

From only £6,398 what's more.

The other partner? A Subaru estate, of course.

Marries all the practical virtues to sheer desirability.

With seven models to choose from. Starting at just £8,899.

Which means you can both be in Subaru four-wheel drive for around £15,000.

A small price to pay for lasting marital harmony, don't you think?

4   Polo

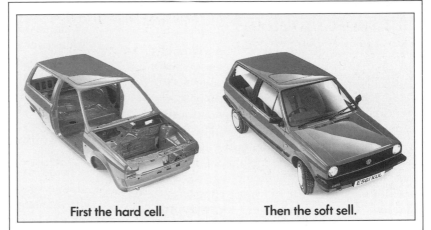

First the hard cell.   Then the soft sell.

Accidents will happen.

But in a Volkswagen Polo at least you'll be steeled for the worst.

Our rigid safety cell sees to that. Giving better all-round protection to passengers and driver alike.

Besides your good self, we have something else to protect: our reputation.

Which is why we still give our bodyshells not one, not two, but, in crucial areas, three rust-inhibiting coats.

Still inject it with 300 litres of niche-seeking wax.

Still lavish on it a full 7 lbs of thick, lustrous paint.

A car, then, whose beauty is many skins deep.

As for its looks is there not just a hint of panache, a soupçon of chic to those crisp, clean lines?

Aerodynamically, it certainly puts the wind up most of its rivals.

Inside, too, it couldn't be anything but a Volkswagen.

Here, cosy is not another word for cramped.

25 sq.ft of passenger room say as much. While, with the rear seats, 41 cu.ft for luggage speak volumes more.

So, whether you buy a Polo for its strength, its styling or its spaciousness, it's safe to say you won't be sorry.

5   Citroën AX

At its launch, every newspaper and magazine that tested the sensational new Citroën AX gave it rave reviews.

Great economy, at 72 m.p.g., the AX 10E is unrivalled by any other petrol car on the market.

Great performance, the new AX's unbeatable combination of power to weight gives 100 m.p.h. plus performance without sacrificing economy.

Great space, with the best level of interior space for a car of its size, you've more than enough room for the kids and the shopping.

GREAT PRICE, FROM ONLY £4,988. And without our special Low Cost Finance scheme, it's hard to find a better-priced 3-door hatchback.

Add to this less than 2 hours servicing in the first 15,000 miles, Citroën's legendary comfort, ride and roadholding then it's small wonder that 'Motor' declared the new AX, 'The most important Supermini of the decade…'

E | Speaking

Structured discussion

Transport Problems

1 In the final stage of this activity you will hold a structured discussion regarding the best ways of getting about in a big city.

In your presentations in Unit 11, you needed functional language for expressing relationships between facts and ideas. For the discussion in this activity, you will need this language again, but you will also need a further dimension of language. Since any discussion must be interactive, you will certainly want to do the following things.

to present an opinion   to agree   to disagree
to interrupt or to resist interruption
to ask for clarification

Below is a list of useful language for performing these functions. Discuss the language with your teacher. Which items seem more certain and which seem more tentative?

Presenting an opinion
It seems to me (that...)
In my view...
It cannot be denied that...
There is no doubt that...

Agreeing
I agree entirely.
Absolutely.
Of course.
I take (your) point.

Disagreeing
(I agree) up to a point, but...
I can't accept that.
(I'm afraid) I disagree entirely.

Asking for clarification/'pinning down' what somebody means
How do you mean?
I'm not sure I understand.
Are you saying that...?

Interrupting
Can I just say something here?
Hang on.

Resisting interruption
No, let me finish please.
Just a moment, please.

2 Practise the language in small groups, using the ideas below. The opinions in List 1 contradict the opinions in List 2. One group member should choose an opinion and express it. Others should agree, disagree, express other opinions, etc.

List 1
Certain crimes, such as rape, should be punished by the death sentence.
Private health care is immoral.
Women drivers really aren't as good as men drivers.
Democracy is a sham. What we need is efficient, one-party government.
Children turn to drugs because they are misunderstood by their parents.
Working on your own, without a teacher, is an effective way of learning a language.
Things like ghosts and poltergeists don't exist.

List 2
The death sentence is brutal and primitive, and does no good.
Private health care is a practical way of using available resources economically.
There is no difference between women and men drivers in general.
One-party government is inefficient by its nature.
Children turn to drugs because drugs are fashionable among young people.
The best way of learning a language is studying in a class with a teacher.
It's quite possible that ghosts and poltergeists exist.

3 You will now have a structured discussion about the relative advantages of the following means of getting about in a big city.

Walking   motorcycle   tube   bicycle   car   bus   taxi

Draw lots for the items on the list. Working in pairs, prepare your defence of the item you have drawn. Bear in mind the following factors
time taken up in travelling
privacy
boredom
health
protection from the weather
cost
time wasted on waiting, parking, etc.
comfort
getting exactly where you want to go
safety
fresh air
harm to the environment/other people

The debate need not be entirely serious, so your arguments can be fairly imaginative. Bear in mind the likely arguments people will produce against your means of transport and prepare yourself to counter these. Also prepare arguments against the methods defended by others. Make a brief note of everything you intend to say.

4 Hold the discussion. Everyone in the class must have a chance to speak. Your teacher will be the chairperson.

F Listening

In the driver's seat

Discussion

● What is the worst experience you've ever had on the road? Tell your group about it.
● Discuss each experience. Whose was the worst experience? Who (if anyone) acted wrongly or made a mistake?
● If you are a driver, what is the thing that other drivers do which most annoys you? When was the last time you did something really stupid while you were driving?

Listening exercises

1 Listen to Tony and Psyche talking about experiences while driving. As you listen, note down what it is that makes each account 'uncanny' or strange. After listening, discuss your answers with another student.

2 Listen again, take notes, and answer the following questions as fully as you can.
a How many accidents did Tony have altogether?
b Where is Tony from?
c Who was responsible for each of Tony's accidents? In what way?
d Which accident was the most serious? What happened to Tony?
e What impression do you get about each of his parents?
f How many vehicles did Psyche drive in the story she tells? What kind of vehicle?
g In what way were the faults in the two vehicles similar?
h How do Tony and Psyche seem to feel now about the stories they tell?

3 Write a true or imaginary story entitled 'The worst experience I've ever had on the road.'

G Writing

Guided work: manipulation exercises

1 Combine each group of sentences to form one sentence, using the connecting words and expressions which follow. Check with another student.

a People were driving fast.
People were driving too close to the car in front.
They couldn't see where they were going.
There was thick fog.
This caused the motorway pile-up.
was caused   and   even though   because of

b There are enormous urban problems.
They result from private vehicle use.
Examples of the problems are pollution, stress and the loss of working hours.
The loss of working hours is caused by traffic-jams.
Because of these problems, the government has decided to subsidise public transport.
The purpose of this is to bring fares down.
This will make tubes and buses a more attractive alternative to driving.
Because of   including   in order to   and

2 Provide the five missing sentences in the following paragraph. _____
_____ . _____
_____ .

I wouldn't need to use any energy at all if I drove a car, for instance, whereas riding a bicycle gives me all the exercise I need and means I don't have to run or do gym. _____
_____ .

If I didn't have a bike, I would have to use public transport, which would mean a lot of waiting for buses and so on. Another reason is that riding a bike means I'm not polluting the atmosphere. _____
_____ . _____ .

To tell the truth, I just couldn't afford to run a car, with petrol being so expensive.

3 Put the following fragment into four different contexts, using four of the connecting words and expressions listed beneath it.
Example:
. . . he drives an expensive sports car . . .
However
The suspect holds a low-ranking job in the organisation, and certainly does not earn the sort of salary which would enable him to own expensive possessions.
***However**, he drives an expensive sports car, which leads us to think that he may be involved in corruption.*

. . . he drives an expensive sports car . . .
whereas   on top of that   although   in order to   for
example   as a result   however   not only . . . but also

UNIT

13

Travel, holidays

A Reading 1
Extracts from a brochure and a
travellers' guide:
United Arab Emirates and Amsterdam

B Grammar
'Fronting' for emphasis

C Speaking
Role play: An international party

D Reading 2
An account of a journey:
Making tracks for Thailand

E Vocabulary
Phrasal verbs 2

F Listening
An anecdote: Gentlemanly guys

G Writing
Guided work: review of formal letters

A ▏Reading 1

Discussion

● What were the best and the worst holidays you have ever had? Why? Do you remember any incidents?

● Note down, in order, the three most important factors in a good holiday. Do the tastes of other group members agree with yours?

● If you had a fixed sum of money to spend, would you prefer a long holiday on which you spent little per day, or a short luxury holiday?

● Tell your group anything you know about Amsterdam and the United Arab Emirates. What would be the good and bad points of a holiday in each?

Reading exercises

1 Read the two texts opposite and discuss the following questions in pairs.

a From which sort of publication was each extract taken?

b What is the purpose of each? For what sort of reader is each intended?

c What are the differences between them in terms of language and the information offered?

2 a Find the ways in which the text about the United Arab Emirates gives advice.

b The writer uses rather formal, indirect language. Rephrase the following extracts in informal English:
  i   For the ladies . . . pools (para. 2)
  ii Around . . . appropriate (para. 2)
  iii Although . . . so be it (para. 3)
  iv All . . . anywhere else (para. 3)

3 Which hotel in Amsterdam should you stay at if you fall into each of the following categories:

a You definitely don't want noise late at night.

b You want to spend as little as possible without sharing a room.

c You are a group of four who can't spend more than $15 or $16 each.

d You want lots of advice about the city.

e You intend to stay out very late at night.

f You want to save money by not eating lunch.

g You are travelling with four or five children.

h You insist on your room being spotlessly clean.

i You like to have a last drink when you come in late.

United Arab Emirates

1 CHILDREN AND INFANTS

The prices shown for children (aged 2–11 inclusive) in our price panels are based on one child for every two adults sharing the same room. A child requiring its own room would be treated as an adult and the single supplement would be applicable. Prices for infants will be available on request.

2 CLOTHING

Spring and autumn are the most pleasant seasons in the Middle East. Probably the most comfortable garments are those made of cotton with perhaps something a little warmer for early morning or evening. Summers are hot and humid so light cotton or a predominantly cotton mix is advisable. During winter a combination of light and warm clothing is necessary, as early mornings and evenings can be quite chilly. Dress is generally informal. For the ladies bikinis, but nothing less than both halves thereof, are quite acceptable on beaches and around pools, as are shorts and T shirts. Around the town skirts or slacks, with tops that at least leave something to the imagination, are considered appropriate. Gentlemen, as is the way of things, may wear shorts and T shirts just about everywhere, but hotel restaurants prefer something slightly smarter. Above all, comfortable shoes are essential for everyone.

3 FOOD AND DRINK

Throughout the UAE there is an astonishing variety of restaurants featuring just about every type of cuisine. Many people will wish to try local dishes, which most hotels offer. Seafood is particularly recommended in the UAE. Alternatively, you can explore the delights of Greek, Malay, Chinese, Japanese, Indian, American or English cookery. Even the ubiquitous hamburger and finger licking good chicken are available. Although the UAE is a Muslim country whose religion forbids its adherents the consumption of alcoholic beverages, it is accepted that others of different religious persuasions do not necessarily feel the same way. If they elect to ruin their livers then so be it. Consequently hotels have bars, night-clubs, discotheques and restaurants where drinks may be consumed — generally at reasonable prices. All we would suggest is that your libations do not exceed what would be considered a socially acceptable level in your own country. The effects of over indulgence are about as popular here as anywhere else.

Emirates Holidays brochure

Amsterdam

On the quiet Leidsegracht (the Leidse Canal), a short walk from the important Leidseplein (Leidse Square, one of the two major entertainment areas of Amsterdam), you should find adequate rooms (some recent complaints) at the **Hotel de Leydsche Hof,** 14 Leidsegracht (phone 23-21-48), where most rooms rent for 45 guilders per person (with nearby baths and showers always available at no extra charge), including service charge and tax. A beautiful oak staircase here, unusually large wood-paneled rooms, and special prices for children.

2 **He Witte Huis Hotel,** at 382 Marnixstraat (phone 27-07-77), offers 24 inexpensive rooms (8 singles and 16 doubles) at 50 guilders ($25) single, 40 guilders ($20) per person double or twin, 35 guilders ($17.50) per person in triples and quads, including a remarkable breakfast of coffee, tea or milk, an egg, cheese, ham, sausage, marmalade, chocolate-spread and four types of bread (two slices of white, one each of brown and biscuit bread). Owner is a Mr Damian, helpful and friendly; the hotel itself is only 200 yards from the Leidseplein, an exceptional location.

40 to 48 Guilders ($20 to $24) per Person, Breakfast and Service Included

3 For family travelers to Amsterdam, the **Hotel Kap** at 5B Den Tex Straat (phone 24-59-08) in the Leidseplein-Rijksmuseum area, offers several four-bedded rooms at 48 guilders ($24) per person, into which they'll place additional children at much-reduced rates. I saw a family of seven in residence in May of 1987. The price includes a Dutch breakfast with egg any style other than poached; the bonus features include free showers and a scale, next to the ground floor staircase, on which you can check your weight free.

4 Ten minutes by tram 9 from the center, in a pleasant and quiet residential area near the Zoo, the **Hotel Olszewski** at 89 Plantage Muidergracht (phone 23-62-41), is owned and managed by a friendly but somewhat strict retired police officer of Polish descent, Viktor Olszewski, who rents bath-

less rooms (showers are free) at 50 guilders ($25) per single, 40 guilders ($20) per person double, 42 guilders ($21) per person for twin beds, all in well-furnished and impeccably clean rooms — but ones in which you can't hold a noisy party at night (you'll be asked to leave the next day)! There's also a 1.15 a.m. curfew. And downstairs, the lounge and bar are decorated with flags, badges and postcards from fellow police officers all over the world. Here's one for readers seeking order and security in a turbulent world.

36 to 40 Guilders ($18 to $20) per Person, Breakfast and Service Included

5 An entire collection of extremely cheap hotels (again with near-perpendicular stairs, but satisfactory rooms) is found in an almost unbroken line, composed of half a dozen establishments, on the Raadhuisstraat — which is a three-minute walk from the Dam Square, between the Herengracht and the Keizersgracht. My favourite here is the **Hotel Westertoren,** 35B Raadhuisstraat (phone 24-46-39), owned by a young Dutch-British couple, Tony and Chris van der Veen, both excellent hosts who make a point of explaining the history and layout of the city to their guests. Their charge per person is 40 guilders per night; and their hotel is best for use in the off-season, when central heating and Dutch TV are both on full blast, and Tony and Chris can give you their full attention and advice.

27.50 to 35 Guilders ($13.75 to $17.50) per Person, Breakfast (sometimes) and Service Included

6 Now the price is again lower, but the location this time is the awesomely lovely Prinsengracht canal, where the **Hotel de moor** is an old, old canal house at no. 1015 (phone 23-16-66). For rooms quite tastefully decorated and furnished, the price without bath (and at least 60% of the 40 rooms here are without bath) is only 35 guilders ($17.50) per person in a twin, 34 guilders ($17) per person in a triple, 32 guilders ($16) per person in a quad, only 31 guilders ($15.50) per person in a five-bedded 'dorm', inclusive of free showers and a ham-and-egg breakfast. One or two singles sell for an astonishing 45 guilders ($22.50), and you should try to get the particularly attractive room 14 if you're traveling alone. After enjoying that room, you'll take the morning meal in a street-level dining area serviced by waitresses dressed in traditional apron-frocks and white lace caps; and the amenities also include a small bar kept open until the last guest comes home (beers and genever for 2.50 guilders), tended by a young Dutch woman named Irmelin. Owners are a friendly Dutch couple. From the Central Station, take tram 4, 16 or 25 to the Prinsengracht stop (one of the major, semi-circular canals coursing through Amsterdam), and walk two minutes from there to this highly recommended choice.

Arthur Frommer *Frommer's Europe on $30 a day,* © 1988 Prentice Hall

B Grammar

'Fronting' for emphasis

It is common in formal English to emphasise certain adverbs or adverbial phrases, particularly those with a negative or restrictive meaning, by placing them at the front of a sentence.
Examples:
Seldom *will you find a better bargain.*
Only when *I had got on the bus did I realise that I'd left my purse at home.*
In no circumstances *must this door be left open.*
This stylistic device is called 'fronting'

1 Discuss the following questions in groups. Check your answers on Study page 181.
a What other adverbs or adverbial phrases are used in this way?
b How does the structure of the rest of the sentence change when we use fronting?
c What examples of fronting are used in less formal English?
d Why do these sentences sound strange?
   Only when the bus came did I get on.
   Seldom have I eaten broccoli.

2 For each sentence, write another with the same meaning, using fronting and the word in italics. Sometimes you must write a pair of sentences.
a It was never guaranteed that the swimming pool would actually be full of water. (*time*)
b We arrived and it stopped raining. (*sooner*)
c You must book with a reputable holiday company. That's the only way you can be sure of a good holiday. (*this way*)
d I've never met such an idiot! (*life*)
e Whatever you do don't book a holiday with a company that hasn't been recommended to you. (*account*).
f Our holidays are all top quality establishments, and also they are in beautiful locations. (*not*)
g We didn't realise what we'd let ourselves in for until we actually got to the hotel. (*not*)
h You won't find better, cheaper accommodation anywhere. (*will*)
i This certainly doesn't prove a lack of honesty on the part of the holiday company. (*way*)

j Never open the door of your hotel room unless you know who is outside. (*circumstances*)
k 'Everybody out!' bellowed the driver. That was when I realised the hotel was ours. (*Only then*)
l The only way to be sure of getting a seat on the plane is by arriving at the airport well before time. (*by*)
m I had no idea that no-one would be waiting for me at the airport. (*little*)
n They said absolutely nothing about airport charges. (*word*)

Another form of fronting involves adverbials of direction or place. These sentences are usually formed with verbs of movement or position.
Example:
Down the hillside tumbled the entire contents of the lorry.
Down the hillside is the adverbial phrase, and the verb is *tumbled.*
The inversion of verb and subject only happens when the verb phrase is one word only, i.e. with the present simple and past simple.

Note that *to be* can be used instead of a verb of movement or position.
Example:
Here are those books you lent me the other week.

Note that no inversion occurs when the subject of the verb is a pronoun.
Example:
Out you go!

3 Place the adverbials of place or direction in the following sentences in the front position, and make any other changes which are necessary.
a Fred, Bill, and John walked round the corner.
b He walked into the forest.
c Get in.
d The Ministers for Health and Education go out. Two new faces come in to replace them.
e The children went away at high speed.
f The rain poured down.
g An imposing house stands at the end of the long driveway.
h The Government will come down like a house of cards.
i They ran off.

C | Speaking

Role play

An international party

You are going to do a role play involving the entire class. The place is London, and the situation is a party. Two or three students will be the hosts, who know everybody. The rest of the class are the guests.

1 Role play situation

Divide into groups of three or four. Each student must invent not only a new name for himself or herself but also an imaginary background. If you prefer to remain basically yourself, change only a few facts. If you want to be more creative, the changes you make can include such things as: family, job or profession, nationality, past life, ambitions, reasons for being in London, beliefs and opinions, and anything else which might make your new 'character' convincing and interesting. Explain all this to the other members of your group, who now 'know' you. Do not tell anybody else at this stage.

The hosts should circulate from group to group, making a note of important information, and getting to know as many of their 'friends' as possible.

2 Acting the role play

The room should be arranged as suitably for a party as possible. To make the activity especially realistic, you could play some music (quietly!) on a cassette recorder. Another idea is to get hold of some paper or plastic cups, and some soft drinks to serve.

Guests arrive (singly or in pairs/groups), knock at the door, and are greeted by the hosts. The job of the hosts is to chat, introduce guests to each other (making sure they circulate), offer drinks, and generally keep the party going. Guests should find out each other's reasons for being in London, talk about themselves, and introduce new acquaintances to each other. Ideally, conversations will develop, but don't get so involved in talking to one person or group of people that you lose the chance to talk to everybody in the class.

Show and tell

For your next lesson, bring to class any photographs or souvenirs (which could be anything from handicrafts to a bus timetable or a hotel bill) that you have from previous holidays or trips. Choose things which have a special importance for you, perhaps because the holiday was especially enjoyable (or awful!), or because of the people you spent it with.

Speaking in groups, talk about your souvenirs and photographs, explaining the people and places which they remind you of. When other students are speaking, ask questions to keep them talking and get information, not only about their personal experiences and memories, but also about practical matters, such as the cost of the air fare, the price of meals in restaurants and so on.

D | Reading 2

Discussion

● When you are on holiday, what are the good and bad points of travelling by public transport?

● Would you like to travel in this way around South-East Asia? Why/Why not?

Reading exercises

1 Read the account of a journey and answer the following questions in groups.

a Which countries did the writer travel through?

b What kinds of transport were used? List them in order.

c What was strange about the prison in Kuala Lumpur?

d Why do you think the writer mentions the fact that they slept under blankets at the Merlin Hotel?

e What effect is AIDS having on the Malaysian economy?

f What was surprising about the Malay/Thai border?

g How can Malaysian snakes make you lose your clothes?

h Why might it be dangerous to play golf in Hua Hin?

i What method have Thais found to solve the problem of picking coconuts?

j What effect did the writer's first sight of Bangkok have on him?

2 What do you think the following words and expressions mean?

a glinted (para. 1)

b permeated (para. 1)

c startle (para. 1)

d scrambling to get out of it (para. 6)

e herons (para. 10)

f dozing (para. 10)

g good as his word (para. 11)

h roused (para. 11)

i pug marks (para. 11)

j trishaw (para. 12)

k toyed with the notion (para. 14)

Making tracks for Thailand

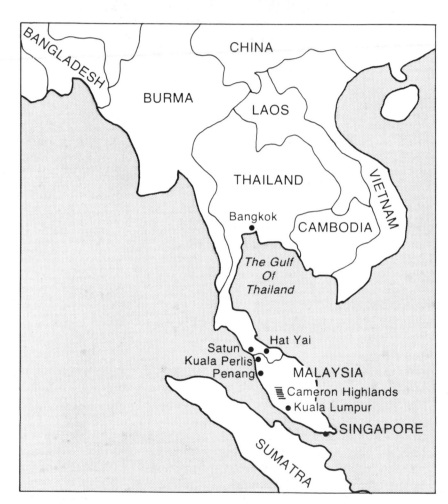

As we crossed the causeway linking Singapore with the Malaysian mainland a crescent moon sailed out from behind heavy clouds and glinted on the sea. In the corridor two ticket inspectors stood smoking clove-scented cigarettes, and the odour soon permeated the whole carriage. At 2.30 I awoke to find the train, dark and silent, standing in a forest clearing which gave off a smell of candlenut. There was a sudden wrenching, rumbling noise nearby, loud enough to startle me. 'Probably a tree falling over,' said the guard in the morning. 'They grow old, sir, and drop down dead just like you and me.'

2 Kuala Lumpur, a clean, spacious city set in wooded hills, was founded by itinerant Chinese miners who discovered tin at the grassy confluence of the Klang and Gombak rivers. Today, the most colourful building in town is the jail where the several dozen men and women awaiting the hangman bide their time. The

exterior walls have been painted with gaudy escapist murals, fantastic landscapes as cheery as illustrations from a children's picture book. The artist was one of the prison's inmates, and these murals were such a hit that he had now been commissioned to beautify the walls of Malaysia's other major prisons as well.

3 Next day we caught a bus through rolling green country to the Cameron Highlands. At the Merlin Hotel, set in the heart of this cool, misty plateau, a monsoonal downpour drummed on the roof and made the drainpipes boom and clang.

4 That night we slept, contentedly, under blankets, then pushed on to Penang through flat, dusty country badly in need of the rain which, even now, was unfurling like a black umbrella over the mauve hills of the Cameron Highlands.

5 Penang was crowded with Australian families having a final fling at the end of the school holidays. We had already made arrangements to cross the Thai border next day, hiring one of the specialist operators who ferry people back and forth in huge old sixties cars with supercharged smugglers' engines. There is no bus over the border, and taxis haven't the documents. Two trains a day go through, but the halt for frontier formalities can take hours. A long-tailed country boat runs from Kuala Perlis to Satun, just inside Thailand, but Kuala Perlis was even more complicated to reach than the border itself.

6 The car collected us at 5 a.m. We had hoped for one of the extravagantly finned and chromed Chevrolets the run is famous for, but instead found ourselves in a big 20-year-old Datsun with a throaty, rumbling engine that could have powered a light aircraft. The driver, a heavy-set, watchful man in a worn aviator's jacket, set off at Formula One speeds through stands of rubber trees planted in precise, mathematical rows. Rubber, he said, was in decline until a few years back. Everyone had been scrambling to get out of

it but now, with the advent of Aids and the worldwide revival of the condom, they were all scrambling to get back in again.

7 In open, sparsely wooded country walled in on one side by hills, we halted at a roadside canteen for a quick noodle breakfast. The driver took our passports into a tiny room behind the kitchen where, surprisingly, a languid, good-looking girl stamped them with the Malaysian exit permits...

8 At the Southern Star Tour Company in Hat Yai, Thailand's southernmost town, a charming Burmese couple sold us tickets for the afternoon train to Bangkok...

9 At the station an unshaven young Dubliner carrying a backpack and guitar told us he was heading for the Himalayas. He had come over that morning in one of the Chevrolets, his driver boasting that certain Malaysian snakes could travel faster than a running man. 'They'll chase you for bloody miles,' said the Dubliner, 'and the only way to slow them down is to tear off your clothes, one by one, and throw them behind you for the snake to attack.'

10 The train was carrying numbers of Thai army officers, small, dapper chain-smokers with graveyard coughs. We passed a succession of curious hills shaped like wet sand tipped from upended beach buckets. As the evening drew in, clamorous flocks of white herons began roosting in the branches of dead trees. On board, affable young men rushed about taking orders for dinner, or selling beer and fiery Mekong whisky. We decided to break our journey at Hua Hin, a small resort on the Gulf of Siam; I found the conductor dozing on his sleeping mat in the corridor and woke him to ask that he, in turn, wake us at the ungodly hour the train was due in.

11 We slept fitfully. A hot, smoky wind blew out of Burma, its border lying only a few miles to the west of the track. Once, when the train halted, I heard the harsh cries of predatory birds. The

conductor, good as his word, roused us at 3.30 and put us off opposite the pretty Royal Waiting Pavilion built for King Kama VII, when he established a summer palace and golf course here in the twenties. (The pug marks of tigers down from the Burmese hills may be seen occasionally in the sandy bunkers.)

12 A cycle trishaw pedalled us through the darkness to the old colonial-style Railway Hotel, latterly famous for its inclusion in *The Killing Fields*. As the sun rose we saw scores of small, sway-backed fishing boats with pagoda-like superstructures putting out across a choppy, sparkling sea. Family groups, all dressed to the nines, processed gravely along the beach beneath brilliantly coloured lacquered umbrellas.

13 We completed our journey next day aboard a waddling little local train that made its leisurely way to Bangkok through tea woods, paddy fields and groves of coconut palms where the nuts were being picked by trained monkeys. The young driver's pretty wife and baby were aboard, seated just behind his cab. He talked to me constantly through the open door and, during the numerous village halts, stepped back to hold the baby in his arms.

14 Then, all at once, our rural service became a suburban service. The countryside began to fill with houses, and we took aboard homebound secretaries, clerks, merchants and severe-looking men with document cases who may have been writ-servers. Entered through its back door, the city presented a sprawling, grimy aspect of flyovers, freeways and smogbound traffic jams. John remarked that it was difficult to think of this unlovely place as the capital of the serenely beautiful land through which we had been travelling. He was right, and, for a brief moment, battling through the crowds, we toyed with the notion of turning around and going back again.

The Observer Colour Supplement

E Vocabulary

Phrasal verbs 2

1 In groups, note down all the two and three-part
verbs you know which could be connected in any
way with travel or holidays.

2 Working in pairs, try to fill the spaces below with
phrasal verbs in the correct tense or form. Each
line represents a word. For the moment, cover the
list at the end of the exercise. When you have
done all you can, check with another pair.

'Talking about holidays, you wouldn't believe the
trouble we had with a package holiday last year.
It's a familiar story, but quite true; ask my husband
and he'll (1)_____ _____ what I say. We'd been
meaning to go abroad for ages, but had always had
to (2)_____ it _____ to the following year because
we never had enough money. But last year we'd
managed to (3)_____ _____ quite a lot of money, so
we decided this time we were really going to
(4)_____ _____ _____ it.
'Well, we knew enough not to book a holiday
with the first agency we walked into, so we
(5)_____ _____ a bit, picking up lots of holiday
brochures and taking them home. I was (6)_____
_____ one of these one day, looking for something
in our price range, when I (7)_____ _____ what
seemed like a marvellous holiday. Four weeks in a
luxury hotel on the Mediterranean! It was a lot
more money than we'd wanted to pay, but then my
husband (8)_____ _____ _____ the idea of getting a
bank loan, which we could (9)_____ _____ over the
following year. I was still very nervous, but my
husband said we deserved to (10)_____ _____ for
once in our lives, and he finally (11)_____ me
_____ it.
'As the time came closer and closer we got more
and more excited. We got books out of the library
and (12)_____ _____ _____ the country where the
hotel was. We found out that it wouldn't be too
expensive, especially since we only had to
(13)_____ _____ expenses on drinks, presents and
so on, since all meals were included. Finally, the
day arrived, and off we went, (14)_____ _____ the
sun!
'Well, what a disappointment the holiday was!
The first shock was the hotel bus, which was nearly
falling to pieces, it was so old. We were a bit
(15)_____ _____ by that, but the hotel was even
more of a shock! What a dump! When the driver

(16)_____ _____ outside it I thought he'd stopped
to buy some cigarettes or something; it was only
when he told us to get out that it (17)_____ _____
us that this was our 'luxury hotel'. After all our
dreams, we'd (18)_____ _____ in a fleapit like this!
The town itself was beautiful, and the weather was
marvellous, but not even this could (19)_____
_____ _____ our disappointment with the hotel.
Nothing worked, the rooms were filthy, the pool
was empty because the pump was broken, and the
food was awful. Apparently the owner used to be
shopkeeper; I suppose he must have noticed that
more and more holidaymakers were coming to the
town every summer, and had decided to (20)_____
_____ _____ the tourist boom by (21)_____ _____ a
hotel himself. And this was the result!
'Well, of course we complained to the travel
agent when we got back, but it was no good. They
just tried to (22)_____ _____ all our complaints,
without promising anything. We argued and
argued, but what it all (23)_____ _____ _____ was
that we weren't going to get any money back. We
could have taken them to court, but what good
would that have done? The law always (24)_____
_____ companies, rather than individuals, in this
country. And of course we couldn't (25)_____
_____ _____ paying the money back to our bank, so
we can't afford a holiday this year!'

3 The missing verbs are listed below. In groups, use
them to fill more gaps.
explain something away   bear something out
come across something   pull up   dawn on
head for something   flick through something
make up for something   end up   side with someone
cash in on something   set something up
put something off   put something by
pay something off   read up on something
shop around   talk someone into something
follow through with something   take someone aback
allow for something   boil down to something
come up with something   get out of something
splash out on something
Now turn to Study page 182, where the verbs are
matched with their meanings, and fill any
remaining gaps.

4 Working in pairs, write a short dialogue containing
six of the phrasal verbs you have been using.
Practise your dialogue, then perform it for another
pair. Listen to the other pair's dialogue. Are the
phrasal verbs being used correctly? Use your
teacher as a consultant.

F Listening

Gentlemanly guys

Discussion
● Note down anything you know about the Amazon region.
● What would make it an interesting or a difficult place to travel in?
● How many different ways do you know of catching fish? In the monologue you are going to hear, the speaker talks about some Amazonian Indians he went fishing with and describes the method they used. What do you think it might be?

Listening exercises

1 Listen to David talking about part of a trip through the Amazon region. Take notes so that you can answer the following questions as fully as possible. Discuss the questions in groups.

a What were David's two hosts doing in Brazil? Why did they invite David to their encampment?

b 'I suddenly realised this was it.' What was that?

c 'One of the most wonderful experiences I've ever had.' Why was it so wonderful?

d What did David have for breakfast? How did he feel about it?

e What was being mined? What was the method? How did David feel about it?

f How did David feel when the Indians turned up one morning? What made him feel that way?

g Who was the 'very gentlemanly guy'?

h Why did he follow the men, at the pool?

i What was the job of the men on the fishing expedition?

j What was the job of the women?

2 Listen again, and discuss the following questions in groups.

a Where had David been talking about just before the extract begins?
Venezuela
Brazil
the North of Brazil

b What part of the anecdote gives you the strongest feeling of what it felt like to be in Amazonas?

c What was the attitude of the Indians to David? How did they communicate?

d David twice uses the 'fronted' expression 'Little did I realise . . .'. Why does he use it each time?

e With what emotions does David seem to look back on his experience now?

f On two occasions, David seems to feel he was, or looked, or bit silly. Which ones?

3 Describe the Indians' method of fishing, using four or five sentences.

G Writing

Guided work: review of formal letters

Generally speaking, we write formal letters either to ask for something or to reply to somebody who wants something from us. Examples are:
letters of application for jobs, scholarships, etc.;
letters asking for information about courses, services, etc.;
letters demanding money (which will include complaints, in the case of a demand for a refund);
letters of reply to all these.
Formal letters should be as brief and as clear as possible. They should be well-organised, and laid out very clearly, in fairly short paragraphs. The style need not be very formal, but on the other hand it must not be too informal or chatty.
Apart from these rough rules, how you write a formal letter is up to you. However, certain useful expressions come up regularly.
Examples:

Saying why the letter is being written
I am writing in order to . . .
I would like to apply for . . .

Referring to previous contact
With regard/reference to your letter of 15/8/89, . . .
I am writing in reply to your letter of 15/8/89.
I apologise for my delay in replying to your letter of 15/8/89.
Thank you for your letter of 15/8/89.
Further to our conversation/my telex of 15/8/89, . . .

Making a request
Would you be so kind as to . . . ?
I would be very grateful if you would/could . . .

Sending something with the letter
I enclose (my curriculum vitae).

Rejecting/accepting applications
We regret to inform you that your name has not been placed on our short list for the post of . . .
I am pleased to inform you that your application for . . . has been approved.

Looking forward to the reply
I look forward to hearing from you . . .
Thank you in advance for your help . . .

Threatening
If/unless/should . . . , I shall be obliged to take legal action.
Otherwise, I shall be obliged to refer the matter to my solicitor.

Conventions regarding layout vary considerably, but the layout of the letter in Exercise 2 would be acceptable anywhere.
If you know the name of the recipient, use it. Note that married women are usually addressed as Mrs, and unmarried women as Miss. However, if you do not know the recipient's marital status, write Ms. Many women prefer this anyway.
If you do not know the recipient's name or sex, begin, 'Dear Sir/Madam'. If you use the recipient's name, end by saying, 'Yours sincerely'. If you do not, end with, 'Yours faithfully'.

1 The following is an essay set for Cambridge Proficiency. In groups, discuss how you would write it, considering how many paragraphs you would use, what would be in each, and connecting expressions which could be used.
For the moment, cover the letter below.

You are Mr Pungent, who has just returned from the holiday abroad described in your telegram below. Write the promised letter to your local travel agent. Your answer should not exceed 200 words.

INCREDIBLE DELAY AIRPORT NO HOTEL TRANSPORT. ROOMS FOOD SERVICE SERIOUSLY SUBSTANDARD. GOOD HALF HOUR FROM SEA IN RUNDOWN NEIGHBOURHOOD. TOURS COURIER AND OTHER EXTRAS NON-EXISTENT. BROCHURE MISLEADING TO FRAUDULENT EXTENT. INSIST ON COMPLETE REFUND OR ELSE. LETTER FOLLOWS. G. PUNGENT.

2 Read the letter. Take notes, putting them in the flow diagram. Some notes have been taken for you.

3 Do one of the following tasks.
a Reconstitute the letter from your notes.
b Write a similar letter, complaining about a disastrous cruise.
c Write the reply from the manager of Sunnytours. Plan the letter carefully, considering content and organisation. Your letter should be about 200 words.

15 Cedars Road,
Worthing
Sussex
10 September 1989

The Manager,
Sunnytours,
3 High St.,
Worthing

Dear Sir,
further to my telegram of 4/9/88, I am writing to complain in the strongest possible terms about the Sunnytours holiday (ref. 59823-4), from which I have just returned. I have been going on package holidays for over thirty years, and never in all this time have I spent such a disagreeable fortnight.

My troubles started at the airport, where I and other guests were obliged to wait for over an hour for a hotel bus which never arrived. Having made my way to the hotel by taxi — at my own expense — I found it to be in a run-down neighbourhood a good half-hour from the sea — quite different from the 'pleasant suburb within easy reach of the sea' promised in your brochure. From then on, things got worse. Not only was my room a disgrace, but the food and service were also seriously substandard. In addition to this, other extras, including tours and a courier, proved to be non-existent.

In view of the foregoing, I would say that your brochure is misleading to a fraudulent extent. Therefore I insist on a complete refund. Should this not be forthcoming, I shall be obliged to refer the matter to my solicitor.

Yours faithfuly

[signature]

CUP Book of Practice Tests 1

Flow diagrams for Exercises 2 and 3a

Paragraph 1
Topic sentence for letter: *Further / telegram / complain / holiday*
Amplification:

Paragraph 2
Problem 1:
Problem 2:
Introduction of other problems:
Problems 3, 4, 5:

Paragraph 3
Conclusion:
Demand:
Threat:

Study pages

UNIT **1**

Organising your learning

1 To study effectively at an advanced level requires a little financial investment. You should buy:
a good advanced learner's dictionary;
a good practical grammar, and a book of grammar exercises;
a notebook for use in class;
a proper file for storing, organising and working on the language which you acquire during your studies. Divide this file into sections for grammar work, corrected written work, vocabulary, etc.

2 It is not easy to be aware of what you need to do to improve your English, but you can make a start by thinking about your strengths and weaknesses. Consider the questions below. You may not be able to give complete answers, but thinking about the questions will be helpful.
Vocabulary
Do you feel you know plenty of words? Can you use many of them? What problems do you have in learning new words and expressions?
Grammar
What areas of grammar do you find confusing?
Listening
Do you feel you are a fairly efficient listener? What do you find easy and what difficult when you listen to English?
Reading
Is your reading effective? What do you find easy and what difficult when you read?
Writing
Do you write in a well-organised way? Can you only use simple sentences correctly? How is your spelling? Can you write in fairly formal as well as informal style?
Speaking
Are you a fairly fluent speaker? Do you make lots of

mistakes or do you speak fairly correctly? Can you only use simple language when you speak or is your speaking quite creative?

3 You can't learn to use a language really well by just turning up for lessons regularly. You can learn good English much more quickly if you use it and work on it at other times as well. Make a list of all the things you could do outside the classroom to improve your English. Do you do any of these things? If not, why not?

Projects and assignments

1 Write in an organised way about your reasons for studying English, what you feel you need to learn/improve (and why), and any ideas you have for improving your English outside the classroom.

2 If you are studying in your own country, interview two foreign teachers (not yours) about being there. Record the interview or prepare a questionnaire. Prepare the questions you will ask.
Write a report of your findings, comparing, contrasting and concluding. If the interview is recorded, note down any adjectives used and add useful ones to your file. Play the interviews to your class, adding any further information about the speakers which is useful.

3 Visit three language schools (not your own), and get information about them. Consider: interviews (permission will be needed); leaflets, etc.; your impressions. Write a report comparing the schools. Which one seems the best value/do you like best?

4 Write the first letter from an English teacher new to your country to a friend in England. Keeping the language natural, try to include some of the structures and vocabulary you have covered in this unit.

B | Speaking

Finding a flat

2 Role play situation

Student C

> You work in an accommodation agency. You are determined to let a flat to someone today. You work partly on a commission basis (i.e. the more expensive the accommodation you let, the more you earn). You have the following flats to offer.
>
> **A flat in Ealing**   Occupies the top floor of a semi-detached house. Two bedrooms. Tiny sitting room. Kitchen. Bathroom. TV. No telephone. Shares a large garden with the ground-floor flat. 3-month let. Ealing is a pleasant residential area about seven miles from the centre. There is a bus service from near the flat to a tube station, two miles away. £100 p.w.
>
> **A flat in Stockwell**   One bedroom, two single beds. Large sitting room. Kitchen. Bathroom. No telephone. Bills included. 6-month let. Stockwell is only two or three miles from the centre, with a tube station (cheap central-fare zone) and regular bus service. It is considered a rather tough, down-market area, suffering from poverty and some racial tension, but more well-off people are beginning to move in. £90 p.w.
>
> **A large bedsit in Chelsea**   Sitting area, two beds, small stove, sink. TV. Coin-box telephone outside (in hall). The bathroom (reached through the hall) is shared with two other bedsits. 4-month let. Chelsea is a central, very fashionable area with a lot of night life. £85 p.w.
>
> **Two small bedrooms in a shared flat in Streatham**   Sitting room. Kitchen. Bathroom. Telephone. TV. Central heating. Bills: all shared with existing tenant. Streatham is a fairly pleasant residential area, four or five miles from the centre, which can be reached by bus and then tube from Brixton. It lies between two big commons (open parks). £40 p.w. (per person).
>
> **A flat in Islington**   Two large bedrooms. Small kitchen-diner. Luxurious bathroom, with sunken bath. No sitting-room. Telephone. Central heating. 6-month let. Islington is an increasingly fashionable area just outside the centre, with quiet streets and beautiful Victorian terraced houses. The flat is five minutes by bus from King's Cross Station (tube and overland trains). £500 p.c.m.
>
> You cannot be flexible about rent, but you might be able to alter the length of lets. Try (fairly honestly) to make each flat sound as attractive as possible.

D | Reading 2

1 London, a tourist trap that lives up to its name

> d   Sir,
> There is much alarm about the declining tourist figures in London this year: various reasons have been put forward including the strength of the pound and the oil shortage.
>
> f   I spend my working hours with tourists and foreign students, and I can give another reason for the tourist decline: it's a growing awareness among foreigners of what a voracious and insatiable tourist trap London is.
>
> j   If you look at London from a foreigner's point of view, it isn't really a holiday city, more a type of steeplechase in which the tourist has to jump over a set of hurdles at the same time as fighting off the clutches of some of the more unscrupulous inhabitants.
>
> l   The first hurdle is Immigration, a service not renowned among foreigners for its tact and diplomacy. The UK and the USA apparently have the worst reputation in the West for the belligerence of their immigration officers.
>
> h   When the tourist has fought his way through Immigration Control, his next problem is accommodation. If he arrives after 9 p.m., then he's just had it. All the hostels and B&B places are full.
>
> k   I arrived with two German students at Euston at 11 p.m. last Thursday. After half an hour's working through Yellow Pages, we still hadn't found them anywhere to stay. We tried the BR information office: 'Ask a policeman,' they said.
>
> c   The Germans (and myself) found it amazing that there was no useful information service available — not even some central clearing house we could telephone to find a bed for the night. Surprising though it may seem, trains and planes do arrive outside office hours.
>
> e   If the tourist manages to find an accommodation agency, the next hurdle is the price. I spent an hour telephoning agencies advertised in the Evening Standard for an Argentinian student,

whose maximum was £50 a week. 'Oh, no,' said the agencies, 'we haven't got anything for £50: don't you know this is the tourist season?' One agency offered me a double bedsit for £40. I know the floors of London are paved with gold but this is ridiculous.

i And next, the 'language' schools. A lot of people come here because they want to learn English since in many countries a sound knowledge of English is very useful for job promotion. But you don't need a licence to open a language school; there are 400 language schools in London, some of which are quite reputable and others which are downright atrocious. Tarzan could come over to London and open the 'Me Tarzan, You Jane School of English' and no one would blink an eyelid.

a I worked at a language school once where the principal was a retired actor with no educational qualifications; the teachers were completely untrained, the students were not graded into different language levels (so you had nearly fluent students in the same class as people who could just say, 'Hello, how are you?') and the language laboratory, though advertised, didn't exist. And the students were each paying £110 a month.

g Do you remember the feeling of relief when you're abroad, on guard against being ripped off and you see the sign on the wall of a restaurant or hotel 'This establishment is subject to Touristic Control'; in other words, the price and conditions offered are regularly checked?

b Until we have a similar system in London, or until we at least make an effort towards looking after our tourists, then the numbers coming to London will continue to decline. The word is being passed back along the line: 'Don't go to London — it stinks.'

Yours,

Steve Elsworth
London N5

E Vocabulary

Neutral and strong adjectives

1 Language description

a *Downright* is the strongest adverb; *quite* is the weakest

b *atrocious*

c *Quite* could be replaced by *fairly*, which is slightly weaker. Neither is very enthusiastic.
Very could be replaced by *extremely*, which is more informal.
Downright could be replaced by *utterly*, which is slightly formal, or *absolutely*. As a rule, use *absolutely* for any strong adjective

d

surprising	amazing
bad	atrocious
useful	indispensable
angry	furious
silly	ridiculous
hungry	starving

e Each adjective on the right is a stronger version of the one to its left.

f The adjectives on the right follow strong intensifying adverbs like *downright*, *utterly*, *absolutely*. Those on the left follow the weak adverbs.
Rather is an adverb used with neutral adjectives to mean *more than usual* or *more than expected*, or *more than I like*.

F Writing

Listing and adding; recommending; explaining purpose

2 Language description

a Listing and adding

Paragraphs are connected by: *The first objective is . . .; the second question is . . .; the final way is . . .*
Sentences are connected by: *First of all . . .; On top of that . . .; Furthermore . . .; Lastly . . .; The most important question . . .; In addition to this . . .; Last but not least . . .*
Expressions connecting information within one sentence are: *and; apart from; not only . . . but also; or.*

b Explaining purpose

to *learn*; **in order to** *be able to.* To (do) and *in order to (do)* are used when the subject is the same for both verbs (the young people both *come* and *learn*). *In order to* is more formal.
a bar **for** *socialising*. The purpose of a thing (e.g. *a bar*) is indicated by *for doing*, unless the user is specified, when the infinitive is used.
so that *students don't.* So that is normally used when two different subjects are involved (*a school* and *students*).

c Recommending

Directly: *should; must; ought to; it is important that . . . should.* Although *must* is theoretically stronger than *should* or *ought to*, in practice they all often have the same strength. In speech *must* is often stressed to show greater strength.

Indirectly: *it is convenient for students if a school. . .; a responsible school will. . .; in good schools there is . . .; it is part of a school's responsibilities to . . .*

G Grammar

Used to do; be (get) used to doing; present simple with frequency adverbs

2 Language description
Used to do

This structure is employed to refer to a state of affairs or habit/custom in the (usually distant) past, which no longer exists.

Notes

1 In formal or literary English, we can use *would* rather than *used to* for past habits, but not for past states of affairs.
Example: *As a child, young Margaret would often help to serve customers in her father's shop.* This is correct literary style when describing a past habit.
Example: *I used to live in Luton when I was a kid* It would be wrong to use *would* here as this sentence describes a past state of affairs, not a habit.

2 In the interrogative and negative forms, the *d* is *deleted from* used.
Example: Did you use to dream of escaping?

Get/be used to something/doing something

This structure is employed to refer to something one has done or experienced so often that it isn't strange any more.
Example: *I'm used to getting up early.* (It's not new to me.)
The structure is also used when a state of affairs is strange.
Example: *I'm used to getting up whenever I want.* (Not to getting up early, as I have to now.)
The contrast in meaning is shown by the way we pronounce the sentences. This will be practised in Exercise 4).

Notes

1 *Get used to* means *become used to.* When we use a perfect or progressive tense we usually use *get.*
Examples:
He's getting used to it.
I've got used to it now.
2 We say *can't get used to*, not *don't get used to.*
3 The gerund (e.g. *getting up*) must be used because *to* is a preposition.
4 In formal style, *accustomed* can replace *used.*
5 This structure is only used to say things are (or are not) new or strange to us.

The present simple with frequency adverbs

This structure is used for habits in the present.
Example: *I go for a run every morning.*

UNIT

Organising your learning

1 Take time to study corrected written work carefully. Are errors just carelessness, or are they caused by confusion about spelling, some area of grammar, etc.? Note the latter. Make a list of habitual errors, refer to your grammar, and do extra work from your grammar exercise book. Before you hand in any homework, check that you haven't made the same errors again. Ask your teacher if you may re-do corrected work for a second correction. Always make sure that any work you hand in is as error-free as you can make it.

2 When you write, try to use new language which you have learnt in or out of class.

3 For each area of vocabulary in your coursebook open a list in the vocabulary section of your file. Transfer to this list new items you have studied, with the phonemic transcription (where this will be helpful) and an example sentence. Add to your lists new items which you come across in or out of class. It is a good idea to make additional lists according to some area of meaning which makes sense to you (e.g. shops, crime, persuasion, anger). Transfer items to these lists. The advantage of such lists is that items more easily 'call up' one another from your memory. The thinking you do in compiling lists and transferring items will also make items more memorable.

Projects and assignments

1 If you are studying in Britain and staying with a host family write a description of its members, and the relationships between them. At the end of your stay in the UK reread your description. Does it still seem fair and accurate to you? Write about anything new you have learnt.

2 If you are studying in your own country, get hold of any leaflets, etc. produced by the government regarding the drug problem. Describe the leaflet's style and apparent intention, summarise its content, and compare it with the extract in Reading 2. If there is no such official information, explain why you think this is.

3 Write a realistic dialogue between a young person and her/his parents, who have discovered that she/he takes drugs.

B Grammar

Conditional sentences

1 Language description

First conditional

Example: *If he does that again, I'll complain to the manager.*
Both parts of the sentence are considered to exist in future time.

Second conditional

Example: *If you were a woman you would know what I mean.* Both clauses are considered to be impossible. The time frame is the present for both.
Example: *If they offered me a job in London, I would consider moving.* Both clauses refer to a hypothetical possibility. The time frame is neither present nor future, in the definite future sense of the first conditional.
The two examples are similar but the difference can be seen more clearly if one follows each with *but*.
Example: *If you were a woman, you would know what I mean, but you **aren't** so you **don't**.*
Example: *If they offered me a job in London, I would consider moving, but they almost certainly **won't**, so I almost certainly **won't**.*

Third conditional

Example: *If I hadn't pulled you out of the way, that car would have hit you.* Both clauses refer to a hypothetical past possibility: a past that didn't happen, in fact.

Zero conditional

Example: *If you forget to say 'please' when you ask for something, English people think you're being rude.* The meaning is not hypothetical, or past, or future. We are talking about what always or usually happens.

D Reading 2

Reading exercises

1 *Extract 1*

THE DRUG PROBLEM

h Just because someone takes a drug it does not mean they will become addicted to it.
At times in our life, almost all of us turn to drugs of one sort or another.

c Cigarettes and alcohol are, of course, the most common ones.
But many of us also turn to sleeping tablets, tranquillisers or anti-depressants to help relax and cope with the stress and tension of everyday life.

i In many ways children turn to their drugs for just the same reasons.
Adolescence, as we all know, can be a difficult period.

a Often it's a time when we don't get on with our parents.

d There are also many pressures at school, from parents, and from friends.
It is a period of change when many choices must be made.

j And at a time when work can be a major problem, there is also frustration and boredom.

g All of which means that when someone, perhaps a friend, offers a child something which is supposedly 'fun' and 'everybody else' is taking it, the pressures and curiosity are so great they may try it themselves.

e Fortunately, most children say 'no'.

k Unfortunately, though, a disturbing number are saying 'yes'.

f Most children grow out of it. Or simply decide they don't like it and then stop. But a few go on to have a serious drug problem.
That's why we all need to tread carefully when talking to a child we suspect may be taking drugs.
A wrong word at the wrong time can sometimes make a child even more rebellious.

l But the right words of understanding can reinforce their decision not to take drugs.
This booklet hopes to help you find those right words, and to make you better informed.

b Because the most important people when it comes to coping with the drug problem may not be the police, doctors or social workers.
They could be parents ... like YOU.

2 *Extract 2*

HOW PARENTS CAN HELP

It is natural for parents to feel hurt and angry when they discover that their child is taking drugs.

The problem is that these reactions won't solve anything.

So here we'd like to (1) show you how some parents have helped solve their child's problem.

Mike, for example, told his parents how a friend had been caught smoking cannabis at school and how he'd been offered a joint once or twice.

Understandably worried, Mike's parents (2) talked to teachers at the school and then to other parents.

As a result the school took action — (3) drug education was included in classes and meetings were arranged to tell parents about drugs and their effects.

Helen, like many teenage girls, had become depressed after breaking with a boyfriend. So she started taking her mother's tranquillisers, which she knew her mother had taken on prescription for a short time following her grandma's death.

Discovering this, perhaps not surprisingly her mother and father reacted angrily. But this (4) only made Helen even more upset.

So, shortly afterwards, when a friend offered her heroin, (5) she took it, and became entangled in the drug world.

On reflection Helen's parents realised that (6) getting angry didn't help and that Helen needed love and understanding to cope with the problem.

The lesson of many similar stories from children of all kinds of background is that (7) it's better to try talking to young people calmly.

E Vocabulary

Phrasal verbs 1

3 *run away*, leave home without telling your parents
get on with someone, have a good relationship with someone
stand for something, accept something which is unacceptable
put something forward, propose something

getting on, progressing, managing
let someone off, excuse someone
get over something, recover from something
(not enough to) go round, insufficient quantity/number for everyone
grow up, become adult (*not bigger*)
frown on something, disapprove of something
catch up with someone, achieve a position of equality with someone
live up to something, correspond to (*expectations/a reputation*)
tell someone off, rebuke, reprimand someone
long for something, think of with keen nostalgia/anticipation
go without something, deny yourself something/manage without something
let someone down, disappoint/betray someone
work something out, find a way of solving a problem
fall behind someone, opposite of 'catch up with'
take after someone, resemble (*a parent/uncle, etc.*) in character
get away with something, escape punishment for something
go off something, stop liking something

F Speaking

Informal criticism

Language study

Dialogue 1

MOTHER: Oh no, I don't believe it! John, look at this!
JOHN: What's up?
MOTHER: I wish you wouldn't leave your mess lying everywhere. Just look at the state of this kitchen!
JOHN: Eh? Oh, yes, sorry about that. I was cleaning my shoes.
MOTHER: Well, you might have put everything away again.
JOHN: Er, yes, I suppose you're right. I'm sorry. It won't happen again.
MOTHER: That's not good enough! You're always doing it. The trouble with you is you're just lazy and inconsiderate! And look at that floor! Oh, I might have known it!
JOHN: What about it?
MOTHER: It's got boot polish all over it, that's what! Oh, I've had enough of this. Why couldn't you have put some newspaper down? Why can't you take a bit of care with things?
JOHN: It wasn't my fault. There wasn't any newspaper.
MOTHER: Well then, why on earth didn't you take more care?

JOHN: Well, I did try. I'm terribly sorry, Mum.
           Shall I try and clean it up?

MOTHER: Oh don't bother, I'll do it. I just wish you
           would be a bit more careful, that's all.

JOHN: OK Mum. Sorry, Mum. Oh, Mum, have
           you pressed my suit yet? I left it out this
           morning.

MOTHER: Pressed your suit? That does it. That really
           does it. I've had enough of this.

JOHN: Oh so have I. I don't know why I don't
           leave home.

MOTHER: Neither do I. I wish you would!

Dialogue 2

FATHER: John, I hear you've been rude to your
           mother again.

JOHN: Rude? Me? She's the one who's always
           complaining and moaning at me. It's not
           my fault if she's neurotic!

FATHER: That's a nasty thing to say.

JOHN: Yes I suppose you're right. Sorry.

FATHER: I mean, I don't like to criticise, but it was a
           bit thoughtless of you, you must admit. You
           really should be more careful, and you
           certainly should have kept your temper with
           your mother.

JOHN: Yes, you've got a point. I suppose. But the
           trouble with Mum is she never knows when
           enough is enough.

FATHER: I know John. But put yourself in her shoes.
           It wasn't very diplomatic of you to ask if
           she'd pressed your suit, was it? That was
           really a stupid thing to do in the
           circumstances.

JOHN: I must admit it was a bit tactless.

FATHER: Couldn't you have pressed it yourself?

JOHN: Well, I did try, but I don't know how to
           press things properly.

FATHER: Well it might be an idea to learn, and also
           remember to clear up after yourself, and be
           more considerate to your mother. I mean,
           I'm sorry to have to say this, but you're
           becoming a very difficult person to live with.

JOHN: Yes, all right. Point taken. Sorry Dad. It
           won't happen again, I promise.

G Writing

Supporting a statement

1 Language description

Amplification

One way of supporting or clarifying a statement is to
follow it with another which says more about it, or
amplifies it.

Example: *Beating a naughty boy will make him as violent
as his parents. Studies have shown that people who have
been beaten during childhood tend to be brutal themselves.*
Such amplifying sentences are sometimes introduced
by *in fact* or *indeed* (more formal), when they are
emphatic.

Example: *I get on really well with my Dad. In fact, I
could almost say he's my best friend.*

Exemplification

Support for a statement can also be achieved by
giving examples.

Example:

Drugs **such as** *glue*
Such *drugs* **as** *glue* } can be obtained easily by children.
Drugs **like** *glue*

Here, the information is expressed economically, in one
sentence.

Example:

Not all dangerous drugs are hard to find, or even illegal.

For instance,
For example, } *children can buy ether-based glue anywhere.*

Here, the example requires a separate sentence of its own.

Example:

Not all dangerous drugs are hard to find, or even illegal.

Take the case of *ether-based glue.*
Ether-based glue is **a case in point**.
One example *is ether-based glue.*
Take *ether-based glue,* **for instance**.

} *This is available in any
hardware store, and it is
practically impossible to
prevent youngsters
looking for a cheap 'high'
from buying and sniffing
it.*

In this case, there is even more information in the
example, so it is introduced with one sentence, and
the details are given in a second, amplifying
sentence.

Rephrasing

A third way of giving support to a statement is by
rephrasing it to make it clearer or more forceful. At
the start of a second sentence, we use such
expressions as: *That is to say, . . .; In other words, . . .;
To put it another way, . . .*
To rephrase a statement in the same sentence, we
use: *. . ., or rather, . . .*

UNIT **3**

Organising your learning

1 List compound verbs in your file according to the divisions of meaning described in G Vocabulary.

2 In the reading tests in this unit there are many words concerning violence. Find them, use your dictionary, and open a list in your file.

3 Whenever you want to say or write something, but don't know how in English, make a note and build up a list in your own language. These could be items of vocabulary, idiomatic expressions, grammatical structures, appropriate language for performing functions (e.g. interrupting, disagreeing, offering, etc.). Use your teacher, other native speakers, other students, and your dictionary or grammar to help you with these doubts and transfer the language you learn to the lists of things you do know.

Projects and assignments

1 If you are studying in your own country, interview a member of a minority ethnic or racial group. Prepare your questions beforehand. Summarise the answers in writing, saying also what you have learnt that you didn't know before. If you can tape the interview, translate important parts into English and include them as quotations.

2 If you are studying in Britain, interview five local people to discover attitudes to foreigners and to the British themselves. Plan your questions carefully. Be careful to be extremely polite. If you record the interviews play them in class, commenting on age, apparent class, appearance, etc. of person interviewed. Note these shortly after each interview. Summarise your findings in writing.

3 Find three advertisements (in English preferably, but not necessarily) which seem sexist to you. Cut them out and display them alongside your explanation of why they are sexist.

B Grammar

Story-telling structures

Past tense review
1 Language description
a iv, vi and viii.
b The first situation is described by i, ii, and iii.
The second situation is described by v.
The third situation is described by vii.
c ii is the activity at the time the action started.
i and iii are a state of affairs and an activity before the action, which are relevant to the situation.
d i Past perfect simple. The past perfect simple tells of events/actions before the moment being described. With verbs not normally used in a progressive tense (e.g. i *to be*) it tells of previous situations.
ii, v and vii Past progressive/continuous. The past progressive sets a situation, in which the events occur.
iii Past perfect progressive/continuous. The past perfect progressive tells of recent continuous activities before the moment being described.
iv, vi and viii Past simple. The past simple tells of consecutive actions/events.

Ability in the past
3 Language description
a i to vii refer to ability in a particular sequence.
viii and ix refer to the general past.
b i and ii.
c iii, iv, vi and vii (*he was able to slap*).
d *Was able to. Managed to* is used when the action is more difficult.
e Verbs of involuntary perception: *hear, sense, smell, taste, feel.*

Notes
1 For an ability which existed in a past period (not considered as part of a sequence of events), use *could*. Example:
I could speak French when I was young. This is not saying that you did so on a particular occasion.

2 For ability in a particular situation use:
was/were able to when you actually did what you were able to;
could have (done) when you didn't do it;
could with verbs of voluntary perception.

3 *Couldn't is always acceptable as a negative form.*

4 *was able to* can precede verbs such as *see* when they required an effort.

5 In very formal style, the *able to* structure can be used for any situation, past or present.

E | Writing

Time expressions in story writing
1 Language description
a The point in time when something happened

At the beginning, at the end (of the day, a film, a party).
At that point, just then, at that moment relate an
event/action precisely to the sequence of events.
Meanwhile relates a continuous activity *to a point in the
sequence of events.*

b How long something took

In next to no time (amazingly soon), *straight away,
shortly afterwards, at first.*
Finally, at last, in the end, after a while.

Notes

1 *At last* is used more than *in the end* to express a feeling
of relief, excitement, or happiness.
2 *At first* distinguishes between the way things were
before and the way they were afterwards.
Example: *At first the weather was quite nice, but it soon
clouded over.*
3 *At first* and *at last* do not tell the order in which things
happened.

c The order in which things happened

First, after that, lastly, last of all, finally.

F | Speaking

Formal complaints

Language study

Dialogue   Part 1

RECEPTIONIST: Can I help you?
GUEST: Yes I hope so. The air conditioner in
my room isn't working. Would you
send someone to repair it please?
RECEPTIONIST: Well, I'm very sorry, but the
electrician has just left, and it will be a
bit difficult to get hold of him again.
Are you quite sure it isn't working?
GUEST: Of course I'm sure. Are you telling me
my air-conditioner can't be repaired
until tomorrow?
RECEPTIONIST: I'm afraid not. It's rather difficult
really.
GUEST: Well I'm afraid this isn't good enough.
I insist that my air conditioner is
repaired tonight. This is ridiculous.
RECEPTIONIST: Well, as I say, I'm very sorry, but
there's nothing I can do. The problem
is we haven't got anybody here who
could repair it. The electrician goes

home at eight o'clock, you see.
Perhaps you could leave your window
open.
GUEST: Look. I don't think you understand. I
don't care when the electrician
finishes, I want my air-conditioner
repaired tonight. Otherwise I shall
have to speak to the manager.
RECEPTIONIST: All right, I'll see what I can do, but I'm
not promising anything.
GUEST: Very good of you.
RECEPTIONIST: Don't mention it. Only doing my job.

Part 2

RECEPTIONIST: Oh, hello, is it about the air
conditioner?
GUEST: Yes it is. It is now 9.30, and nothing
has been done.
RECEPTIONIST: Yes, well, we tried to get hold of him,
but he wasn't there, so we tried
another one, but he wasn't there
either.
GUEST: Would you be good enough to call the
manager please?

Part 3

MANAGER: Good evening, Madam.
GUEST: Good evening. Are you the manager?
MANAGER: I am. What can I do for you?
GUEST: I have a complaint to make. In fact,
two complaints. The first concerns
the air-conditioner in my room, which
isn't working. The second concerns
your reception clerk, who doesn't seem
to be taking my complaints very
seriously. I cannot help feeling that
his attitude would be rather different if
I were a male guest.
MANAGER: Oh, I'm sure that isn't so, Madam.
Our clerk has told me of the problem.
I'm extremely sorry for the
inconvenience you have been caused.
The matter will be dealt with
immediately.
GUEST: Well that's what he said, more or less,
but nothing was done.
MANAGER: Don't worry, Madam, leave it to me, I
will attend to it. Once again, Madam,
please accept my apologies for any
inconvenience.
GUEST: Oh, well, in that case, thank you very
much. I'm much obliged to you.
MANAGER: Not at all, Madam, my pleasure.

4 Improvisation

Student B

You are a badly-paid male receptionist in the Service Department of a garage. You have had a hard day, in which you have been treated rudely by various customers, who seem to have more money than manners. The problem is that two mechanics are off sick, so cars have not been repaired on time. Some cars will have to be left until tomorrow. Among them is a silver-grey Saab, registration number F123 ABC. You must ask the owners of these cars to return tomorrow. If they refuse to leave, they may wait, but it is very unlikely that their cars will be repaired today. Your manager only wants to see angry customers in extreme cases.

Student C

You are the manager of the Service Department of a garage. You have had a hard day, because two of your mechanics are off sick, and repairs have been delayed, in some cases until tomorrow. You have told your receptionist that the owners of these cars must be asked to come back tomorrow. You will only speak to a customer if s/he is VERY insistent, as you are finding it more and more difficult to be courteous. It is possible to move a car to the 'front of the queue', but you don't like to do this.

UNIT **4**

Organising your learning

1 Transfer the verb lists in B Grammar to a 'Gerunds and Infinitives' section in your file. To clear up doubts about meanings, use your dictionary or ask your teacher or another student. Keep adding to your lists.

2 Think again about the strengths and weaknesses you considered in Unit 1. Have your ideas become any clearer? Do this continually as you study.

3 Open lists in your file for language you want to remember from the Focus on function Speaking sections in your coursebook (in Units 2, 3, 4, 6, 9). Write short dialogues using items of the language. Perform and record them with another student and have your teacher listen to them. Do this for every Focus on function Speaking section.

Projects and assignments

1 Go to a restaurant, play, film, etc. and report back to your class on it, recommending or warning off. Alternatively, write a report or review and display it in your classroom.

2 If you are studying in your own country, work with one or more students to prepare a 'Guide to (your town) at night', which can be as general or specific as you like. Plan how to organise it, think about the layout, which information to include, whether to add photographs and personal experiences, etc.

3 If you are studying in Great Britain, prepare a guide as above, but of the town where you are studying. If your guide is especially useful and attractive, ask your teacher if it could be displayed somewhere in your school, to help new students.

B Grammar

Verb patterns using the gerund and the infinitive

3 The verbs should be grouped as follows.
1a Example: *Do you fancy* **going** *for a walk?*

enjoy	miss	practise	face	deny*
detest	mind*	resent	suggest*	avoid
delay	postpone	escape	imagine*	risk
admit*	finish	entail*	involve	stop

1b
Examples: *Please forgive* **me for being so rude**.
He apologised **for being rude**.

prevent (him) from	persist in
discourage (her) from	thank (her) for
congratulate (him) on	blame (him) for
accuse (her) of	stop (her) from
dissuade (him) from	insist on*
succeed in	praise (him) for

2a Example: *I decided* **to apply** *for the job.*

pretend*	bother	learn*	threaten*	tend
appear*	volunteer	hesitate	afford	arrange*
happen	manage	long	attempt	refuse
agree*	fail	swear*	hope*	consent
pretend*				

2b Example: *I order* **you to fire**.

encourage	permit	empower	tell*	compel
enable	cause	challenge	instruct	persuade*
get	command	advise*	remind*	teach*
force	entitled	oblige	allow	invite
forbid	tempt			

2c Example: *I dared* **her to do** *it.*

beg	promise*	expect*	intend*	claim*
choose				

3 Example: *It began **raining/to rain** at ten.*

continue	prefer	forget	help
bear/stand	need	regret	mean
hate	remember	try	consider

Notes

1 Verbs marked * may also be followed by a clause beginning with *that*, sometimes with a slight change in meaning.

2 Of the verbs in group 3, *need, remember, forget* and *regret* change their meaning slightly according to whether they are followed by a gerund or an infinitive. *Try, help, mean* and *consider* change their meaning completely. The other verbs suffer negligible changes in meaning.

F | Speaking

Inviting; accepting and refusing

Language study

Dialogue 1

PETER: David, Freda and I were wondering if you and Mary would like to have a night out with us sometime.

DAVID: All right, we'd like that very much. What did you have in mind?

PETER: Well, perhaps we could go and see a play, and then have something to eat afterwards.

DAVID: That would be great. When?

PETER: We were thinking of Friday.

DAVID: That should be OK. I'll have to check with Mary, but I don't think we're doing anything.

PETER: All right, perhaps you could let me know tomorrow?

DAVID: OK. Or I'll phone later. See you then! And thanks for the invitation.

Dialogue 2

JOHN: Hello.

MICK: Hello, John?

JOHN: Yes. Mick.

MICK: Hi. Fancy coming out for a drink?

JOHN: I can't really. We're having dinner in a few minutes. How about a bit later?

MICK: All right. Would about 9 o'clock be OK?

JOHN: Fine by me. Do you want to come round, or shall I see you in the pub?

MICK: I'll pop round first.

JOHN: OK see you then. About 9.

MICK: Right you are. See you.

Dialogue 3

PETER: Hello.

DAVID: Hello Peter?

PETER: Yes. Is that David?

DAVID: Yes, how are you?

PETER: Fine. Have you spoken to Mary?

DAVID: Yes. I'm afraid we're busy on Friday. We're going to a party, apparently. What are you doing on Saturday?

PETER: Freda's parents are coming over.

DAVID: Oh, that's a pity. Some other time then.

PETER: Yes. See you tomorrow, then.

DAVID: Yes, see you.

Dialogue 4

MONICA: Hello.

ANDREW: Hello, is that Monica?

MONICA: Yes, who's that?

ANDREW: It's Andrew. Andrew Thomas.

MONICA: Oh. Hello, Andrew.

ANDREW: I'm phoning because I was wondering if you might like to come out with me tonight.

MONICA: Tonight? With you?

ANDREW: Yes. I thought we could go out for dinner.

MONICA: Oh. Well, thank you for the invitation, but I don't really feel like going out tonight, actually. I've got a bit of a headache.

ANDREW: OK. Some other time then? When would suit you? Are you free tomorrow?

MONICA: No I'm not. I'm . . . er . . . going out with some friends from work.

ANDREW: Oh, that's a shame. How about Thursday?

MONICA: No, really. I'd rather not, if you don't mind, Andrew. Look, I must go now. Thanks for calling. See you.

Dialogue 5

ROGER: Charles, I must speak to you about the sales figures.

CHARLES: Certainly Roger. When did you have in mind?

ROGER: Well, when would be convenient for you?

CHARLES: Well, I'm tied up all day tomorrow, but I'm free on Wednesday morning.

ROGER: No, Wednesday morning's rather difficult for me. Would the afternoon be convenient?

CHARLES: No, I'm afraid not. I have a meeting.

ROGER: Hmm. Well, that leaves Thursday afternoon, as far as I' concerned. Are you free then?

CHARLES: No, I'm tied up every afternoon this week, as a matter of fact. Do you have anything arranged for Friday morning?

ROGER: Yes, I'm afraid I do. That leaves Friday afternoon. But you say you're busy.

CHARLES: Well, I was going to see Perkins, from Marketing, but I could put it off.
ROGER: I'd appreciate it if you would.
CHARLES: Very well, I'll see to it.
ROGER: Shall we say Friday afternoon, then?
CHARLES: Very well. Until Friday.
ROGER: Until Friday.

4 Improvisation
Student B

a It is Saturday afternoon, and you have nothing to do. The weather is nice, so you are thinking of going out. You are broke, and would like to just go and look round the shops, but not alone. Phone Student A to ask her/him to accompany you. You met her/him recently, and like her/him. You would like to become her/his friend.

b You are a businesswoman/businessman. You manage a small department and have to speak to one of your staff (Student A) about a project, report, etc. Arrange a meeting with him/her. Today is Tuesday. You are tied up every morning this week but free every afternoon except Thursday.

UNIT **5**

Organising your learning

1 Open a list of *-ion* nouns in your file. Transfer the ten groups of nouns in B Vocabulary. Three of the exceptions on Study page 168 form another group. Find out what this group is and add it to your file. Find the verbs for the other exceptions. If you know other nouns derived in the same way, open new groups.

Re-read A Reading, noting abstract nouns not ending in *-ion*, which are derived from verbs or adjectives. Group them according to their derivation (from verbs or adjectives), and their suffixes (endings). Keep adding to your groups.

2 If you are not reading something in English in your spare time, start now. Short stories are a good idea, novels if you are ambitious. How about magazines concerning a personal interest? Sport, music, current affairs, etc. Take out a subscription to such magazines or newspapers. Tell your teacher what you are reading. Recommend good reading matter to other students.

Projects and assignments

1 If you are studying in a developing country, find out as much as you can about one of the following: health; education; the foreign debt. Write a report, or give a short talk to your class about the topic.

2 Scan a good (English-language, if possible) newspaper every day this week for articles about developing countries. Cut out or photocopy the most interesting articles and prepare them for display. Write in two or three sentences what each article is about.

3 In F Speaking, the activity ended with your group choosing an imaginary desert island to be shipwrecked on. Either write an explanation of your group's choice of island and the things you brought from the ship, or write an account of your first few days on the island. In either case, include a careful map of your island.

B Vocabulary

Abstract *-ion* nouns derived from verbs

1 **a** *-ute*, *-ate*, *-ete* verbs: Drop final *e*, add *-ion*.
  b *-ct*, *-pt verbs:* Add *-ion*.
  c *-duce* verbs: Drop final *e*, add *-tion*.
3 **d** *-ise* verbs: Drop final *e*, add *-ation*.
  e *-de* verbs: Drop final *de*, add *-sion*.
  f *-fy* verbs: Drop final *y*, add *-ication*.
  g *-mit* verbs: Drop final *t*, add *-ssion*.
  h *-ss* verbs: Add *-ion*.
  i *-scribe* verbs: Drop final *be*, add *-ption*.
  j *-pose* verbs: Drop final *e*, add *-ition*.
  Notes
1 The last syllable of *-ion* nouns is pronounced /ʃən/, except for nouns in group **e** (*decision*, etc.), where it is pronounced /ʒən/.
2 The penultimate (second-to-last) syllable is stressed in all *-ion* nouns.

5 Each word is followed by the letter of the group in which it belongs. Exceptions are marked *.

toleration	a	subscription	i
maximisation	d	destruction*	
imposition	j	submission	g
contraction	b	commission	g
decision	e	imagination*	
satisfaction*		attraction	b
simplification	f	impression	h
suppression	h	obsession	h
complication	a	combination*	
inscription	i	permission	g
intrusion	e	inclusion	e
omission	g	suspicion*	
minimization	d	repression	h
qualification	f	seduction	c
victimisation	d	invasion	e

eruption	b	extension*	
reduction	c	consumption*	
information*		intensification	f
prescription	i	possession	h
contribution	a	exploration*	
completion	a	exaggeration	a
contradiction	b	admission	g
specification	f	supposition	j
deducation	b/c	oppression	h
depression	h	exception	b
opposition	j	inflation	a
construction	b	proposition	j
realisation	d	examination*	
hesitation	a	reception*	
prediction	b	adaptation*	

Note
Both *deduce* and *deduct* have *deduction* as their abstract noun.

E | Grammar

Present perfect; past simple

1
a	ii	e	ii	i	i
b	ii	f	i	j	ii
c	i	g	i	k	i
d	i	h	i	l	ii

2 Language description

1a The present perfect simple is used for actions or events considered as occurring (or not occurring) during a period of time which still continues. (My life, today, since March, human history.)
Example: *I haven't seen him at all this week.*
1b The past simple is used for actions or events considered as occurring in a past period of time (last year, before lunch, the Stone Age), or at a past point in time (at 10 a.m., when I got up).
Example: *I went to the theatre last night.*

2a The present perfect simple is used for actions or events (or their absence) considered as causing a present state of affairs.
Example: *They haven't come* means they aren't here. Thus it is used for announcing news and for commenting on changes.
Examples:
The Princess has given birth to a son means she now has a son.
Hasn't Eric got fat? means: Isn't Eric fat now?
2b The past simple is used for actions or events considered as items in a completed sequence, often connected by sequencing expressions such as *just then, straight away.* Thus it is used for telling stories.
Example: *After lunch we went for a walk.*

3a The present perfect simple, or the present perfect continuous, is used for the duration of present states of affairs (or ones which have just finished). The present perfect simple is used with verbs which do not usually have a continuous form (e.g. *own, belong, know*). Otherwise the present perfect continuous is used.
Example: *We've known each other for a long time now.*
3b The past simple is used for the duration of past states of affairs.
Example: *I lived in Athens for three years during my childhood.*

Notes

1 Depending on the context, a single use of the present perfect may be an example of more than one category.
Example: *I've been to Poland* illustrates 1a if I am talking about my life (present period). But in an argument about Poland, it might be an example of 2a, i.e. the present state of affairs is that I know Poland.

2 The present perfect continuous is also used to refer to continuous actions in the recent past.
Example: *Have you been sunbathing? You look tanned.*

3 It can also refer to progressively changing states of affairs, when these still continue. These sentences are from Reading 1.
Examples:
Infant mortality has been rising in some areas.
Primary school attendance has been falling.
São Paulo school failures have been increasing.
There is a difference between these sentences and the following.
Examples:
In Jamaica, the percentage of children passing examinations has dropped, i.e. it is lower than it was.
In Jamaica, charges have been introduced, i.e. people are now charged, though they weren't before.
These do not say if the changes are still continuing, but emphasise the states of affairs resulting from them. They are examples of 2a.

G | Writing

Cause and effect

1 The following list contains most of the ways of indicating cause and effect in English.

Sometimes the cause is mentioned first, so that the focus is on the effect, i.e. *higher rents.*

Using one sentence

a **One consequence** } of greater demand for accommodation
   The result } is that rents have risen.

b **Owing to**
   As a result of } greater demand for accommodation, rents have risen.

c Greater demand for accommodation has **led to** / **caused** / **resulted in** } higher rents.

d Demand for accommodation has increased, **so** rents have risen.

Using two sentences

e Demand for accommodation has increased. This has **led to** / **caused** / **resulted in** } higher rents.

f Demand for accommodation has increased. **Consequently** / **As a result** / **Therefore** / **For this reason** } rents have risen.

Sometimes the effect is mentioned first, so that the focus is on the cause, i.e. *greater demand for accommodation.*

Using one sentence

g Higher rents are **the result of** / **due to** / **caused by** } greater demand for accommodation.

h Rents have risen **because** demand for accommodation has increased.

i Rents have risen **as a result** / **because** } of greater demand for accommodation.

Using two sentences

j Rents have risen. This is **the consequence of** / **the result of** / **due to** } greater demand for accommodation.

UNIT 6

Organising your learning

1 How many areas of vocabulary have you listed in your file? How many words are in each? If your answer to either question is 'not many', why is this?

2 It is important to keep your file alive by continually renewing it, testing yourself on vocabulary, etc. It is also important to keep your file fairly lean, or it becomes difficult to use. Is each sheet in it still useful to you? If not (e.g. a newspaper article you will never read again, comprehension questions for a photocopied text, a grammar exercise you found easy, a list of words you have learnt well), transfer whatever you want to keep and throw the rest away. Do this continually.

Projects and assignments

1 If you are studying in Great Britain, interview a British person about the NHS. Prepare your questions beforehand. Summarise the interview. If you record it, include direct quotes in the summary. Play it to your class, commenting on the age, apparent social class, etc. of your subject.

2 If you are studying in your own country, visit three sports or gymnastic clubs, and get information about them. Decide beforehand what information you will want. Write a report comparing them. Which seems the best value?

3 Scan an English-language newspaper for articles concerning health. Choose the one that interests you most and prepare it for display, with a summary of five or six sentences. Note in your file vocabulary associated with health.

B Grammar

Making comparative structures more informative

1 Language description

-er, more

This construction can be modified in the following ways.

To show a big difference

Put *much, a lot, far,* or *a great deal* (more formal) in front.
Examples:
There is far less disease in Africa than in Europe.
Drugs are a great deal more expensive than they used to be.

When comparing number, we cannot use expressions of quantity, like *much,* or *a great deal.* Therefore, always use *far.*
Example: *There were far more people than I had expected.*

To show a small difference

Put *a bit* (informal), *a little,* or *slightly* in front.
Example:
There is a bit less disease in Europe than there was.
The operation was slightly cheaper than we'd feared.

Notes

1 Use *slightly* or *a few* when comparing number.
2 Note how *even* is used by comparing these two sentences.
Examples:
Nurses earn less than lawyers.
Nurses earn even less than teachers.
Even tells us that both nurses and teachers earn very little, but does not tell us if there is a big or small difference between their earnings.

Not as ... as

This construction can be modified in the following ways.

To show a big difference

Put *nearly* before the first *as.*
Example: *I don't know nearly as much about AIDS as I should.*

Notes

1 A common informal alternative to *not nearly as* is *not anywhere near as.*
Example: *I don't know anywhere near as much as I should about . . . .*
2 With comparisons involving adjectives, and *there are/is* it is also common to use *nowhere near as.*
Examples:
There are nowhere near as many hospitals in Africa as in Europe.
He's nowhere near as sick as he pretends to be.

To show a small difference

Put *quite* before the first *as.*
Example: *I don't feel quite as bad as I did yesterday.*

With **measurable differences,** one can be more precise.
Example: *He earns £5,000 more per year than she does.*
There are also constructions involving *twice, three times,* etc.
Examples:
He earns three times as much as she does.
She runs twice as fast as he does.
With words like *size* and *price,* another construction is possible.
Examples:
London is twice the size of Manchester.
This one is twice the price of that one.

F | Speaking

Getting information tactfully; giving opinions and advice

Language study

JACK: Good Heavens, Gladys, you're getting really fat, you know. You'd better do something about it.

GLADYS: Yes, perhaps I should. Do you really think it's that bad?

JACK: Do you mind if I ask how much you weigh these days?

GLADYS: Oh, you know, Jack, a bit more than last year.

JACK: Seriously, Gladys, I wouldn't laugh about it, if I were you. How much do you weigh, in fact?

GLADYS: About 14 stone.

JACK: That's an awful lot, Gladys. I mean, I hope you don't mind my saying so, but you are dangerously fat. How old are you, if you don't mind my asking?

GLADYS: 34. What do you mean, dangerously?

JACK: Well, heart attacks of course. I hate to say it, but that's a lot of fat for one heart to carry. I really think you ought to lose weight.

GLADYS: Yes well, I see your point, and I have tried a few diets, but nothing seems to work. What do you think I ought to do?

JACK: Well, if you want my opinion, complicated diets don't work. How many times a day do you eat?

GLADYS: Well, I hardly stop, really.

JACK: Well, have you tried just eating less often? Why don't you just eat twice a day?

GLADYS: I've tried that, but it's no good; I just can't resist the temptation.

JACK: Well, the way I see it, you've simply got to resist it.

GLADYS: Well, it's easier said than done, isn't it? I mean it's all right for you, you're thin anyway. It's easy for you to talk. The thing is, I've got so much weight to lose that it hardly seems worth starting.

JACK: Well, you've got to start, if you want to know what I think.

GLADYS: I suppose you're right. Perhaps I'd better.

JACK: Have you tried doing exercises?

GLADYS: Oh yes, I tried keep-fit classes, but they didn't do any good.

JACK: How many times did you go, if you don't mind my asking?

GLADYS: Oh, you know, a few. Well, three or four.

JACK: Well, what do you expect? You've got to keep it up!

GLADYS: Oh, I'm sure you're right, but what's the point?

JACK: Look, Gladys, if you don't mind my saying so, I think you're being rather negative. It's simple. If you don't lose weight you're going to have problems.

GLADYS: All right, you've got a point I suppose. I'll try again.

Organising your learning

1 To improve your listening, see at least one English-language film (even with subtitles) per week. Films on videocassette are particularly useful, since they can be used for intensive as well as extensive listening, and useful expressions and vocabulary can be picked up. Also listen to the BBC World Service on the radio.

Projects and assignments

1 Write the story your group planned in B Speaking.

2 If you are studying in Britain, note down any signs you see (e.g. road signs, warning, etc.) and express them in informal English.
If you are studying in your own country, translate signs in your own language into formal English signs.

3 Watch an English-language film concerning crime. Write a review of the film, describing the crime, commenting, recommending or advising against it. If the film is on videocassette, choose a scene, listen carefully and write down the dialogue. Add stage directions according to what the characters do or what happens as they speak. These should be brief and in the present simple tense.

4 Scan a tabloid newspaper (or the equivalent in your country) for articles concerning crime. Prepare them for display and place each next to a summary of two or three sentences.

5 If you are studying in Britain, show the advertisement in E Reading 2 to a varied selection of British people, and ask for their comments. (Or work out questions beforehand, regarding their attitude to the police.) Record the comments. Play the recording to your class, commenting on the age, apparent social class, etc. of the speakers.

6 If you are studying in Britain, telephone your local Crown Court and arrange to attend a trial. You will not be allowed to take photographs or notes. Write a report on what you see there.

E | Reading 2

Reading exercises

1

Brothers-in-law

f   As you can see, the Police have changed in recent years.

l   But the way they've changed is simply a reflection of the way Britain itself has changed.

Just as individuals who make up our society come from every imaginable background, from every walk of life, so do our Police Officers.

a   But where some communities may be divided, the Police are not. And it's not just the uniforms they wear that unites them.

They share the same basic principles. Otherwise they would never have wanted to join in the first place.

g   And those are the same principles of law and order that existed twenty years ago and more.

Ask any Policeman or Policewoman why they applied for the job, and you'll get the same answer. 'To get involved with people.' To get involved with the community they patrol. To understand it. Safeguard it. Unarmed, remember.

e   And what all Officers have in common is that they are dealing daily with human problems.

h   With different sorts of people. Who rarely behave predictably.

There are few situations in which an Officer has a textbook solution to the difficulties he faces.

j   For example, he's called in to sort out a rumpus on a housing estate.

It has been reported that a man is beating up his neighbour.

k   He discovers that there's only been a slanging match. Even so, the peace has been disturbed.

Technically he could arrest either or both of them. But a better solution might well be to talk the problem out.

n   You see, it's a grey area with no easy answer.

And every Officer will tell you that it's like that time and time again.

b   He needs to be something of a social worker on the one hand.

m   Yet, on the other, he is invested with the authority of the law.

He sees the seamy side of life, the sordid and the unpleasant.

i   Yet he'll also see human nature at its best.

d   When members of the public are helpful, kind and selfless.

The two officers we've pictured here both have breadth of experience few of us could match.

c   And it's the experience that makes them mates. Knowing they can rely on each other in times of crisis.

If you think you are the kind of man or woman who could cope with the rigours as well as the rewards, write to:
Police Careers

POLICE

OFFICER

UNIT **8**

Organising your learning

1 After the list of compound verbs in your file, open a list of compound nouns such as *knock-out, takeover*.

2 Keep all your extensive written work in a section in your file. From time to time, read through it to see if you are still making the same errors, or if there has been an improvement. If there hasn't, why do you think this is? What problems do you still have?

There are no more **Organising your learning** sections. Keep on organising your learning.

Projects and assignments

1 If you are studying in Britain, work with other students to interview local people about the current situation in the UK. Prepare questions or a questionnaire. Write a report on your findings. If interviews are recorded, play them to your class, with comments on the speakers. Add direct quotes to your report.

2 Choose a newspaper article about politics, note new words, and look them up. Write out phonemic transcriptions and example sentences for those you want to remember.
Note down words specifically associated with politics and open a list of 'politics' words in your file.

3 If you are studying in Britain, write a brief description of the political situation in your country, or prepare a short informal talk to your class. If there is someone else from your country in your class, work together.

4 If you are studying in your own country, write about the most important problems your country faces. What are the causes? Can you suggest any solutions? Alternatively, prepare a short informal talk to your class on the subject, inviting debate.

B Vocabulary

Compound nouns

2

```
    a b c d e f g h i j k l m n o p q r s t
 1  X V O U T L O O K M B S T Q O O P V W Q
 2  E O U U V J K U P D O W N P O U R E O H
 3  O U T P A Q O T L G I N C O M E F X V O
 4  U J C B O F I S N S E T P S W E T M E U
 5  T F A R U O V E R S I G H T A E O C R T
 6  L O S I T F Z T Y X O U T P U T U O T S
 7  A U T N C D O W N F A L L A S W T U I K
 8  W T T G O U T B R E A K G Y S H B T M I
 9  N L D I M P E N O D V L C Z A J U L E R
10  T E S N E Z X V C H P O V E R D R A F T
11  G T R G M N V J Q O U T R A G E S Y Q S
12  H A W R J O V E R H E A D S E H T A S L
```

ACROSS		DOWN	
outlook	downfall	outlaw	outset
downpour	outbreak	outlet	outburst
income	overdraft	outcast	outlay
oversight	outrage	upbringing	overtime
output	overheads	outcome	outskirts

Explain words you know, if your partner doesn't know them, and try to guess the meanings of others.

F Grammar

Relative clauses

3 ***Student A***
a chest of drawers   a fork-lift truck   a roof-rack
a kettle   a quill

G Writing

Comparison and contrast

1 Language description

The words and expressions are used in the following ways.

Comparison

Within one sentence
Examples:
Both communism ***and*** democracy claim to represent ordinary people.
Neither does so with 100% success.
Neither communist governments ***nor*** democratic governments admit that they violate human rights.
In fact, ***both*** do so whenever necessary.
Like the Soviet Union, China is trying to change to a different style of communism.

Note
Neither and **both** can be used without nouns when
these are understood. When **neither** is used alone
or with singular nouns, the verb is singular. **Both** is
always used with the plural of the verb.

Over more than one sentence
Example: *The USA has Latin America as its sphere of
influence.* **Similarly/In the same way,** *the Soviet
Union has influence over Eastern Europe.*

Contrast

Within one sentence
Examples:
*Left-wing governments spend a lot of money on the
welfare of ordinary people,* **whereas/while** *conservative
governments consider this to be less important.*
Unlike *the USSR the USA has easy access to*

the Atlantic ocean.
Over more than one sentence
Example: *Democracy aims to govern sensibly through the
opposition of different political opinions. Communism,* **in
contrast/on the other hand/however,** *assumes that
there is only one way to achieve this aim, and allows little
political debate.*

F Grammar

Relative clauses

4 Student B
   a wheelbarrow   a holepunch   a colander
   a filing cabinet   a fan

UNIT

Projects and assignments

1 Read the short story written in English. Summarise
the plot, and rewrite the ending of the story.

2 Translate into English all the expressions you know in
your language which in some way compare people to
animals.
Examples: *He eats like a pig; He is an ass.*
Show your list to a native English speaker to find out:
which expressions are similar to English ones; other
English expressions of this type.
Open a list of such English expressions in your file.

3 Choose a simple poem or song from your own country
which you like.
Translate it into English. Your translation should try
to capture the spirit of the original, but should not
stick so closely to it that the English is unnatural.
Explain what the song or poem is about, and why you
like it.

4 Write a poem in English. Remember, poems need
not rhyme, nor need they have a regular rhythm.

5 Find a poem or other piece of literary writing in
English which describes an animal. Identify the
language which is most effective in making the
description vivid.

B Vocabulary

Verbs of movement and posture

2

```
    a b c d e f g h i j k l m n o p q r s t
 1  W P T H U N C H S W A E T K L P O U N W
 2  C S O O S T R O L L S T R I D E T O P A
 3  R T I P T O E C L A L O I N A R D O T N
 4  A A B S O R E C G H I C P O S C I A L D
 5  W G Q U P T P A B D P L O D H H A T R E
 6  L L G O A P N O C K L E A G E N C E U R
 7  T E A L L O U N G E R M U N K L E M S T
 8  P R I N E G A S T U M B L E R U M B E R
 9  S P R I N T O P O L E E S H U F F L E K
10  W I A K L P R E W N D R E L E A W E J X
11  L I M P F J K L E A P W R I G G L E O P
12  S T R A N T S T R U T R I P P L A N G E
```

ACROSS		DOWN	
hunch	sprint	crawl	clamber
stroll	shuffle	stagger	trip
stride	limp	hop	dash
tiptoe	leap	topple	perch
plod	wriggle	creep	tumble
lounge	strut	tower	jog
stumble		slip	wander

Explain any words you know to other group
members. Then, using your dictionaries if necessary,
choose one of the verbs for each definition below.
You will not need all of them.

a sit with rounded shoulders and bent back
b go with no direction, destination
c walk unhurriedly, for pleasure
d climb using hands and feet
e jump energetically from one place to another
f sit, stand in a lazy way

g hit your foot against something, nearly falling
h walk energetically, with long steps
i fall, quickly, or down a hill
j sit alertly, like a bird on a branch
k run quickly, suddenly
l walk with small steps, hardly lifting the feet
m move the body around like a worm
n move unsteadily, from weakness, drunkenness, etc.
o walk putting most weight on one leg
p walk arrogantly
q hit your foot against something and fall forwards
r run easily, slowly
s fall over, usually slowly, heavily
t be tall in relation to surroundings

C Listening

3 Language study

Snake

A snake came to my water-trough
On a hot, hot day, and I in pyjamas for the heat,
To drink there.

In the deep, strange-scented shade of the great dark
    carob-tree
5 I came down the steps with my pitcher
And must wait, must stand and wait, for there he was
    at the trough before me.

He reached down from a fissure in the earth-wall in
    the gloom
And trailed his yellow-brown slackness soft-bellied
    down, over the edge of the stone trough
And rested his throat upon the stone bottom,
10 And where the water had dripped from the tap, in a
    small clearness,
He sipped with his straight mouth,
Softly drank through his straight gums, into his slack
    long body,
Silently.

Someone was before me at my water-trough,
15 And I, like a second comer, waiting.

He lifted his head from his drinking, as cattle do,
And looked at me vaguely, as drinking cattle do,
And flickered his two-forked tongue from his lips, and
    mused a moment,
And stopped and drank a little more,
20 Being earth-brown, earth-golden from the burning
    bowels of the earth,
On the day of Sicilian July, with Etna smoking.

The voice of my education said to me
He must be killed,
For in Sicily the black, black snakes are innocent, the
    gold are venomous.

25 And voices in me said, if you were a man
You would take a stick and break him now, and finish
    him off.

But must I confess how I liked him,
How glad I was he had come like a guest in quiet, to
    drink at my water-trough
And depart peaceful, pacified, and thankless,
30 Into the burning bowels of this earth?

Was it cowardice, that I dared not kill him?
Was it perversity, that I longed to talk to him?
Was it humility, to feel so honoured?
I felt so honoured.

35 And yet those voices;
If you were not afraid, you would kill him!

And truly I was afraid, I was most afraid,
But even so, honoured still more
That he should seek my hospitality
40 From out the dark door of the secret earth.

He drank enough
And lifted his head, dreamily, as one who has
    drunken,
And flickered his tongue like a forked night on the
    air, so black,
Seeming to lick his lips,
45 And looked around like a god, unseeing, into the air,
And slowly turned his head,
And slowly, very slowly, as if thrice adream,
Proceeded to draw his slow length curving round
And climb again the broken bank of my wall-face.

50 And as he put his head into that dreadful hole,
And as he slowly drew up, snake-easing his shoulders,
And entered farther,
A sort of horror, a sort of protest against his
    withdrawing into that horrid black hole,
Deliberately going into that blackness, and slowly
    drawing himself after,
Overcame me now his back was turned.

55 I looked round, I put down my pitcher,
I picked up a clumsy log
And threw it at the water-trough with a clatter.

I think it did not hit him,
But suddenly that part of him that was left behind
    convulsed in undignified haste,
60 Writhed like lightning, and was gone
Into the black hole, the earth-lipped fissure in the
    wall-front,
At which, in the intense still noon, I stared with
    fascination.

And immediately I regretted it.
I thought how paltry, how vulgar, what a mean act!
65 I despised myself and the voices of my accursed
    human education.

And I thought of the albatross,
And I wished he would come back, my snake.

For he seemed to me again like a king,
Like a king in exile, uncrowned in the underworld,
70 Now due to be crowned again.

And so, I missed my chance with one of the lords
Of life.
And I have something to expiate;
A pettiness.

Taormina
D.H. Lawrence

Study the text in pairs.
a Underline language which:
makes the snake seem human;
gives a clear visual impression of the snake.
b Comment on the sound of words like 'sipped',
'straight', 'softly'. What other sounds have the same
effect in suggesting a snake?
c Why 'in the gloom'? (line 7)
d How is what happens in lines 55 to 60 different in
feeling from the rest of the scene? What is the effect
of the words 'clumsy', 'clatter', 'convulsed', 'writhed'?
e What is the poem's clearest image for you?
f Which lines do you like best?

4 Listen to the poem again, reading as you listen. Mark
any lines you particularly like, because of the way
they are read. Do other class members agree?

E Speaking

Permission; requests; apologising

Language study

Dialogue 1

JOAN:	Do you think you could lend me £10, Sue?
SUE:	I can't actually. Sorry but I've only got £20 for the weekend.
JOAN:	OK. Thanks anyway.
SUE:	Sorry about that.
JOAN:	It's OK. Don't worry about it.

Dialogue 2

BOB:	Can you give me a lift tonight, Harry?
HARRY:	Sure, I'd be glad to. I'll be leaving about 5. Is that OK?
BOB:	That's great. Thanks a lot.

Dialogue 3

KEN:	Peter, would it be all right if I left the lesson early tonight?
PETER:	Yes, I think so. Do you mind if I ask why?
KEN:	I've got to go to the dentist.
PETER:	OK then. Yes, that will be all right.
KEN:	Thanks.
PETER:	That's all right.

Dialogue 4

MR THOMPSON:	Jackie, I was wondering if you would mind working late tonight?
JACKIE:	Oh. Well, I'm afraid that's rather difficult, Mr Thompson. I've got to pick my children up from school.
MR THOMPSON:	Oh dear. Well, it is rather important, I'm afraid. Would it be possible for someone else to pick them up? I'm sorry to put you out like this, but it really is rather important.
JACKIE:	Well I could ask a friend, I suppose. I'll see what I can do.
MR THOMPSON:	Would you? I'd be very grateful if you would.
JACKIE:	All right, Mr Thompson. I'll do my best.
MR THOMPSON:	Thank you, Jackie.

Dialogue 5

JACKIE:	Hello, Anne, it's Jackie. Listen, can I ask you a favour?
ANNE:	Of course, what is it?
JACKIE:	Well, I've got to work late tonight, so I can't pick my kids up. I don't suppose you could pick them up for me, could you?
ANNE:	Oh dear, that's a bit tricky actually. I'm going to the hairdresser's at 3 o'clock.
JACKIE:	Oh, dear. You couldn't pick them up afterwards, I suppose? About 4 o'clock.
ANNE:	Let me see. Yes, I think I could manage that. All right.
JACKIE:	Great. Thanks very much, Anne. Sorry to put you out.
ANNE:	That's all right. No trouble.

Dialogue 6

MAN: Hello, excuse me. Sorry to bother you. Would it be possible for me to leave my bags here for an hour or so?

WOMAN: I'm very sorry, but I'm afraid that's impossible. We can't be responsible for anything left here, so I'm afraid we can't allow passengers to leave baggage.

MAN: Oh I see. Oh well, thanks anyway.

WOMAN: I'm sorry I can't be more helpful.

MAN: It's all right, I quite understand.

G Grammar

Passive voice

Simple variations
1 Language description

a How the passive voice is formed

The object in the active voice is the subject in the passive, at the front of the verb phrase.
Example: *I want John to be invited.*
Passive meaning is shown by *to be*, in any tense, infinitive or gerund.
Example: *Having been born in the USA, he's entitled to US citizenship.*
The main verb is in the past participle form.
Example: *I would prefer to have been told in advance.*
The agent is introduced by *by* when it is important information.
Example: *He was killed by his best friend.*

b When the passive is used

We use the passive voice when we don't know, don't care, or want to hide who did something.
It is used to add formality. Any passive-voice construction is more formal than its active-voice equivalent.

c What constructions replace the passive

I'm going to have my car serviced this afternoon.
Used when an action is done to something of ours, usually a service. (Not always, however: we can also say, *He had his car stolen.*)
My car needs servicing.
This is more colloquial than the passive *needs to be serviced.*

Advanced variations

4 a It is thought that he is living in Leningrad.
He is thought to be living in Leningrad.
b It is thought by many that Steven Spielberg is an underrated director.
Steven Spielberg is thought by many to be an underrated director.
c Nowadays, it is agreed that Galileo was a genius.
Nowadays, Galileo is agreed to have been a genius.
d In his lifetime it was thought that he was evil.
In his lifetime, he was thought to be evil.
e It was suspected that he had sold his soul to the devil.
He was suspected to have sold his soul to the devil.

Language description

These constructions are extremely common in reporting what people say, believe, allege, etc. They are often found in news reporting and discussion of an academic kind.
The following verbs can be used with either construction: know, think, say, believe, allege, announce, claim, report, feel, find, suspect, assume, fear, consider, recognise, understand, assume.
In the infinitive construction, the present infinitive (*to be*) is used when there is no difference in time between the main verb (think, believe, suspect, etc.) and the rest of the sentence.
Examples:
In his lifetime, he was thought (past) *to be evil* (past).
Spielberg is thought (present) *to be an underrated director* (present).
The perfect infinitive (*to have done*) is used when there is a difference in time.
Examples:
Nowadays, Galileo is agreed (present) *to have been a genius* (past).
He was suspected (past) *to have sold his soul to the devil* (previous past time).

Notes

1 *Not known* is followed by *whether*, instead of *that*, and cannot be used with the infinitive construction.
Example: *It is not known whether anyone survived the crash.*
2 If the agent is mentioned in either construction, it is placed straight after the passive verb phrase.

UNIT **10**

Projects and assignments

1 Write the story your group planned in B Speaking.

2 If you are studying in Britain, find a native English speaker who has had some experience or knows a good story involving ghosts, the supernatural, divination of some kind, etc. If possible, record the person telling the story.
Write out part or all of what the person actually says. Underline expressions which are typical of oral story telling (e.g. *anyway, you know*). What other features are typical of oral story telling?
Summarise the story in writing.

3 Watch an English-language film concerning the occult. Write a review of the film, summarising the plot, commenting, recommending (or warning off). If the film is on videocassette, choose a short scene, listen as many times as you need to, and write down the dialogue. Add stage directions according to what the characters do and what happens as they speak. These should be brief and in the present simple tense.

4 If you are studying in Britain, read your horoscope in a tabloid newspaper every day for a week. Cut out the horoscopes. At the end of the week prepare the horoscopes for display and write under each your comments on how accurate they were.

B Speaking

Miming game

The fortune teller

Pair A
Message 1

You will join the Navy and travel all over the world. In a hot, dangerous country you will meet your husband/wife, and you will live there for many years, in a house with a swimming pool and many servants. You will have eight children, but you will be alone when you are very old.

Message 2

I see a tanned, very strong man, with long hair. He is wearing only the skin of a leopard. He is riding an elephant through a dense jungle, looking for you. He is very worried.

D Grammar

Conditionals

Variations on *if* clauses
4 Language description

First conditional

Unless means *if not*
Example: *Unless you give me the money, I'll shoot.*
Provided, on condition that and *as long as* emphasise the importance of the condition being fulfilled, often when negotiating or making a deal. All refer to things that we want to happen. *Provided that* and *on condition that* are more formal.
Examples:
Provided you let us know in advance, there'll be no problem.
As long as you're careful, you'll be OK.
Should, happen to, and *by any chance* emphasise the improbability of the condition being fulfilled, often to reassure the listener. All are common when making a request in the main clause. The *should* variation is the most formal.
Examples:
If you should see Mr Jenkins, would you ask him to call the office, please?
If you happen to see Dave, can you ask him to give me a ring?
If by any chance it goes wrong again, let us know straight away.
Will is used for formal requests.
Example: *If you will wait a moment, the manager will see you shortly.*

Second conditional

Would is used for more polite formal requests.
Example: *I would be grateful if you would send me further details.*
Were to is used to emphasise the improbability of a hypothetical condition being fulfilled. It is also used to make suggestions more careful and polite.
Examples:
If you were to be told that you only had a year to live, what would you do?
If you were to dress a little better, you might have more luck with girls.
Weren't/wasn't for is used when the noun alone is enough to suggest the hypothetical meaning, so it is unnecessary to say the whole clause.
Example:
If it weren't } *for the kids, I'd ask for a divorce*
If it wasn't } *tomorrow.*
It is often further shortened, by using *but for.*
Example: *But for the kids, I'd ask for a divorce tomorrow.*

Third conditional

Hadn't been for is the same as the last example, except in the past. The *but for* construction can also be used.
Example:
If it hadn't been } *for John, I would have*
But } *drowned .*

Inversions

The inverted constructions below increase formality.
Examples:
If it should happen . . . ──▶ *Should it happen . . .*
If it were to happen . . . ──▶ *Were it to happen . . .*
If I had done . . . ──▶ *Had I done . . .*
If I hadn't done . . . ──▶ *Had I not done . . .*

UNIT 11

Projects and assignments

1 Find out all you can about an important environmental issue in your country. Write a report about it.

2 If you are studying in Britain, scan a serious newspaper every day this week for articles concerning the environment. Note down new words concerning the environment, look them up and open a list in your file.
Choose the article which interests you most, prepare it for display, and write a summary underneath.

3 Imagine yourself in the year 2000. Write a letter to one of your present classmates, telling her/him about your home, family, work, hobbies, etc. Have they changed? Are you happy?

B Speaking

Miming game

The fortune teller

Pair B
Message 1

The first half of your life will be ordinary. You will work in a bank and be happily married. You will have two children, a dog and a canary, and you will live in a small flat near the top of a high-rise block. When you are about forty years old, you will leave all this and go to Tahiti to live on a beach and write very bad poetry.

Message 2

I see a crowded theatre, and a beautiful ballerina on the stage. She is not dancing at the moment, but watching others dance. I see you in the audience, wearing evening-dress. You are staring at the beautiful dancer. You have a gun in your pocket.

D Vocabulary

Sound-words

3

	a	b	c	d	e	f	g	h	i	j	k	l	m	n	o	p	q	r
1	R	T	G	U	R	G	L	E	S	W	A	N	V	O	C	K	L	V
2	A	G	R	O	A	N	P	T	C	O	B	C	O	D	R	I	P	T
3	V	S	O	H	T	L	M	B	R	L	D	R	T	S	A	W	R	O
4	H	O	W	L	T	Z	F	E	E	T	S	U	I	S	S	X	U	S
5	I	R	L	A	L	S	W	Q	E	U	S	N	T	H	C	M	A	A
6	S	N	L	P	E	C	H	O	C	L	I	C	K	R	J	R	B	A
7	S	Q	U	A	N	T	I	D	H	I	G	H	L	P	S	A	L	R
8	S	C	L	A	N	G	N	R	U	S	T	L	E	W	Q	C	E	A
9	A	O	K	U	C	R	E	A	K	X	A	Q	U	E	U	K	R	N
10	P	S	Q	U	E	L	C	H	A	B	P	D	G	R	E	C	M	C
11	M	O	A	R	L	S	W	I	N	T	O	F	R	O	A	R	N	E
12	B	A	R	K	F	R	O	B	L	A	R	E	N	S	K	R	O	T

ACROSS
gurgle rustle
groan creak
drip squelch
howl roar
click bark
clang blare

DOWN
hiss growl
lap rattle
whine screech

tap rumble
crunch tinkle
crash squeak
crack

Explain to your group the sounds you know from the list. Use your dictionaries for unknown words. Each group member should be responsible for a few words, and explain these to the group.

179

F | Grammar

Future arrangements and intentions; predictions

1
a ii	d ii	g iii	j i
b ii	e iii	h iii	k i
c ii	f i	i i	l i

2 Language description

Although it is almost impossible to formulate watertight grammar rules for talking about the future in English, there are certain regularities. These are as follows.

a Arrangements and intentions

Will/shall do is used: for intentions which are expressed as they are formed, and for offers; also when we have no special plans (with verbs like *suppose* and *guess*).

Going to do is used for intentions already formed before the moment of speaking.

Was going to do is used to talk about past intentions. The *present continuous* is used for definitely arranged future activities, often involving other people and usually in the near future.

The *future continuous* is used to talk (especially to ask) politely about intentions.

Am/is/are to do is very formal language for talking about definite arrangements.

b Predictions

Going to (do) is used to talk about things we can see are sure to happen.

Will/shall do is used to talk about things we believe are sure to happen, with nothing in the present to make us think so. However *going to* is sometimes used to give added emphasis to our prediction.

Example: *I'm **going to** fail, I just know it.*

The *future continuous* is used for future activities expected to happen, in the normal course of events (like routine actions); for an activity which will be in progress at a point in future time.

Example: *Call at around 10.30. I'**ll be having** a break.*

The *future perfect* is used to refer to processes or events which will be finished before, (or by) a future point in time.

Examples: (I don't know exactly when the destruction of the tropical forests will be completed, but I can say that) *Unless urgent measures are taken the tropical rain forests **will have disappeared** by the time our children are adults.* .

(We are going to a concert and are stuck in traffic.)
*Oh, no! The concert **will have started** by the time we get there.*

Should means the same as *will probably* and we use it only to talk of things we want to happen.

Example: *If the traffic isn't too bad, we **should** get there in time.*

Bound to is used for emphatic prediction, especially when someone doubts it.

Example: *I think the conservatives will win the election. Why do you say that?*

*Well, they're **bound to**, aren't they? The opposition are so disorganised that nobody would vote for them.*

3 *Student B*

a On page 131 is a page of your appointments book for the next week. Fill it in as you like, imagining things you intend to do and things you have definitely arranged to do.

b Student A calls you. It is Sunday evening. Improvise a telephone conversation with your partner, bearing in mind the following information.

You study at the same university as Boris, a friend of yours and Student A's, and always see him on Tuesday afternoons at a seminar. You don't have his telephone number.

You and Student A both know Betty, who lives quite close to you.

Alan, another mutual friend, left his wallet at your house the other day. Perhaps Student A, who works with him, could give it to him.

You haven't got Anne's telephone number, and would like Student A to check with her if she is still coming round for dinner on Thursday evening, as you arranged last week.

You want to invite Student A to accompany you on one of the things you intend or have arranged to do this week.

UNIT **12**

Projects and assignments

1 If you are studying in your own country, look in a newspaper for car advertisements. In what ways are they different/similar to English ones? Choose one advertisement and translate it into English.

2 Write an essay comparing and contrasting the USA and the UK, or the Americans and the British. If you have been in both countries, give personal impressions.

3 Choose three parts or controls of a car and explain as fully as you can what function they perform.

4 If you are studying in Britain, interview five native English-speakers about: the things which annoy them most when driving; the last time they did something which they feel was bad driving.
Write up your findings, pointing out anything interesting or instructive. If interviews are recorded, play them to your class, commenting on the speakers. Note motoring vocabulary and open a list in your file.

B Grammar

Modal auxiliaries used for logical deductions

1 Language description

a i I know for a fact it is.
  ii I'm sure it is because of its appearance.
b i I know for a fact he isn't.
  ii I'm sure he isn't; maybe he isn't answering his phone.
c i It's possible that's what they're doing.
  ii I'm sure they are.
d i I'm sure he didn't.
  ii It's possible he didn't.
e i I'm sure you are.
  ii I'm sure you were.

f i I'm sure they are.
  ii I'm sure they aren't
g i I know for a fact they were.
  ii I'm sure they were.
h i It's possible that she was.
  ii I'm sure that she wasn't.

Statements of this kind, using *must* and *can't*, are the result of logical thinking, not expressions of known fact. They are not always, however, less sure or less true than factual statements.
Example: Someone commits suicide, and we say, *She can't have been very happy.*
This is said, not because we are less than 100% sure (it is 100% certain that she wasn't happy), but because we didn't know her, and so have to rely on logical reasoning.
She committed suicide. People who commit suicide aren't happy. Therefore: *She can't have been happy.*
We use *must* when we are sure something is so.
We use *can't* when we are sure it isn't so.
When we are not sure, we use *might*.
Talking of the past we use *must/can't/might/have done* rather than *do*.
Talking of an action in progress we use the present participle of the verb after *be*: *must/can't/might be doing* (present); or *have been*: *must/can't/might have been doing* (past).

UNIT **13**

Projects and assignments

1 If you are studying in Britain, prepare an itinerary for a holiday in your country. You should be able to find information and pictures in a travel agent's. Most will let you take out brochures. If there is somebody else from your country in your class, consider working together. Describe the holiday to your class, and answer any questions that come up. (Anticipate these, and prepare accordingly.) If more than one student describes a holiday, each class member should decide which holiday she/he would prefer, giving reasons.

2 If you are studying in your own country, interview five (not necessarily native) English-speaking tourists about their holiday in your city. Prepare questions or a questionnaire. (Also offer to answer any questions they may have about your city.) Write a report on your findings. If interviews are recorded, play the recording to your class, commenting on the speakers.

3 If you have a primitive community (like the Indians in F Listening) in your country, write a description of them, their lifestyle, etc.

4 If you are studying in Britain, spend a weekend in London, or another large city, staying in at least one

hotel within your price range. Write a report on the hotel(s), like that in A Reading 1.
If a number of students do this, prepare an information sheet or wall-display for students new to Britain.

5 If you are studying in your own country, write a piece recommending the sights, museums, etc, in your city which you personally feel shouldn't be missed by tourists.

B Grammar

'Fronting' for emphasis

1 Language description
a **Adverbs and adverbial phrases used in the 'fronted' position**

Never   Hardly ever   Rarely   Nowhere
Examples:
Hardly ever has there been such interest in a Royal visit.
Nowhere has there been more interest than in the schools.

Hardly . . . when   No sooner . . . than
Only then   Not until

Examples:
Hardly had we arrived when things began to go wrong.
Not until I had got on the bus did I realise that I'd left my purse at home.
The driver asked for my fare. Only then did I realise that I'd left my purse at home.

In no circumstances   On no account   In no way
At no time
Examples:
On no account should this door be left open.
At no time was any warning given by the police.
In no way are my comments intended as a criticism.

Only by (doing)   Only in this way   Only if
Examples:
Only by examining all the facts can we be sure of a fair verdict.
We must examine all the facts. Only in this way can we be sure of a fair verdict.

b How the sentence structure changes

The verb phrase following the adverbial is inverted.
Not until is an exception: the verb in the main clause is inverted.
In story-telling, *Hardly*, *Not until*, and *No sooner* are usually followed by a verb in the past perfect tense.
On no account and *In no circumstances* can also be followed by the imperative form.

c Examples of fronting in less formal English

There are more than is sometimes imagined.
Examples:
Never in my life had I seen such a mess.
Not only did he borrow my car without asking, he also brought it back covered in mud.
Of course, no sooner had she left than Doris rang, asking for her.
No way would you find a house for that price in London.
(The last example is still considered sub-standard English by many.)

d Why fronting sometimes sounds strange

There is no reason to use an emphatic stylistic device to say banal, ordinary things. Don't use fronting indiscriminately.

E Vocabulary

Phrasal verbs 2

3 *explain something away*, dismiss complaint, etc. by giving explanation
bear something out, confirm story, statement, etc.
come across something, find by accident
pull up, stop (*vehicle*)
dawn on someone, be realised (*It dawned on me that...*)
head for something, go towards a place
flick through something, look at book, etc. while turning pages quickly
make up for something, compensate for something
end up, conclude a series of actions in a certain state, place, etc.
side with someone, be on someone's side in a disagreement
cash in on something, take advantage, make a profit for yourself from something
set something up, establish
put something off, postpone
put something by, save (*usually money*)
pay something off, pay money back in instalments
read up on something, inform yourself about something by reading about it
shop around, compare prices, quality, etc. before buying
talk someone into something, persuade someone to do something
go through with something, actually do something you've promised, threatened, planned, etc. to do
take someone aback, startle, surprise someone
allow for something, include something in your calculations
boil down to something, may be reduced to something (*an essential fact*)
come up with something, discover, invent, provide, a suggestion, solution, idea, etc.
get out of something, avoid doing some unpleasant duty, etc.
splash out on something, spend a lot of money on something you want but don't really need